John Henry Newman

Volumes of the *Continuum Library of Educational Thought* include:

John Henry Newman

JAMES ARTHUR AND GUY NICHOLLS

Continuum Library of Educational Thought

Series Editor: Richard Bailey

Volume 8

continuum

Continuum International Publishing Group

The Tower Building   80 Maiden Lane
11 York Road   Suite 704
London   New York
SE1 7NX   NY 10038

www.continuumbooks.com

© James Arthur and Guy Nicholls 2007

British Library Cataloguing-in-Publication Data
A catalogue record for this book is available from the British Library.

ISBN: 0-8264-8407-7 (hardcover)
ISBN: 978-0-8264-8407-9 (hardcover)

Library of Congress Cataloguing-in-Publication Data
Arthur, James.
John Henry Newman / James Arthur and Guy Nicholls.
p.   cm.
Includes bibliographical references and index.
ISBN-13: 978-0-8264-8407-9 (hardcover)
ISBN-10: 0-8264-8407-7 (hardcover)
1. Newman, John Henry, 1801–1890.   2. Educators–England–Biography.
3. Cardinals–England–Biography.   4. Education–Philosophy.   5. Religious
education–Philosophy.   I. Nicholls, Guy.   II. Title.

LB675.N452A78   2007
370.92–dc22
[B]
2007018460

Typeset by Aptara Books Ltd.
Printed and bound in Great Britain by Biddles Ltd, Kings Lynn, Norfolk

Contents

Contents

Series Editor's Preface

Education is sometimes presented as an essentially practical activity. It is, it seems, about teaching and learning, curriculum and what goes on in schools. It is about achieving certain ends, using certain methods, and these ends and methods are often prescribed for teachers, whose duty it is to deliver them with vigour and fidelity. With such a clear purpose, what is the value of theory?

Recent years have seen politicians and policy makers in different countries explicitly denying *any* value or need for educational theory. A clue to why this might be is offered by a remarkable comment by a British Secretary of State for Education in the 1990s: 'having any ideas about how children learn, or develop, or feel, should be seen as subversive activity'. This pithy phrase captures the problem with theory: it subverts, challenges and undermines the very assumptions on which the practice of education is based.

Educational theorists, then, are trouble-makers in the realm of ideas. They pose a threat to the *status quo* and lead us to question the common sense presumptions of educational practices. But this is precisely what they should do because the seemingly simple language of schools and schooling hides numerous contestable concepts that in their different usages reflect fundamental disagreements about the aims, values and activities of education.

Implicit within the *Continuum Library of Educational Thought* is an assertion that theories and theorizing are vitally important for education. By gathering together the ideas of some of the most influential, important and interesting educational thinkers, from the Ancient Greeks to contemporary scholars, the series has the ambitious task of providing an accessible yet authoritative resource for a generation of students and practitioners. Volumes within the series are written by acknowledged leaders in the field, who were selected both for their scholarship and their ability to make often complex ideas accessible to a diverse audience.

It will always be possible to question the list of key thinkers that are represented in this series. Some may question the inclusion of certain thinkers; some may disagree with the exclusion of others. That is inevitably going to be the case. There is no suggestion that the list of thinkers represented within the *Continuum Library of Educational Thought* is in any way definitive. What is incontestable is that these thinkers have fascinating ideas about education, and that taken together, the *Library* can act as a powerful source of information and inspiration for those committed to the study of education.

Richard Bailey
Roehampton University, London

Foreword

The public signposts of Newman's life and of his spiritual and intellectual *oeuvre*, since the centenary of his death, have been manifested in a plethora of books, monographs and articles. There have been few important studies, however, that have attempted to lace together a schema of Newman's educational philosophy since the publication of Dwight Culler's assessment of his views on higher education in *The Imperial Intellect* (1955). The production for the general reader of this volume by James Arthur and Guy Nicholls is thus particularly timely. It concentrates upon the abiding principles of Newman's educational thought and practice and locates his strengths and varying degrees of success in his practical endeavours firmly within the intellectual context of his time. Furthermore, the authors show that the interplay between issues of authority and freedom were as characteristic of nineteenth-century debate as they are in the context of our own day.

In 1879, Newman asserted his entire life had been a struggle against that liberalism defined by Mark Pattison as having the characteristics of a religion: 'a temper, a habit of mind – not so much anything *per se*, as a form under which we can think our thoughts and live our life' (*Mind, I*, 1976, p. 83). In the central chapters of this book, Professor James Arthur and Fr Guy Nicholls take up this theme by showing how religious and moral training was the integrating factor in Newman's concept of sound intellectual formation. He would have concurred with Augustine that the final reward would be a measure of happiness emerging from a commitment leading to self-giving and service.

Newman, of course, was able to build upon the work of contemporaries who propagated a similar message. Antonio Rosmini, for instance, was writing in 1825 (at twenty-eight years of age) an epoch-making study of education. He gave wide currency to the philosophy that the true education of a person necessitates a concept of perfect unity of which religion is the catalyst. It is a great mistake, Rosmini taught 'to believe that physical, intellectual and moral education are three separate and independent things'. Hence 'the first law of education is that of unity' (R. P. O'Leary, *Rosmini's Educational Thought*, 1973, p. 21).

The subscription to unity (or 'wholeness' as it is often called) rapidly passed into the apologetic of Christian education. Arthur and Nicholls emphasize that Newman has an important place in the dissemination of the view that inner harmony can only be achieved by the creation, in the educational sense, of the conditions needed for the Spirit to function. The book measures the congruence between aim and unity in education at all levels of Newman's conviction of the practical effects that would emerge for the life stance of an individual exposed to it. Perhaps there was something prophetic in the view of Newman's contemporary, Manning, when he declared in 1876 (*Miscellanies*, II, p. 310) that it was 'to rectify and to restore the intellect of [the] day' that formed a major task of the Church in the twentieth century. Newman would have been emphatic to Manning's view in the same passage that the sanctification of the intellect was to be 'the proper work of those who have the light of faith and of men who desire the welfare of their fellows' (*Ibidem*, pp. 9–10). Two sermons printed for the first time in the Appendices to this new study of Newman's educational thought copper-fasten this philosophy. In that of 1826, Newman declared 'All education should be conducted on this principle – that it is a means towards an end, and that end is *Christian holiness*' (Appendix A, p. 207). A year later, Newman was even more precise '. . . Let the subject before us be metaphysics, physics, moral or political philosophy, rhetoric, history or general literature, a spirit of faith and Christian principle should leaven them all' (Appendix B, p. 217).

V. Alan McClelland
Emeritus Professor of Educational Studies
University of Hull

Acknowledgements

We have received much help and encouragement in the writing of this book. We should like to express our thanks to the Fathers of the Birmingham Oratory who gave permission for us to publish for the first time two early sermons as appendices to this book, and to Fr Dermot Fenlon and Fr Philip Cleevely who provided helpful comments on various drafts and provided us with valuable information at crucial stages. We would also like to acknowledge the encouragement and comments of Dr Ian Ker and the reviewers of this series.

Moreover, we owe a particular debt of gratitude to Professor Katherine Tillman of the University of Notre Dame who kindly agreed to read through the whole typescript and made many useful suggestions as well as correcting the occasional error. Her kindness and scholarly expertise have been invaluable to the completion of this work.

Finally, we are most grateful to Professor Alan McClelland for agreeing to write the Foreword to this book.

Introduction: Newman the Educator

The influence of John Henry Newman on education both in his lifetime and since has been great. It is over fifty years since Dwight Culler made the last comprehensive assessment of this contribution in *The Imperial Intellect*. Many other articles, chapters and monographs on Newman's educational work have been published in the meantime, and various aspects of it have been well treated, but a review of his entire *oeuvre* is overdue. We hope that the present work will help to fill this gap. Our purpose is to introduce the general reader to Newman's educational thought and practice, not restricted to any particular phase, but interpreted broadly as it is found in his contribution to primary, secondary, higher and lifelong education.

Newman was deeply involved in educational work throughout his life. He was to be a teacher in several different kinds of educational institution, and to be the founder of more than one of them. Yet beneath the diversity of his educational projects there lay a single aim. Newman was above all a pastor who cared for the souls of those whom God had put in his personal charge. All of Newman's educational projects were pastoral. His work as an educator, an academic, a writer and a thinker is all an expression of his priesthood, whether as an Anglican in the first half of his life, or as a Catholic in the second. The consistency of Newman's thought on education is remarkable when one considers both the length and variety of his life and the fertility and suppleness of his mind. His first sermon on education, which he preached to a congregation of poor parishioners in Oxford in January 1826, when he had not yet reached his twenty-fifth birthday, anticipates many of the themes he was to develop later in his career. Although it still awaits a critical edition, we have included the text of this sermon (see Appendix A) in order to demonstrate how early in his career his thought on morality and education had begun to develop. This thought was to mature fully in the 'Tamworth Reading Room' letters of 1841, and in Discourse IX of *The Idea of a University* of 1852. The sermon shows a maturity and insight well beyond his years, and perfectly illustrates the holistic approach, which characterizes Newman's educational thought, wherein virtue, intellect and religion are treated as intrinsically united in every human being.

The following year Newman preached another sermon in which he showed that he was not afraid to engage in controversy and to oppose what he saw as the prevailing trend towards secularism in education. In this sermon, which we publish for the first time (see Appendix B), Newman warns against the danger posed by state involvement in what we would recognize today as faith schools. This danger he sees as the tendency to treat religious education in school as a 'bolt-on' extra rather than as the soul of the whole enterprise. He connects religion with rationality and opposes it to excitement and sentiment, themes he further develops in *The Idea of a University*. Many of the concepts contained in these two early sermons were used repeatedly by Newman throughout his life as we show in this book. They will be discussed in detail as they occur in connection with Newman's life and projects.

The structure of this book does not follow any division of material made by Newman himself. We have chosen to treat Newman's thought and practice thematically in six chapters according to our own categorization of his ideas.

Part One is an educational biography in which Newman's thought and practice may be more clearly appreciated in the context of his life and work. In addition to describing his own educational background we survey his writings, the controversies he engaged in together with both the difficulties he had to face and his achievements. It can be seen from this historical overview that although many of his projects either did not come to fruition, or did not survive him, the reason lies not with Newman himself. Newman was not a theorist as such, but rather a man of action, whose thought was integrally connected with his projects, and arose from his reflection upon them.

In Part Two, Chapter 2 explores the religious dimension of education in Newman's thought. It should be recognized that this does not mean 'religious education' as this term is commonly understood today, but rather the religious philosophy which underpins Newman's entire work and which was of enormous significance and originality. Newman's contribution to the philosophy of religion is to be found in his treatment of conscience and faith, and is still of profound importance. Chapter 3 focuses on the moral purpose in education. In Newman's practice this is integral to the religious aspect of education, but we treat it separately in order to show the role of conscience and its formation in the young. We also draw attention here to Newman's approach to character formation at various stages of a person's development.

Chapter 4 deals with the centrality of the idea of liberal education in Newman's thought and explores the way in which he put this into effect as a teacher at both school and university level. In contemporary debates about education, Newman is often referred to as one of the great exponents of liberal education, but he is also frequently misunderstood. Modern notions of education are predicated on the need for people who are trained in useful skills, in contrast with education for its own sake, which is often mistakenly identified with liberal education. For Newman, the purpose of liberal education was not so much to introduce the student to high culture, such as the study of great books, but rather to help him learn to think. Chapter 5 examines Newman's attitude to professional and vocational education. We show that Newman positively valued all forms of professional education. He was opposed to a simple training in skills which ignored personal and intellectual development. Newman developed vocational courses at his university in Dublin and prepared boys at his school in Edgbaston for mercantile trades and the professions. We also show that Newman did not subscribe to a false dichotomy between teaching and research. In fact he both pursued and promoted research at Dublin. Part Three explores the relevance of Newman to contemporary education, particularly to questions of religious education, teaching and learning.

Part 1

Intellectual Biography

Chapter 1

Newman: Educational Biography

Introduction: Historical Background

John Henry Newman (1801–1890) was one of the most important churchmen of the nineteenth century. In his own lifetime he was recognized as a powerful religious leader and theologian, known both as a man of action and an original thinker. As a clergyman he was involved for most of his life in various forms of pastoral work and in a variety of educational projects. Gifted with a highly original mind, he made significant contributions to many areas of philosophical, theological and educational debate. Not only intelligent and extremely well read, he possessed an intense self-awareness and power of reflection on his own experiences. This influenced him in terms of both his practice and theoretical perspectives, in particular shaping his thought and actions as an educationalist. Most of his written works arose from, or were influenced by, his projects as a priest and educator. Newman continues to have a profound influence on subsequent generations. Today, for instance, we can find numerous tributes to Newman and his educational ideals by scholars from all over the world. His reputation as an educator is such that many institutes of higher education, schools and university chaplaincies are named after him.

Newman spent the first half of his life as an Anglican, principally as a don and clergyman in Oxford, where on account of his preaching and writing he had great influence as one of the founders of the Tractarian Movement in the 1830s, of which he was arguably the greatest exponent and apologist. The Tractarians were so named after the *Tracts for the Times* which they wrote, printed and distributed to many of the clergy not only in Oxford but around the country, in order to revive a sense of what they claimed to be the original catholicity of the Church of England, obscured by Protestantism and the Enlightenment. Newman's own interpretation of Anglicanism in the Tracts was not only to be the source of increasing conflict within the Church of England, but also within his own soul and mind. After much prayer, reading and reflection, Newman was received into the Catholic Church in 1845 and left both Anglicanism and Oxford for good. Newman was to remain a controversial figure after becoming a Roman Catholic, both in English society and in the Catholic Church.

Together with several companions who also converted to Catholicism at this time, Newman studied briefly in Rome before his ordination as a Catholic priest. Returning to England in 1847, he set up the first English Congregation of the Oratory, a community of secular priests modelled on that founded by St Philip Neri in Rome in the sixteenth century. Together with his fellow Oratorians, Newman undertook a great variety of pastoral works in Birmingham and the surrounding districts, including the establishing and running of several schools. His own most important contributions to education as a Catholic priest were to be the Catholic University in Dublin which he founded and ran throughout the 1850s, and the school he founded at Edgbaston in 1859 for the sons of his fellow-converts from Anglicanism.

Newman was a prolific writer whose complete list of works is too long to recount in full here. During his Oxford years the most important of his published works include *Arians of the Fourth Century* (1833) in which he first explored the continuity between ancient and modern forms of Christian faith; the *Lectures on Justification* (1838) in which he brilliantly expounded scripture and theology in order to try and resolve a major *casus belli* of the Reformation era. Between 1833 and 1842 he also published eight volumes of *Parochial and Plain Sermons,* and one volume of *University Sermons* exploring the relationship between faith and reason. His *Essay on the Development of Christian Doctrine* (1845) was the work he produced out of the research which finally brought him to conversion from the Anglican to the Roman Catholic Church. From 1833 to 1841 he not only edited but also wrote the greater part of the series of *Tracts for the Times* (1833–1841).

As a Catholic he continued to write, producing *Lectures on Certain Difficulties felt by Anglicans in submitting to the Catholic Church* (1850);

Lectures on the Present Position of Catholics in England (1851) addressed principally to his Oratorian lay confraternity in Birmingham; *Discourses on the Scope and Nature of University Education* (1852) which, together with other lectures delivered in Dublin, was published as *The Idea of a University* (1859); *On Consulting the Faithful in Matters of Doctrine* (1859) in which he showed how the laity in the Church have a vital role in transmitting the faith; his autobiographical masterpiece, the *Apologia pro Vita Sua* (1864) which he wrote in self-defence against the charge of dishonesty levelled against him by Charles Kingsley; the *Grammar of Assent* (1870), his most important philosophical work in which he explored and defended the nature and grounds of religious faith, and besides these major works two novels and countless other lectures, discourses, sermons and articles. He is also remembered as one of the great Victorian letter writers. His edited *Letters and Diaries*, which contain much important material relating to the development of his opinions and activities, occupy no less than thirty-two volumes.

Newman's thought can be difficult for a modern reader to interpret. In the first place, his was an age in which religious faith and language could still be taken more or less for granted in debate. In his educational discourses he makes assumptions in both his premises and his conclusions which frequently differ from those of our own time. Newman was unusual as a Catholic thinker in not following a Thomist approach in his writing. Although he had studied Aristotelian logic at Oxford, his religious thinking was influenced more by the method and content of the ancient Church Fathers and by his own intuitive and literary style of analysing and developing arguments. Newman is also recognized as one of the greatest prose writers in English of the nineteenth century. Biographer Ian Ker, even refers to his style of writing in the *Idea of a University* as 'Victorian hyperbole' and says that it would have been read by his contemporaries as a kind of 'approximation to the truth'.[1] Yet Newman actually took great pains to try and express his meaning accurately, frequently writing 'chapters over and over again, besides innumerable corrections and interlinear additions' in order to achieve 'what is so difficult – viz. to express clearly and exactly my meaning'.[2] Of all his writings, it was the *Idea* that cost him the greatest effort in this regard. He continued to adjust and revise it until the year before he died.

In addition to being charged with untruthfulness, Newman was accused of regretting his conversion to Catholicism, of being a sceptic, of being hyper-sensitive, and of being a social elitist in education. Newman vigorously defended himself against all such attacks and his creation as cardinal by the newly elected Pope Leo XIII in 1879 is the mark of his ultimate success in establishing his orthodoxy. By that time Newman had spent most of his life as a priest involved in educational projects, both as teacher and administrator at school and university level. Because of their originality and subtlety his writings have sometimes been misinterpreted posthumously as inclining towards modernism in the Roman Catholic Church. It is therefore appropriate that we begin with a critical review of the kind of education and training that shaped Newman and an account of his educational thought and projects before we proceed to an appreciation of his educational philosophy.

Early Life and Education

John Henry Newman was born in London on 21 February 1801, the eldest of six children. His father, also called John, was a man of modest background who had become relatively wealthy as a banker. His mother, Jemima (née Fourdrinier), was of French Huguenot descent and deeply pious. It was from her that young John imbibed a thorough knowledge and love of scripture as the basis of religious life and faith.

When he was seven years old, Newman was sent to Great Ealing School, which was 'conducted on the Eton lines'.[3] There were two to three hundred boys at the school, and Newman's schoolmaster, the Revd George Nicholas, recognized that he was unusually bright. He was to say that 'no boy had run through the school, from the bottom to the top, as rapidly as John Newman'.[4] Newman himself writes autobiographically in *The Idea of a University*, disguising himself as the character Mr Black, 'At school I was reckoned a sharp boy; I ran through its classes rapidly.'[5] Nor should this be taken as indicating that Newman was simply a bright boy at a small school, because it was noted that many of the boys at the school 'got on'.[6] It included two lord chancellors among its past pupils, as well as Thackeray and W. S. Gilbert. Among Newman's own contemporaries was Philip Westmacott the sculptor, who was to remain a lifelong friend.

Although initially somewhat shy, Newman emerged as a leader among his peers. He founded a club and a satirical magazine, *Spy*, most of which he wrote himself. He even wrote a counter-blast to *Spy*, *Anti-Spy*.[7] Newman had an engaging and intriguing personality, and these characteristics were to play an important part in the development of his future work as an educator. It was during his school days that Newman began to keep a diary which he was to continue throughout his life, and to supplement in later years by his collected *Autobiographical Writings*. Clearly a studious and methodical boy, whom one of his sisters was to describe as 'very philosophical . . . always full of thought, and never at a loss for an answer',[8] he even kept much material from his school and university days which is still preserved in Birmingham.

What kind of education Newman received at Dr Nicholas's school can be ascertained from his own notebooks.[9] From 1810 he began to study Latin and Greek grammar and literature, and verse and prose composition. Style in writing was to become an important aspect of Newman's pedagogy. He was not interested in elegance for elegance's sake, but in clarity of expression and the mark of personality which good Latin style embodied. Newman also took up the violin in 1811, at which he was to become very proficient, and which was to remain a life-long pleasure. Music features in Newman's own reflections about the nature of thought.[10] French he had at least begun by 1814, possibly earlier. He learned mathematics from five of the books of Euclid, and was to become extremely proficient in arithmetic and geometry.[11] Although Newman did not study history, geography, biology, chemistry or physics, it should be noted that there was nothing unusual about the method or content of this curriculum at the time, or for many years before or after. Indeed, it seems that Dr Nicholas was able to attract a number of highly capable and interesting members of teaching staff to his school.[12]

Extracurricular activities also featured in Ealing school life, especially in the form of a Latin play twice yearly on three consecutive evenings known as 'Grand Nights'. On the third day it was also customary for the boys to deliver speeches for which prizes, chosen by the boys themselves, were awarded. Not surprisingly, Newman excelled in every way. He played leading roles in several plays, and many years later was to include Latin plays edited by himself in the activities of his own school at Edgbaston.[13] As prizes for proficiency at speechmaking, Newman chose Lamb's *Tales from Shakespeare*, Milton's poems, Cowper's translation of Homer, and *Travels in Upper and Lower Egypt* by Vivant Denon, which indicates the range of his interests at this age.

In addition to all this organized study and play Newman was highly self-motivated. In his spare time he read much eighteenth-century poetry and essays and imitated their style in his own 'poems, satires, burlesque operas, romantic dramas, and vast cabalistic periodicals such as *Spy* and *Anti-Spy*, the *Portfolio* and *Beholder*, which combined the style of Addison with the materials of Mrs Radcliffe'.[14] Newman himself says that he 'had some idea of the style of Addison, Hume and Johnson'.[15] At this time he also began a lifelong love of Walter Scott, reading his novels 'in bed in the early summer mornings when they first came out'.[16]

Oxford – The Undergraduate

By the time he was fifteen, Newman said that 'my masters had nothing more to teach me, and did not know what to do with me'.[17] Despite his youth, Newman was considered sufficiently well-prepared and able to continue his education at a university. This was a new departure for a member of his family, and since John Newman senior had not been to university himself he was unsure whether to send young John up to Oxford or Cambridge. It was only when he was actually about to take Newman to the coach that he happened to consult a clergyman of his acquaintance, the Revd John Mullens who was a graduate of Exeter College, Oxford. He warmly recommended that John Newman should send his son there. But when they reached Oxford, they found that Exeter had no room for young John, so they were directed across the road to Trinity College. This was a small college at the time, with about sixty undergraduates and, from an academic point of view, not among the most distinguished colleges. It was here that Newman was accepted to begin studies as soon as a place could be found for him.

The universities of Oxford and Cambridge were at that time not only exclusively Anglican, but also predominantly clerical foundations. They were also exclusively male preserves. Their clerical origin continued to influence their courses of studies and their daily way of life. Attendance at daily chapel services was not only expected, but was taken for granted in the same way as daily attendance at dinner in hall. Studies included not only classics and mathematics, but also theology, and subscription to the *Thirty-Nine Articles* of the Anglican Church was to remain a requirement for all students entering the university until 1854, after Newman had left Oxford.

By the time he went up to Oxford, Newman was not only unusually young but also more than conventionally religious, though he had not always been so. When he was fourteen or fifteen, he was to admit in his *Apologia pro Vita Sua* (*Apologia*), he read Paine, Hume and (possibly) Voltaire and 'found pleasure in thinking of the objections which were contained in them' against such Christian doctrines as miracles and the immortality of the soul.[18] He began to espouse the idea that he should like to be virtuous but not religious.[19] Just at that time he came under the influence of an evangelical clergyman of Calvinist views, named Walter Mayers, who was teaching him at Ealing. It happened that Newman's father's bank failed in March 1816, and Newman was obliged to remain at the school for the entire summer vacation while his family made arrangements to move from London to Hampshire. During this time he fell seriously ill, possibly in reaction to the shock of his family's changed circumstances.

As he was recovering, he and Mayers were thrown into each other's company for much of the time, and they discussed religious questions together on long walks. Between August and December Newman underwent a most profound religious conversion. Nevertheless, despite Mayers's influence upon him, Newman was even then convinced that his experience did not follow the usual evangelical pattern of conversions, which were typically reckoned to be almost instantaneous and violent in their force. Newman's experience was quite unlike anything he had read about. But such was his self-awareness and assurance that he had no hesitation in recognizing that it truly was a conversion and that, as he was to say many years later, 'I should say that it is difficult to realize or imagine the identity of the boy before and after August 1816'.[20] So by the time he arrived in Oxford, Newman had experienced both intellectual scepticism and an unusual, though profound, religious conversion.

As he waited to go up to Oxford, Newman studied as much as his poor eyesight would allow. In his *Record of Studies* he describes his daily routine, from which we can judge that he was already very methodical and diligent, reading on average for five hours a day. When Newman finally entered Trinity College on 16 June 1817, the undergraduates were just then going down for the summer vacation. He had been summoned at such an unusual time of year when a room became unexpectedly vacant. He was virtually alone in Trinity and tried to acclimatize himself to his new surroundings. When he had technically fulfilled the requirements for a university term after three weeks' residence he was allowed to go down for the 'long vacation'. Before leaving Oxford, however, he was determined to find guidance for his summer reading. But it was no easy thing to find such guidance at the beginning of the long vacation. Eventually he came across a college tutor who happened already to be leaving the city on horseback. The serious young Newman surprised him by running up and stopping him in the street. Nevertheless, as Newman himself recounts, it was with great kindness that this tutor directed Newman to another colleague.

Newman's *Record of Studies* for that long vacation tells us that he read extensively in Latin and Greek literature and from the Greek Old Testament. He also experimented translating passages of Cicero into English and then back into Latin which he compared with the original. Many years later Newman explained that 'I had no idea what was meant by good Latin style. I had read Cicero without learning what it was; the books said, "this is neat Ciceronian language", "this is pure and elegant Latinity", but they did not tell me why'.[21] Newman absorbed the principles of Ciceronian style after he studied Provost Copleston's Latin addresses to the University of Oxford.

When Newman arrived in Oxford in October 1817 he found that the majority of his fellow undergraduates were very different from himself. Not only were they older than he was, but they preferred dissipation to scholarship. Yet despite his disapproval of their behaviour his contemporaries did not seem to regard him as they might have regarded a more priggish young man. Indeed, there is evidence that he was held in some respect on account of his courage and consistency. Newman was fortunate in his tutor, Thomas Short. Although not noted as a scholar, Short was a good teacher and a conscientious tutor, and as a newcomer to the role he was considered more of a disciplinarian than his predecessor. Newman also found a like-minded fellow undergraduate, John Bowden, who was 'pretty assiduous'[22] and under Mr Short's tutorial guidance the two boys 'fagged' to get ahead of their contemporaries in Euclid, algebra and classics. Hard work was to become a characteristic of Newman's time in Trinity, and indeed of his whole life.

Towards the end of his first full year at Trinity in May 1818, Newman had mastered his classical and mathematical studies so thoroughly that Short urged him to enter the examination for a scholarship. The examination was open to students from the whole university and was very exacting in both classics and mathematics. Despite being the youngest competitor Newman won.

The scholarship was to prove the high-water mark of success in his three years as an undergraduate. Without any doubt he soon afterwards found the responsions, the end of year university examinations, quite undemanding by comparison with the scholarship examination. He himself said that for the long vacation of 1818 and the two following terms '[I] relaxed in my reading for schools, and amused myself with general literature.'[23] He also began to go to concerts and together with Bowden he launched and co-wrote six numbers of a periodical entitled *The Undergraduate*. He even advocated the setting up of a Debating Society which should cover 'the whole range of history, poetry and the fine arts, indeed nothing should be excluded but the politics of the last fifty [altered to 100] years'. Such a society 'would be a school for the future senator or lawyer, it would enlarge and refine the mind, it would be a most agreeable relaxation after the toils of the day'.[24] Since he had entered at Lincoln's Inn in 1820 according to his father's wishes, Newman probably saw himself at this time in the guise of the 'future senator or lawyer' who would sharpen his adversarial skills in such a debating club.[25] Although he was not in the end to follow either of those callings, Newman did later elaborate the principle that enlarging and refining the mind by such means is the true aim and end of a liberal education in *The Idea of a University*.[26]

From spring of 1819 until December 1820, when he took his degree, he renewed his application to hard work with even greater zeal and determination, doubtless intending to make up for time lost in the preceding year. He had to redouble his efforts on account of the decision he took to attempt honours in both classics and mathematics, rather than in only one of them. By the time he had joined Bowden in Oxford once more in October 1819, they were reading eleven or twelve hours daily. They worked together in a way which helped them to achieve much that would have been impossible to them separately. They kept up a variety of subjects constantly, going over them repeatedly to ensure that the material remained in their heads. They devised their own oral and written exercises to complement their reading, including viva voce examinations.

Yet doubts about his readiness began to creep into Newman's mind. He was aware that he had become 'puffed up' with pride on account of winning the scholarship. He also noted that he had lost mental sharpness and clarity, observing that his mind was now 'a labyrinth more than anything else'.[27] By the time he was summoned for his viva voce examination, therefore, Newman no longer expected to get a first in classics, though he was still confident in mathematics. Yet in the Schools he unexpectedly found himself so nervous that he could not think and was unable to answer any questions. Although the examiners were very patient and encouraging, it was to no avail. He came 'below the line' in classics altogether, which is to say that he failed, while in mathematics he did not gain the honours he and everyone else expected.

It is possible to ascribe Newman's failure simply to nervous exhaustion. Doubtless that played a big part at the time. But that would not be a sufficient explanation of this event, nor did Newman himself think so. Apart from believing that he was being punished for being too proud, he also seems to have recognized that he had made the mistake of overfilling his head with facts and insufficiently understanding what he had absorbed. The relation of mind to memory was wrong. The lesson he learned from this was to become a major element of his own educational methodology, whereby he would help others to avoid the mistakes that he had made in his youthful enthusiasm. Newman, writing later, believed that Trinity provided little tutorial assistance or guidance and that he had found himself left almost entirely to his own devices – 'I spent four years with no fruit', only beginning his true education at twenty-one.[28]

That Newman had just about scraped a pass was considered a disaster not only by himself, but also by his college and tutor, who had all expected great things from him. A good degree following on his scholarship would certainly have guaranteed Newman a fellowship. At that time most Oxford and Cambridge colleges appointed their own graduates as fellows, to continue studies until such time as they might resign their fellowship to get married and seek a living as a parish clergyman. During their time as fellows they would take on the care and direction of undergraduate students, assisting them in their own studies, and engaging in scholarly work more or less as they felt inclined. It was a comfortable, and on the whole not too demanding, way of life. Given his academic abilities and turn of character, it is therefore not surprising that Newman should have decided to try for a fellowship. What was surprising, indeed audacious under the circumstances of his less than brilliant degree, was that he decided in 1822 to try for a fellowship not at his own college, but at Oriel.

Oxford – The Oriel Fellow and Pastoral Clergyman

Oriel College at the beginning of the 1820s had the reputation of being the home of Oxford's most formidable minds. The Fellows of Oriel College in particular had sought to raise the intellectual level of their own society by offering fellowships not merely to the graduates of their own college, but to all comers, solely on the basis of proven intellectual ability, even if, as in Newman's own case, their previous examination results might suggest otherwise. Not only did they lead a reform of the intellectual life of the entire university, but they also felt able to take on the challenge of defending their own tradition and method to the world beyond Oxford. Newman's tutor at Trinity, Thomas Short, encouraged him to try for an Oriel fellowship in order to show his true capabilities, and to recover for Trinity some of the prestige lost by his poor showing in the schools. Newman was naturally a diffident person, yet also aware that he had unusual intellectual gifts, so it was with some trepidation that he nonetheless allowed his name to go forward.

The examination was very searching, and he felt despondent about his performance, feeling so ill that he was unable to complete or correct some of his papers. Newman therefore resigned himself yet again to failure. Yet unknown to him, his examination papers were creating a sensation among the Oriel Fellows. They were not necessarily looking for the conventional signs of academic ability, such as were shown in the examination results, but for evidence of intellectual powers. The provost of Oriel, Edward Copleston, commented that Newman 'was not even a good classical scholar, yet in mind and powers of composition, and in taste and knowledge, he was decidedly superior to some competitors, who were a class above him in the Schools'.[29] Newman was clearly first choice, even though many in Oxford had not expected him to win what was seen to be one of the most demanding and prestigious prizes in the whole university. Copleston positively considered it an 'important triumph' when an election to one of his college's fellowships 'discouraged the narrow and almost technical routine of the public examinations' and saw Newman's election as the best example of his contempt for what he called the 'quackery of the Schools'.[30] Copleston's attitude to 'technical routine' had also characterized his defence of the Oxford system against certain attacks launched upon it in the *Edinburgh Review* some twenty years earlier.[31]

On 12 April 1822, a date he was to commemorate gratefully every year of his long life, Newman was playing his violin at his lodgings when an Oriel College servant came to announce in ironic mode the 'disagreeable news' of Newman's election to the Oriel fellowship, and request that he present himself at the college immediately. Thinking this an odd, not to say impertinent, way of communicating such information, Newman answered the servant casually and simply carried on playing. But as soon as the servant had left him, he put down his violin and immediately ran to Oriel, finding Copleston, Hawkins, Keble and the entire fellowship assembled there to meet him. He was to remain one of their number for the next twenty years.

Because Copleston had favoured him over men with better degrees, Newman was rather an unknown quantity and the Oriel Fellows were taking something of a risk in electing him. By his own account Newman was at first extremely shy and gauche in his manner. The Fellows may have begun to wonder if they had made a mistake, but because they did not wish to appear to have blundered in electing him, they determined to work on Newman to 'bring him out'. The man they called upon to undertake this project was Richard Whately. Although he had until recently been a Fellow, Whately had just moved out of the college in order to marry, but was still to be in Oxford for a few more months. Whately's enduring contribution to Newman's development was not only social but intellectual, as he was widely recognized at the time as a specialist in Aristotelian logic. He took Newman out walking and riding, and talked constantly. 'Thus he was the first person who opened my mind, that is, who gave it ideas and principles to cogitate upon.'[32] Whately was in the process of writing his *Elements of Logic* which was to become a standard text on the subject for many years to come, and he liked sounding his ideas out on those around him. He was to say of Newman that he was 'the clearest-headed man he knew' and entrusted to him the task of working on some portions of an article on logic that he had been commissioned to write for the *Encyclopedia Metropolitana*. Such was the effect that Whately had on Newman that he in turn considered dedicating his own first book to Whately "'who, by teaching me to think has taught me to differ from him", or "to think for myself"'.[33]

Meanwhile, Newman began a lifelong involvement in pastoral work. Although it was customary for Oxford dons to take Holy Orders, it was not necessarily seen by many of them as leading to a deeper engagement with ordinary people's pastoral and spiritual affairs. In Newman's case not only did he actively seek to become a parochial clergyman, but did so at the earliest possible opportunity, and in a setting which would bring him hard work for little financial return. In May 1824, a month before he had even been ordained a deacon, he became curate of the very poor and populous parish of St Clement's, situated just beyond Magdalen Bridge. He visited his parishioners assiduously, which was considered unusually zealous for a clergyman in his day. This intense work of visiting and preaching was to affect him in many ways. He realized very quickly that it was out of ignorance that so few people came to church, rather than because they had rejected religion. Therefore he sought to counter this ignorance by setting up his first Sunday school for the children of the parish. Having nowhere to meet, he persuaded friends to contribute to a fund so that he could build a gallery in the church. His friend Edward Pusey contributed a stove.[34] Newman clearly understood that a minimum level of comfort was both conducive to good learning, and necessary to encourage attendance. The overall effect of his work in the parish was that attendance at Holy Communion was vastly higher by the following Christmas.

Although Newman was still under the influence of Calvinist theology, he now began to realize that the standard Calvinist account of conversion and grace just did not fit the way these people lived. He had previously held the Calvinist principle that men were either saved or damned, and were accordingly either simply good or evil in their moral lives. He now saw that reality was far more complex. Moreover, as well as finding his views challenged by working among the people of St Clement's parish, Newman at this time also came under the influence of another older Oriel Fellow and practising clergyman, Edward Hawkins, vicar of St Mary's, the university church. Throughout the long vacation of 1824, Newman and Hawkins were often virtually alone in the hall and common room at Oriel as they went about their duties in their respective parishes.

Hawkins helpfully criticized Newman's first sermon, in which Newman had followed the usual Calvinist line of dividing Christians into two classes, 'the one all darkness, the other all light'.[35] Just as Newman was beginning to find from his own experience, so now Hawkins demonstrated by clear argument and by illustration from scripture that people were not simply either saints or sinners, but that they had elements of both in them, and that it was in reality impossible to draw a neat line between two such classes. It was Hawkins who first taught Newman 'to weigh my words and be cautious in my statements. He led me to that mode of limiting and clearing my sense in discussion and in controversy, and of distinguishing between cognate ideas, and of obviating mistakes by anticipation.'[36] Clearly, Hawkins's influence on Newman's religious ideas was just as crucial to his

educational and intellectual development. Nor should this seem para-
doxical, since Newman himself always appreciated the importance of
intellectual clarity in analysing and discussing religious questions,
within the context of faith in God's revealed truth.

Two of Newman's sermons preached in these early years, still
unpublished (2006), give remarkable evidence both of Newman's
commitment to education at this early stage in his career, and of
the consistency of his educational principles throughout his life. He
preached the first of these, 'On some popular mistakes as to the object
of education', at St Clement's in 1826. To educate, he says here, is
'to work together with God in the salvation of souls'.[37] He anticipates
the 'Tamworth Reading Room' letters when he condemns the proposition 'that in proportion as men *know* more, they will be *better* men
in a moral point of view', for it is one thing to know the truth, and
altogether a different thing to love it. He also warns against the notion
that 'the end of education is merely to fit persons for their respective
stations in life', for 'thus education is robbed of its religious character
and made the mere instrument of worldly ambition'. He reminds his
audience that, as parents, they have a grave responsibility for their
children's education which they must not delegate to schools, but
should rather form in them good habits of 'conscientiousness, diligence, truth and humility' because 'we are tutoring them for ... the
enjoyment of a divine citizenship'.

In the second of these sermons '*on general education as connected with
the Church and religion*',[38] Newman expounds his great principle that
the 'end of education is ... to *affect the heart*', and therefore speaks
of the need to 'take children separately' and to 'address ourselves to
them almost one by one'. He shrewdly observes the ambivalence of
human knowledge in that 'the very best [means] for advancing us in
holiness, *might* prove the very best for advancing us in sin – that every
thing depended on the state of mind worked upon'. He warns against
the error 'of being very eager to bring children forward *rapidly*', and
of being 'too eager to make every subject learned by children *easy
and amusing* ... for to live well in the world is nothing else than
the doing or suffering hard things'. He also speaks of the Church's
special responsibility in education in saying that 'to baptize and not
to educate is a grievous sin', and that although the clergy ought

therefore to be closely involved in educational work, nevertheless they 'are not to be considered as controlling education in their own right; but as representatives and instruments of the general body of Christians'. It is no exaggeration to say that in these two early sermons are contained the seeds of virtually all the major themes of Newman's lifelong educational project.

In March 1825, Whately returned to Oxford as principal of St Alban's Hall, a somewhat decayed institution which welcomed students who could not reach the academic level required for entry into the other colleges. Whately invited Newman to be his vice-principal. As Newman had begun to think that it was more his duty 'to engage in College offices than in parochial duties'[39] , he accepted, without either losing his fellowship at Oriel or resigning his curacy. Since St Alban was a small hall, with only about a dozen students, Newman effectively became tutor to these students as well. Such was the success he felt that he had in this new role that Newman decided to accept the offer of a tutorship in his own college after Easter 1826. In view of the greater workload that this office would bring him in Oriel he decided to resign both the vice-principalship of St Alban's Hall and the curacy of St Clement's. Just as his commitment to parochial work there had already been recorded as remarkable by his parish clerk, so too would his dedication to the tutorship. This was to prove one of the most important aspects of his development as an educational practitioner. The office of tutor was given to a few of the fellows in a college so that they might direct the education and formation of a certain number of undergraduates entrusted to them. But Newman believed that most tutors were not involving themselves adequately in the formation of those entrusted to their care. For Newman more than anyone else at that date, the tutorship represented not only an educational responsibility, but a moral one. He sought to make his students more devout, and this led him to question certain customs which in turn brought him into conflict with the authorities who had appointed him, especially Copleston.

It would be wrong to assume that Newman's attitude to his protégés was puritanical. He simply aimed to influence the character and behaviour of his students as much as their intellectual development. In this he was acting as a priest with pastoral as well as academic

responsibilities in his college. He was also being consistent with the
principle he had begun to espouse that a person's character and
behaviour help to shape his beliefs. In February 1825 he had written to his brother Charles, who had become an unbeliever, that the
rejection of Christianity arises 'not from mere error of reasoning,
but either from pride or from sensuality'.[40] Accordingly, Newman
was never going to be content with a tutorship that only oversaw a
student's academic development, as though that could proceed satis-
factorily without simultaneously caring for the same student's moral
welfare. Nor could he ever have accepted a minimalist interpretation
of his role of tutor as one who exercised only a superficial moral
authority. He would be neither indulgent towards dissipation, nor
sternly remote. In Newman's own words,

> he cultivated relations, not only of intimacy, but of friendship, and
> almost of equality, putting off, as much as might be, the martinet
> manner then in fashion with college tutors, and seeking their society
> in outdoor exercise, on evenings and in Vacation.[41]

In so doing, Newman eschewed authoritarianism, whilst retaining his
authority as tutor.

From the outset he encountered opposition from certain 'young
men of birth, wealth or prospects, whom he considered (of course
with real exceptions) to be the scandal and the ruin of the place'.[42]
He strove to bring about an end to the late night carousing and noisy
drunkenness that was so common among such young men. They in
their turn resented the interference with a way of life that had obviously been taken for granted for many years. As an undergraduate he
had been scandalized by the association of religious celebrations and
drunkenness, and now at Oriel he raised the issue with the provost,
Copleston. It was a rule of the college that students receive Holy
Communion once a term. Many of the students would immediately
go on to a champagne breakfast, which Newman held to be a profa-
nation of the sacrament. Copleston would have preferred the whole
matter to be ignored, but Newman was unwilling to allow such an
important matter to rest unresolved. Characteristically, Newman did
not seek directly to ban such champagne parties. Instead he queried

the rule that required young men to receive a sacrament when they were clearly unprepared for it spiritually. It was Newman's insistence on this that annoyed Copleston and some of the other Fellows, and was to herald his later conflict with the college authorities over his conduct of the tutorship.

But Newman had a few notable successes in his newly enhanced role as a tutor. The level of interest in his students' welfare and the care that he took for their moral, religious and intellectual development won him many devoted friends among them. Many of these remained close to him all their lives. Years later, when some of the former drunken young men attempted to paint the now venerable cardinal as a cowardly figure and the victim of some of their coarser japes, one of those disciples, the distinguished peer Frederic Rogers, Lord Blachford, refuted the falsehoods and spoke up in defence of Newman the tutor's directness, openness and consistency towards all his students. Indeed, when his old mentor Edward Hawkins was elected provost of Oriel in 1827, Newman, who had supported his candidacy, found him at first an ally in carrying through radical reforms in the college, especially in tutoring and teaching. Two years later, Newman was able to rejoice that the number of 'gentlemen commoners' had been vastly reduced. After all, it was from among their number that the opposition to Newman's disciplinary measures had largely come. Moreover, better-prepared candidates were being chosen for admission and examination; the old viva voce examinations were being made more searching by the introduction of paper work; and a Greek composition prize was established.

Most important of all, as far as Newman was concerned, was the reform of the lecture system. Prior to Lent 1829, the tutors had been responsible for college lectures to all the students who were divided between the tutors haphazardly, with no regard to their relationship. Newman thought that the tutors saw too little of the students assigned personally to them, and observed that they even went to great lengths to avoid any knowledge of private irregularities on their students' part.[43] It was this that Newman now sought to change.

The principle now introduced was that each Tutor should in the first place be responsible and consult for his own pupils, should determine what subjects they ought to have lectures in, and should have first choice as to taking those lectures themselves . . . Otherwise they considered the office of Tutor became that of a mere lecturer, and that teaching was not an act of personal intercourse, but an ungenial and donnish form.[44]

Newman consulted the senior tutor, Joseph Dornford, who considered the plan to be worth trying out, though suspecting that it must involve much more work for the tutors. Newman implemented his proposal with the support of two younger allies elected to fellowships at Oriel after himself, and now also appointed tutors: Hurrell Froude and Robert Wilberforce.

The experiment lasted only a term, partly because Newman had failed to consult Hawkins (the provost). For that and a variety of other reasons which were political as well as administrative, Hawkins was already beginning to turn from being Newman's friend and supporter, into his implacable opponent. On the matter of the tutorship, he had no sympathy with what he saw as favouritism towards the clever minority on Newman's part, at the expense of neglecting the less-gifted majority. Of course, the 'less-gifted majority' were almost entirely represented by the wealthy gentlemen commoners who were, in Newman's view, the cause of much scandal, and little interested in learning. Whereas previously all students had attended lectures indiscriminately, Newman was separating them out: 'The bad men are thrown into large classes – and thus time saved for the better sort who are put into very small lectures, and principally with their own Tutors quite familiarly and chattingly.'[45] Newman believed that as a pastoral and religious mentor the tutor had the authority to implement his own tutorial arrangements without the interference of the provost as head of college. Hawkins, on the other hand, was concerned that a tutor who thought of himself in this way might well be implanting unwelcome views in impressionable minds. A war of attrition ensued between the two men, which as provost, Hawkins won. Newman and his supporters were told that unless they reverted to the *status quo ante* they would effectively be starved of future students. Although this is what actually took place, and Newman's experiment was discontinued, it remained important as an indication of his unfolding educational methodology and aims, which he would later be able to implement in a totally different setting in Dublin.

In the end Newman was quite content to lose the tutorship in 1830. He now had more free time in which to study, and he had already established himself personally as a leader and teacher to many of the brightest students, who continued to come to him for tuition and guidance. He was also able to devote more attention to his pastoral work and preaching in St Mary's, the university church, whose vicar he had become the previous year. Over the next ten years he was to make his name within Oxford chiefly as a preacher there. But he was to become well known far beyond Oxford as a controversialist, the principal writer of the *Tracts for the Times* that gave the Tractarian reforming movement within the Church of England its name. The Tracts were the providential means by which Newman and his Oxford friends would revive what they believed to be the truly Catholic nature of the Church of England, driving a *via media* or 'middle way' between Protestantism on the one hand and the 'Romish errors' on the other. The Tractarian view of the Church of England was that it was apostolic and sacramental, and therefore formed a branch of the ancient Catholic Church.

In the meantime, Newman returned to educational controversy with the opening in January 1841 of a new Reading Room in Tamworth, by the town's Member of Parliament, Sir Robert Peel. In his address at the opening ceremony Peel referred not only to the general benefits of wider access to knowledge but to the increase in virtue and awareness of the 'manifest proofs of a Divine intelligence', and that through knowledge men might become 'better qualified to comprehend the great scheme of human redemption'.[46] Peel omitted reference to established religion because he thought it divisive.

Newman was persuaded by some of his friends to answer Peel. Throughout February, seven lengthy letters were to appear in *The Times* newspaper under the pseudonym 'Catholicus'.[47] They were effectively a single treatise criticizing Peel's attitude towards the relationship between knowledge, learning and morality. Newman identified two major problems with Peel's argument. In the first place Peel was taking up utilitarian attitudes to education which had been expressed twenty years previously by the Whig peer, Lord Brougham. Brougham's arguments that education should be useful rather than intellectual had encouraged the establishment of a new kind of further education institution, the University College of London, in which students were no longer to be trained in matters remote from everyday life, such as the classics, but principally in subjects which would fit them for useful contributions to society. Newman here resumed the defence of the Oxford system which his former provost, Copleston, had undertaken against the *Northern Review* some twenty years earlier. He argued in ways that anticipated many of the more developed arguments of the *Idea of a University* that education ought not to be confused with vocational training, however important that might be, but that education was specifically the training of the mind as an instrument of human nature. Just as the body enjoys the benefits of health as a good in its own right and for no further end than itself, so too the mind enjoyed being brought to full strength as a good in its own right, and not necessarily for any further end.

Newman was also concerned about Peel's view of human nature in which education led to knowledge, and knowledge led to virtue. In Newman's opinion, Peel's was not a view that could accommodate the reality of man's fallen moral condition, upon which knowledge itself could have no definitely positive control. Newman by no means accepted Peel's assumption that by reading, by having their minds filled with facts of all kinds, people would thereby simply become more virtuous, or more deeply aware of God and redemption. Newman profoundly disagreed with Peel's view that both faith and moral virtue somehow depended upon knowledge. Newman argued on the contrary that secular knowledge could be a tool of unbelief and that children would not be morally good simply because they were taught some facts or were introduced to the art of doubting.

Later in the same year, Newman became embroiled in controversy following the publication of his *Tract 90*, which was an attempt to reconcile the *Thirty-Nine Articles* of Anglicanism with the very principles of Catholic theology against which they had been devised in the sixteenth century. This argument predictably caused a storm of protest. The Protestant establishment who had long been dismayed at the apparently pro-Catholic tone of the Tracts now declared open war on their authors, especially Newman. Many of the Anglican bishops willingly condemned *Tract 90* in public, and even Newman's own bishop reluctantly did so under pressure. This was a bitter blow to

Newman personally and to his hopes of confirming the Catholic credentials of Anglicanism. He retired from active involvement in Oxford life in 1841 and for the next four years lived at the heart of a small community of clerical companions which he set up at Littlemore, an outpost of his parish of St Mary's. Here he had already built a church which now would be not only his place of quiet prayer and study, but also the means by which to immerse himself in parochial life.

He also became closely involved in the day-to-day running of the parish school. The schoolmistress seems to have been somewhat unreliable, and Newman felt it was his responsibility to make up for her shortcomings by taking on more of the teaching. In March 1840 he wrote to his former curate, Bloxam, that he had begun teaching the children to sing, accompanying them on his violin, 'their voices are so thrilling as to make one sick with love'.[48] In 1840 he was telling his sister Jemima Mozley that 'I have been reforming, or at least lecturing against, uncombed hair and dirty faces and hands'. Although he claimed that he was 'not deep in the philosophy of school-girl tidiness',[49] he was clearly taking his responsibilities as a teacher seriously. This led him to subscribe to the *English Journal of Education* which dealt, among other things, with the running of schools in poor parishes. From the journal it is clear that Newman read a range of articles on educational topics which had immediate relevance to his teaching at Littlemore. This concerned areas such as the teaching of music, discipline and feminine hygiene. Yet he also read more widely in the journal, notably about the history of university education. The evidence of these years disproves the allegation that Newman was socially exclusive in his approach to education and schooling. After several years of anguish, study, deep reflection and above all, prayer, this period came to an end with his reception into the Catholic Church in 1845.

Birmingham: The Founding of The Oratory and Early Educational Projects

After Newman's conversion to Catholicism he asked to be taken on as an ordinand for the Catholic priesthood. His new superior, Bishop

Wiseman, sent him with a friend, another convert from Littlemore called Ambrose St John, to the *Collegio de Propaganda Fide* in Rome where they would train together for the Catholic priesthood. Newman was ordained as a priest there on 30 May 1847 and less than a year later, with a small group of Oxford associates, he returned to England to found the English Oratory of St Philip Neri, by Papal Brief, at 'Maryvale', as he had by now renamed Old Oscott near Birmingham. He was to remain as superior of this community for the rest of his life.

Within a short time of his return Bishop Wiseman persuaded Newman to accept as fellow-Oratorians a small community under the leadership of Fr Wilfrid Faber. Unfortunately, there were strings attached to this offer, in that Faber had already given an undertaking to the Earl of Shrewsbury to staff a large house and church at Cotton in the remote North Staffordshire countryside. Against his will, and contrary to the urban character of the Oratory, Newman therefore found himself obliged to transfer his own community to Cotton where he planned a school to bring financial support and work to the newly combined Oratorians. Although Newman described this plan to Faber as a potential 'Eton of the Oratory', [50] this was more likely an attempt to win Faber's approval than an indication of Newman's own attitude. Shortly afterwards he wrote to his friend Maria Giberne that 'we want to form a little school of possible Oratorians there, but can't find the boys. Our married friends will not turn Catholic.'[51] Far from harbouring an ambitious and socially elitist plan, therefore, it seems that Newman was really thinking about a small school which would provide potential vocations for his Oratory.

Already there was an informal arrangement in operation whereby Newman and his companions had taken in and were teaching some boys, including his godson, George Ryder, and Charles, the son of his old Oxford friend John Bowden. These provided a much-needed income.[52] Since he could not find enough boys to make a proper school, Newman turned to another plan for a college 'for Catholic lay students, when they have completed the ordinary school course, which should be to them what Oxford and Cambridge are to Protestant boys from Eton and Harrow'. This college was described in a prospectus as having a staff of nine Oxford and Cambridge graduates, all but one of whom were Oratorian priests, prepared to teach ancient classical and modern languages, as well as mathematics and general literature.[53] By the time the scheme was advertised, however, it was already doomed to failure as the Oratorians had been divided once again into two communities and had left Cotton.

At the request of the new bishop, William Bernard Ullathorne, Newman now took charge of Alcester Street, a populous mission in central Birmingham, where he and his companions immersed themselves in various pastoral projects. His interest in, and care for the education of the poor had in no way diminished after the radical change brought about in his circumstances by his conversion to the Catholic Church. The people were very poor, hardly of the 'higher class' that the Pope's Brief had specified as their proper sphere of operations. Yet Newman had no hesitation about committing himself to working among them. Uneducated though they were, the parishioners were grateful to Newman for all that he and his fellow Oratorians could give them. On Sunday evenings a congregation of six hundred would try and squeeze into the small church, a converted distillery. Many of them were obliged to kneel outside on the pavement to receive the blessing.[54] Although there was already a mission school here run by a nun, Newman personally taught catechism to a hundred children who turned up in the evening because they were all out at work in the day, and so could not get a normal schooling. He also ran a Sunday school. Twice a week lectures were given to the adults, again in the evening, since that was the only free time people had.

It was while living here that Newman composed his *Lectures on the Present Position of Catholics*. He delivered these to an audience of Catholic adults as the beginning of a programme of adult education in which he envisaged that his work as an Oratorian would largely consist. These lectures show Newman to great advantage as a satirist, wittily lampooning the anti-Catholic bigotry of the day. Yet they were also to get him into his first serious scrape as a Catholic, when he was sued for libel by Giacinto Achilli, a defrocked Catholic priest whose lies and immorality he exposed in the fifth lecture of the series.

Although Newman took on the care of the Alcester Street Mission willingly and carried it out with his characteristic energy and thoroughness, his calling was to be more than just a parish priest, even if it should include working among the poor. The Pope had conferred with him about his future work in Birmingham and Newman not only felt that he should remain faithful to the Pope's decision to settle him in Birmingham, but should look to educate the 'higher class' among the people of the town. Although Newman was happy to live and work there for a time, Alcester Street did not provide many such people as that. He fretted that he was not doing 'any thing with the thinking classes; and as life is so short, this is somewhat painful to me'.[55] This was the motivation behind the decision to find a permanent home for the Oratory elsewhere in Birmingham, where a greater variety of work and of people could be found to serve. Newman and his community therefore finally moved into a permanent new home in Edgbaston in 1851.

But Newman's own part in the early stages of development at Edgbaston was to be interrupted. In 1851, even as he was delivering the *Lectures on the Present Position of Catholics*, Newman was invited by Archbishop Cullen of Dublin to become the rector of a proposed new Catholic university in Dublin. Despite his commitments and the worries about the forthcoming Achilli trial Newman accepted on condition that he would not be asked to live permanently in Dublin, and so have to leave the Birmingham Oratory.

The move to Edgbaston and the decision to accept the rectorship of the university in Dublin may at first suggest that Newman had abandoned his earlier care for the poor. This appearance is misleading. Newman was the superior of a community of priests who took much of the practical work upon themselves. But because Newman was away for much of this period, the intense involvement of the Birmingham Oratorians in the work of running mission schools for the poor can escape the attention of his biographers.

For instance, Newman's commitment to this aspect of his pastorate can be seen from his correspondence during the Dublin years with his deputy in Birmingham, Edward Caswall.[56] Newman encouraged the community to set up mission schools for the poor in Edgbaston and Smethwick. Accordingly, Caswall reported to Newman in 1855 that the mission school which the Oratorian Nicholas Darnell had set up next to the Oratory was to be officially incorporated into the Oratory as its own elementary school. With Newman's approval, the Oratorian Fathers paid out £200 to put the school on a firm financial footing. There was within this one school an infants' department, a boys' school and a girls' school, together with an evening school for adults run by Edward Caswall, before yet a further school was established in Smethwick in 1861. Nancy de Flon says that 'Newman must be credited with allowing and empowering the Oratory Fathers and Brothers to organize an extensive apostolate to the Catholics of Birmingham and the outlying areas for some miles to the West – indeed, to the needy as well as to the well-off'.[57]

Dublin: Newman as University Rector

The university which Newman was now about to create was a highly ambitious project and was to be a Catholic alternative to Dublin's Anglican Trinity College and the non-denominational Queen's Colleges being set up throughout Ireland by Sir Robert Peel's government. In 1852 Newman began a series of lectures and discourses in which he spelt out his educational philosophy for the new university. These nine lectures and discourses were published as *Discourses on the Scope and Nature of University Education Addressed to the Catholics of Dublin*, and in 1858 a second volume containing ten lectures appeared entitled *Lectures and Essays on University Subjects*. It was not until 1873 that Newman brought both volumes together as *The Idea of a University Defined and Illustrated*. As he did with many of his earlier works, Newman continued to re-edit and revise the *Idea* right up until the ninth edition in 1889, the year before his death.

There were initially three pressures that Newman had to keep in balance and consider in setting up the university. These were also to affect his writing of the *Idea*. First, the Vatican urged the establishment of a Catholic university in Dublin for the English speaking world to be modelled on the highly successful Catholic University of Louvain in Belgium. The Vatican was preoccupied at the time with one central idea: the denial by secularists that there is any connection between religion and other academic subjects. In 1854, two years after Newman had written the first discourses, a Brief was issued by the Vatican that included a set of objectives to establish the university. These included: religion to be accepted as the soul of education and all studies to be approached in the light of Catholic principles. Newman accepted these objectives in the Brief, and incorporated them in his subsequent revisions.[58] Whereas the original idea for a university had been interpreted by the Irish bishops as a university for the Irish Catholics, Newman conceived of it from the start as an international university under the presiding power of the Catholic Church. He also went to great lengths in the *Idea* to argue that theology was an essential branch of knowledge. He wrote that one of the objects of the university was 'providing philosophical defences of Catholicity and Revelation, of creating a Catholic Literature . . . of giving a Catholic tone to society . . .'[59]

Secondly, Archbishop Cullen of Dublin wrote to Newman in 1851 describing his expectations for the new university 'What we want in Ireland is to persuade people that education should be religious.'[60] Some of the bishops in Ireland clearly wanted a kind of lay seminary to protect young Irishmen from losing their faith, while others argued that the 'non-denominational' Queen's Colleges should be sufficient, even for Catholics. Cullen and his supporters wanted absolute control over the university. Newman's idea of a university was that it could not be a seminary nor necessarily controlled by Catholic bishops, although he eventually accepted that it would be in the case of Ireland. While Newman struggled with the Irish bishops to retain some control over the university he was able to appoint many laymen to chairs when the tradition in Oxford had been to appoint only clergymen.

Thirdly, Newman was conscious that the Irish laity desired and expected the new university to offer them the opportunity for social advancement through the provision of professional education. Some young Irishmen were pragmatic, and as they harboured a utilitarian conception of the function of a university, they demanded an education that had some 'useful' value. Others were suspicious of the new Catholic university and preferred, if they could, to attend Trinity College instead. Newman responded to this growing intellectual and educational movement of utilitarianism by outlining his classic theory of liberal education. He did not simply argue that liberal knowledge was superior to professional knowledge, but posited a fundamental tension between professional education and liberal education. He was clear in his own mind from the start that he was 'making provision for both the liberal and professional education of the various classes of the community'.[61] Nevertheless, in the *Idea* Newman is clear that the university must not subordinate liberal education to short-term, practical, economic or political considerations.

Newman's Vision of University Education

It is often argued that Newman's vision for the new Catholic university is summed up in his statement that Oxford might be 'imported into Ireland, not in its members only, but in its principles, methods, ways and arguments'.[62] Newman at first sight appears contradictory here since he also said that his vision of the university followed 'the pattern of the University of Louvain'.[63] He was nevertheless careful to distinguish what he did in Dublin from his own English formation and this care resulted in some development and changes to his ideas about the Oxford system of education. Newman used the model of Louvain as a corrective to the Oxford tradition as he combined the advantages of both systems. In particular, Newman appointed many lay professors in Dublin after the model of Louvain, not Oxford. He also sought to entrust the curriculum to the rector and professors, rather than to the heads of colleges, as at Oxford. In any case Oxford was not a stable model for a new foundation in Ireland as it was undergoing changes to its curriculum, governance and teaching during Newman's time there.

The idea of a university education was defined by Newman as 'an essential end' or object. In writing the *Idea* Newman made clear that he was 'investigating in the abstract' and that he was advocating a 'certain great principle'.[64] What he meant was that he was concerned with an abstract idea of a university often different from its real institutional and historical embodiment at any given time. He outlined an ideal of a university as principally a teaching institution guided by the principle of liberal education. In practice the form of a particular university would depend on how these ideals were applied in concrete circumstances. He declares that the object of the university is to teach all knowledge and that such knowledge is 'its own end'. It is not to be reduced to a means of acquiring professional skills, or to moral or religious improvement. Knowledge and understanding are viewed by Newman as a good in themselves, but he recognizes that this does not constitute a barrier to their also being instrumentally valuable.

Newman as a university administrator is accused by M. M. Garland of being contradictory in the *Idea* and of making many compromises: 'With respect to the practical issues to be faced in the founding of the Catholic University, Newman in almost every case espoused the more liberal solution, preferring local clerical control to direction from the papal hierarchy, encouraging the employment of laity on the instructional staff, and denying theology active censorship of the curriculum'.[65] Yet such criticism is hardly justified. Newman simply did not have the conditions to accomplish his vision. He had never agreed to become the permanent rector of the university and, since he was unable to remain permanently in Dublin, had unsuccessfully asked Archbishop Cullen many times for a suitable vice-rector to deputize for him during his necessary visits home to Birmingham.

He was criticized both for appointing what some considered too many Englishmen to academic posts and also for appointing Irishmen who were suspected by Cullen of being anticlerical rebels.[66] Newman lacked support from most of the Irish bishops, many of whom were opposed to Cullen's ambitious plans. He spent much time and effort struggling with the archbishop, who was hesitant and interfering by turns, and always determined to have sole control over the university. He and Cullen both hoped that an Oratory might be established to care for the university, and to that end Newman also went to great trouble to build a very beautiful church which still stands as the monument to his time in Dublin. Yet while Cullen hoped that Newman and his Oratorians would leave Birmingham and migrate to Ireland, Newman was ultimately convinced that his own work lay in Birmingham.

For these and various other reasons, that were in no way Newman's fault, the university was not a great success. His attempt at importing Louvain and Oxford into Ireland was a failure and many would have said the attempt was completely unrealistic. The Irish bishops and laity were divided among themselves as to the purpose of the university, and nobody came from any other anglophone country to make it the truly international body that, as Colin Barr points out, both Newman and Cullen were aiming at.[67] Newman had invested an enormous amount of energy and time in the project, yet it all came to nought. The university was never granted a charter by the British government. Indeed, Newman's vision of a Catholic university did not survive long in Ireland as the later University College and the Catholic part of the so-called Royal University of Ireland bore little resemblance to his vision. The university never succeeded in recruiting more than one hundred full-time students during Newman's rectorship and half of these were medical students. Nevertheless, Newman was able to introduce evening classes in 1857 for the people of Dublin, which was a far-sighted innovation. His writings, addresses and sermons to the University continued to be influential long after he resigned as rector in 1858 and returned to Birmingham.

Return to Birmingham: Another School?

Newman was grateful that, while he was being kept busy with affairs in Dublin, he could count on devoted and able assistance from men of the calibre of Caswall and Darnell, which freed him to deal with the many other issues that clamoured for his attention. Meanwhile, the idea of founding another school remained close to the surface. Newman had invited a married convert to come to Edgbaston and set up a school next to the Oratory, but this was yet another plan which came to nothing.[68] Then, in January 1857, principally at the urging of several of his fellow converts, he began planning another school, which was designed for the sons of converts from Anglicanism who wished it to be run without the narrowness of other Catholic schools of the time. What Newman's associates also sought was a form of education which would resemble that given in the Anglican public schools of the time, rather than the English Catholic colleges. This was because the Catholic schools were, generally speaking, institutions not only run by priests, but whose way of life and curriculum were designed principally to prepare boys for the priestly or religious life, and only for secular life by default, as it were. Newman, as we have seen, was alive to the need for a proper religious formation of those who were destined for professions in the world. In contrast with the established Catholic schools of the day, Newman's new school was to be quite separate from the idea of a seminary, and apart from the headmaster it would have a lay teaching staff. In terms of the ethos of the school Newman emphasized that it would encourage openness and trust and avoid the practices of espionage such as listening at doors.[69]

The school opened in May 1859 with seven boys and this number reached seventy by 1862. However, after initially giving his support to the scheme, his own bishop, William Bernard Ullathorne, began to be uneasy about it and even the Catholic gentry had reservations about its location in Birmingham. Moreover, the school was beset not only by financial concerns but also by a major dispute over the role of the matron, Mrs Wootten, between Newman and the headteacher, Nicholas Darnell. This precipitated Darnell's resignation and that of most of the staff.[70] Newman was subsequently forced to become much more involved with the school in teaching, supervising, administering and governing right up to the time of his death in 1890. Although obliged to take on much of this work as a result of the Darnell affair, Newman found great satisfaction in doing so. While he did not lay out a series of lectures on secondary education, Newman did emphasize that the school would provide a liberal education together with an education that would prepare the boys for the world.[71] Towards the end of his life two Fathers of the Birmingham Oratory proposed the foundation of a grammar school. While this proposal was not supported by Newman through fear of financial liability, he did not directly oppose it and St Philip's Grammar School was founded, under the auspices of the Oratory, in 1885.

'An Educated Laity': *The Rambler* and the Oxford Oratory Plan

As a Catholic Newman was party to a succession of educational schemes which ended either in failure or in his own disillusionment. It was significant that as soon as he had become a Catholic Newman began to look about for opportunities to become involved in new and important educational schemes. His proposal to Bishop Wiseman in 1845 that he found a Catholic theological college had not been taken up with interest, and his view that Catholics in England needed education far more urgently than 'showy' architecture was a source of friction not only between him and the great Gothic revivalist architect Pugin, but also with many other Catholics. His judgement was that, with regard to their educational standards, 'Catholics in England, from their very blindness, cannot see that they are blind'.[72] He had subsequently hoped that the Dublin project would offer him the opportunity to set up an educational institution which might serve English Catholics, but it had failed to attract them.

Since Newman saw education as a lifelong process, then not just the young, but the entire body of the Catholic laity, needed education. Newman therefore sought to raise the general level of education among Catholic lay people. So far in this area he had only delivered his *Lectures on the Present Position of Catholics* in 1851, and had initiated some evening catechetical classes at Alcester Street around the same time. An opportunity to reach a wider lay audience came in 1859 when Newman was asked to become editor of the Catholic journal *The Rambler*, which was seen as the organ of educated lay converts and encouraged lay action. Newman saw this as 'substantially the same work'[73] as his Dublin project. It was about this time that he was having long discussions with some of his fellow converts about the Oratory School which eventually opened in May.

Meanwhile, the English Catholic bishops were making provision for Catholic schools without reference to the laity, whom they tended to regard as a merely passive body. Newman wrote an editorial in *The Rambler* on 13 May, urging that the bishops 'really desire to know the opinions of the laity on subjects in which the laity are especially concerned' and by this he meant education.[74] He wanted the bishops to enter into discussion with the educated laity, as he was currently doing, about the provision of schools. He was criticized for this by a number of fellow clerics who believed that they should have exclusive rights to decide what was educationally best for the laity. The bishops and those clerics who ran Catholic schools at the time had an autocratic tendency and tended in practice to disregard any natural rights of parents over their children. As a direct consequence of the furore created by his views on lay involvement in education, Newman was strongly advised by Bishop Ullathorne to resign the editorship of *The Rambler*. It was another blow to Newman's educational hopes. Moreover, as a result of the controversy surrounding his call on the bishops to consult the laity even on matters of doctrine, he was delated to Rome as a heretic and regarded with mistrust by many of his fellow Catholic clergy for years to come.

In 1864 Newman was asked if he wished to buy a large plot of land in Oxford. He immediately thought of setting up an Oratory and consulted Bishop Ullathorne, who invited him to open a mission. It had not been Newman's intention to return to Oxford, an idea he 'simply disliked and shrank from, but which I could not, as a matter of conscience, when put before me, peremptorily refuse'.[75] The prospect of a Catholic college was raised but Newman was doubtful about the wisdom of such an establishment, which would be regarded with suspicion both by the Anglican establishment and by many Catholics, if it were to be run by Newman. There were, as a matter of fact, numerous Catholic students in Oxford who were receiving no guidance from Catholic bodies. Newman was, therefore, in favour of an Oratory which would be concerned for their spiritual welfare and guidance, well short of being a full collegiate institution. The prospect of Newman's returning to Oxford to lead a mission and build a church for Catholics attending the Protestant university was raised, but in the end even Newman's presence in Oxford was too much for his opponents to accept. As Newman realized: 'the real root of the difficulty is *myself*. There are those who cannot endure the thought that I should have the *forming* of the young Catholic mind at Oxford.'[76] Therefore when it was decided to proceed without Newman the Oxford Oratory plan fell through. It was the last of Newman's educational projects. For the remainder of his life he continued writing and running the Oratory School, his only educational venture to survive him.

Conclusion

Much of Newman's work throughout his life was concerned one way or another with education. Newman's educational thought was primarily formed by his various personal experiences of teaching and learning, within the context of the Oxford classical education, which provided a significant Aristotelian shaping of his epistemology. As a tutor and clergyman in the Church of England, and subsequently as a Catholic priest, the context of much of his work was as a professional educator. Yet, particularly after he became a Catholic, much of this work was given to him by others: the Catholic University which was established at the request of the Pope and the Irish bishops, and the Oratory School which he founded in response to the prayers of his fellow-converts to Catholicism. As an Anglican he had been engaged in well-established educational institutions, while giving them new impetus, for instance as a tutor at Oriel. As a Catholic, however, he found himself in often uncharted waters. Nineteenth-century Catholics in the British Isles had few of the educational facilities and advantages which Newman had known in Oxford and wished to share with his new co-religionists. Newman felt that it was his particular calling to assist them in attaining such standards of education as were enjoyed by the members of the establishment. Yet they were not always as eager to receive them as he was to give, and even lacked the ability to see how narrow their own educational base really was. As he reflected on his first two decades in the Catholic Church he wrote in his journal in 1863:

> to aim then at improving the condition, the status of the Catholic body, by a careful survey of their argumentative basis, of their position relative to the philosophy and the character of the day, by giving them juster views, by enlarging and refining their minds, in one word by education, is (in their view) more than a superfluity or a hobby, it is an insult.[77]

It is immediately after saying this that he goes on to write a line which has since become famous, but the context of which is all-important in understanding Newman's achievements and his frustrations as an educator: 'Now from first to last, education, in this large sense of the word, has been my line.'[78] This explains why it was that he felt he had so much to offer and that the Catholic Church in his own land had so much need of it though it failed to recognize that need.

It is this overarching view of the importance of education in 'enlarging and refining minds' which we will now go on to consider in greater detail. Newman was not a systematic writer; with the notable exception of the *Grammar of Assent* most of his work was written in response to a particular situation or demand. It is therefore often necessary to look in different places and at practical experiences for threads to connect Newman's thought and approach to certain educational matters. Yet it is important to try and unravel some of these threads if we are to understand Newman's educational ideas and achievements more clearly. For this reason we will now separately consider his approach to religious, moral, technical and liberal education as these are to be found in his various works and projects.

Notes

1. v. Ker, I. T. (1990), *The Achievement of Newman (Achievement)*, p. 3.
2. *The Letters and Diaries of John Henry Newman* (LD) vol. xxiv p. 241 and n. 1.
3. An unnamed contemporary of Newman's in *Letters and Correspondence of J. H. Newman*, ed. Mozley, Anne (1891), p. 18, quoted by Dwight Culler in *The Imperial Intellect*, p. 2.
4. v. Newman, J. H., *Autobiographical Writings* (AW) ed. Tristram, Henry (1955), p. 29.
5. v. Newman, J. H., *The Idea of A University (Idea)* ed. Ker, I. T., Oxford (1976) Part II: University Subjects No. 4 'Elementary Studies', p. 299.
6. Mozley, op. cit., p. 18.
7. Ibid., p. 19.
8. Newman, Harriet, *Family Adventures*. These stories were written as children's tales and based on life in the Newman household of her childhood.
9. v. Tristram, Henry, 'The School-days of Cardinal Newman', *The Cornhill Magazine*, N.S. LVIII, June 1925, pp. 666–77.
10. v. Ker, I. T. (1990), *John Henry Newman: A Biography* (hereafter Ker 1990), pp. 573–4, quoting LD xxii, p. 9.

11. In mathematics he also studied a text book by Charles Hutton entitled *The Compendious Measurer* (London, 1812) containing lessons in decimal and duodecimal arithmetic, practical geometry and mensuration.
12. v. Tristram, op. cit.
13. Newman played Hegio in *Phormio*, Pythias in *Eunuchus*, Syrus in *Adelphi* and Davus in *Andria*, all by Terence.
14. Culler, A. Dwight (1955), *The Imperial Intellect: A Study of Cardinal Newman's Educational Ideal*, p. 3.
15. *Idea*, p. 367.
16. Culler, op. cit., p. 3.
17. *Idea*, p. 367.
18. *Apologia pro Vita Sua (Apologia)*, p. 17.
19. Mozley, op. cit., p. 22.
20. LD xxxi, p. 31.
21. *Idea*, p. 367.
22. LD i, p. 47.
23. Personal note of 13 May 1874 on various letters of the time.
24. MS papers relating to *The Undergraduate*, quoted by Culler, op. cit., p. 14.
25. AW, p. 49.
26. cf. *Idea*, Discourse V, 'Knowledge its own End', pp. 94ff.
27. LD i, p. 89.
28. AW, p. 52.
29. Ibid., p. 64.
30. Ibid.
31. v. below, pp. 26–7 and pp. 136ff.
32. LD xv, p. 176.
33. Ibid., p. 178.
34. Gilley, Sheridan (1990), *Newman and His Age*. London: Darton, Longman & Todd, p. 55.
35. AW, p. 77.
36. *Apologia*, p. 21.
37. v. Appendix A for the full text of this sermon.
38. v. Appendix B for the full text of this sermon.
39. AW, p. 205.
40. LD i, p. 219.

41. AW, p. 90.

42. Ibid., p. 89.

43. cf. *Historical Sketches*, III, 75.

44. AW, p. 99.

45. LD ii, pp. 117–18.

46. LD viii Appendix 3, pp. 525–33, contains Peel's original Address.

47. Ibid., v. pp. 534–61 for all seven of Newman's 'Catholicus' letters.

48. LD vii, p. 261 (15 March 1840).

49. Ker 1990, p. 194.

50. LD xiii, p. 143.

51. LD xiii, p. 238, v. Gilley, op. cit., p. 261.

52. Gilley, op. cit., p. 261.

53. v. Shrimpton, Paul (2005), *A Catholic Eton? Newman's Oratory School*. Leominster: Gracewing, p. 32.

54. Gilley, op. cit., p. 261.

55. LD xiii, p. 286.

56. v. de Flon, Nancy Marie (2005), *Edward Caswall, Newman's Brother and Friend*. Leominster: Gracewing, esp. pp. 125ff.

57. Ibid., p. 124.

58. In the original Discourse No. 6, Newman's understanding was not the same as in the Pope's Brief, i.e. that theology is to be related to the other disciplines as the soul is to the body. He eventually decided not to publish that discourse in its original form. However, it is possible that Newman maintained that the soul of the university was 'philosophy', in his broad sense of that term.

59. *My Campaign in Ireland (Campaign)*, ed. W. Neville (1896), p. 9.

60. LD xiv, p. 364.

61. *Campaign*, p. 9.

62. LD xiv, p. 389.

63. *Campaign*, p. 58.

64. *Idea*, p. 24.

65. Garland, M. M. (1996), 'Newman in his own day', in Turner, F. (ed.) *The Idea of a University*. Yale University Press, p. 278.

66. Gilley, op. cit., p. 281.

67. v. Barr, Colin (2004), *Paul Cullen, John Henry Newman, and the Catholic University of Ireland 1845–1865*. South Bend, IN: University of Notre Dame Press.

68. Shrimpton, op. cit., p. 32.
69. Ker 1990, p. 469; LD xviii, p. 314.
70. For the details of the Darnell/Wootten dispute and its implica-
    tions, see chapter 2, p.75 and chapter 3, pp. ??
71. Shrimpton, op. cit., p. 87.
72. AW, p. 259.
73. LD xix, pp. 140–1.
74. Ker 1990, p. 478.
75. LD xxi, p. 206.
76. LD xxi, p. 319.
77. AW, p. 259.
78. Ibid.

Part 2

Critical Exposition of Newman's Work

Chapter 2

The Religious Character of Education in Newman's Thought

Introduction

To begin to understand the central place of education in Newman's life, we need to remember that, first and foremost, throughout his adult life, Newman was a pastor. On his ordination as an Anglican deacon in 1824 he wrote: 'I have the responsibility of souls on me to the day of my death.'[1] Newman's varied educational projects must therefore be seen within the context of this responsibility for souls. Nor was this simply a personal responsibility for himself, but an ecclesial one arising from the sacrament of baptism, by which a person is admitted to membership of the Christian Church and receives the supernatural gift of faith. Yet a true understanding of the nature and consequences of baptism for the individual cannot be acquired without careful and prolonged teaching and learning. That Newman understood the responsibility of educating in the faith to be so serious can be readily appreciated from his statement that 'to baptise and not to educate is a grievous sin'.[2]

Moreover Newman was not only aware of the importance, not to say urgency, of this responsibility, but also of its need for careful management. Education is not simply the imparting of certain kinds of information, nor yet the training in certain kinds of skill. However important these aspects of education may be, they are subsidiary to the main aim and purpose, which is the formation of persons made in the image and likeness of God for their eternal destiny. Educating persons requires far more than merely imparting information. The formation of human persons in this life, by engendering their sense of vocation to eternal life was therefore Newman's work and responsibility as a pastor. Newman the educator and Newman the pastor are always intimately linked; his numerous educational projects and writings bound together in his identity and work as a priest.

Faith and Reason in Newman

In virtually all his written works Newman's starting point and aim were religious. In much of his work Newman examines and reflects the processes by which he had himself grown in faith and understanding, thereby the better to assist others. Absorbed by the question of epistemology, he believed that, as part of God's created universe, humanity has a natural desire for knowledge of the truth, and that the human mind instinctively aspires towards and attempts to achieve knowledge of all that exists. This aspiration manifests itself in the power of the human intellect gradually to assimilate and order its sense impressions and to come to a deeper understanding of the truth that lies beyond those impressions.[3]

Truth for Newman was a unifying characteristic of knowledge. He explains in the *Idea* that the oneness of the reality of the universe meant that knowledge must be understood to be 'a view of things', and that all knowledge therefore constituted a unified whole. In order to understand it properly, a human person must understand the unity of truth in God. This understanding of the truth can be expressed as a natural capacity to know God. Yet this capacity must be properly directed in order to reach the truth, for unless it is carefully nurtured and educated, a person's understanding of the truth will remain distorted.

In Newman's age rapid industrialization was creating economic forces that were changing society and forcing the case for a revision of the traditional ideas of education. Newman consistently sought to counter the intellectual attitudes and rationalism of his time which led, in his judgement, to unbelief. Consequently, he was inspired by a positive view of religious belief and practice. Indeed, one could say that his writing was a product of his own personal quest and long intellectual struggle in explaining how religion is both reasonable and justifiable in the world he knew and experienced.

It is not surprising that, as Thomas Vargish observes, there are many important connections between Newman's philosophy of mind and his general educational thought.[4] Newman saw religious education not as an optional, much less a superfluous extra, but as an essential part of any true education. He makes a strong claim for this when he says that 'Christianity, and nothing short of it, must be made the element and principle of all education'.[5] Even in his own day such a claim would have seemed extravagant, and Newman was all too aware that it was not shared by many among the intellectual elite. Christianity, at least in its Anglican form, in early nineteenth-century England, was still recognized as the basis of the establishment and a requirement for common morality, but its doctrinal content was no longer unquestioned. Not only had the Reformation introduced controversy into many areas of Christian doctrine, but the Enlightenment and the rise of science had gone further and elevated reason above the claims of all forms of revealed religion and Church authority.

Newman identified the relationship between faith and reason as especially important to education. He recognized the tension between them and came to understand that each had its proper role in a person's understanding of the truth. The process whereby this came about fascinated Newman, not only because it posed an intellectual challenge, but because within it lies each person's individual path to maturity in faith and knowledge of God and one's own destiny. For Newman there could be no single 'correct' way of arriving at this synthesis of faith and reason, yet he was no relativist regarding the nature of truth. He understood that while truth is objective, the paths by which a person comes to understand and assimilate it are as individual as are each person's history and personality. Throughout his life as educator and guide, Newman respected those particular characteristics which influence an individual's journey to maturity in religious faith and knowledge. Frederick Copleston succinctly summarizes Newman's thought when he says that Newman 'is more concerned with showing the reasonableness of faith as it actually exists in the great mass of believers, most of whom know nothing of abstract philosophical arguments'.[6]

In the opening chapter of his *Essay on the Development of Christian Doctrine* (*Development*) published in 1845, Newman says:

it is the characteristic of our minds to be ever engaged in passing judgement on the things that come before us. No sooner do we apprehend than we judge; we allow nothing to stand by itself, we compare, contrast, abstract, generalise, connect, adjust, classify, and we view all our knowledge in the associations with which these processes have invested it.[7]

At first sight this sentence might seem more relevant to education than to religious doctrine. Yet it makes sense when we realize that Newman approaches the whole question of development by considering how human beings think concretely.

Oxford University Sermons on Faith and Reason

Newman began by asking why people believe and argue as they do, particularly in religious matters. The answers he gave were first outlined in several of the 'University Sermons' he delivered at Oxford between 1839 and 1841 in which he worked out and described his understanding of the relationship between faith and reason. He wished to counter the growing scepticism of the age which was already challenging the strength of claims for religious knowledge.

Faith follows Reason

Newman sought to defend the intellectual integrity of religious faith from attacks upon it coming principally from two directions within the native empiricist tradition. First, he opposed Locke's claim that the Christian faith could be proved rationally through 'evidences'. The weakness of this position lay in its assumptions about the workings of the human mind which led to the claim that faith and religion must be testable by secular notions of reason. Secondly, Hume rejected Lockean religious reasoning, and dismissed faith as merely illogical feelings and private intuitions. Although many of Newman's contemporaries gravitated towards one or other of these approaches, he insisted instead that the concept of reason should not be restricted to a narrow rationalism and empiricism. He wished to broaden the terms of the debate by adopting an approach to reason which in some ways resembled Hume's rather than Locke's, to explain that in matters of faith, reasoning works informally rather than formally.

Newman's initial idea in Sermon X is that reason approves the evidence for believing and that faith 'follows or not, according to the state of the heart'.[8] Faith and reason are therefore related, though distinct. Newman here expresses two important ideas. First, he realized that a decisive factor in the acceptance or rejection of faith is not so much the arguments of the mind, as 'the state of the heart'. He came to this conclusion when arguing with his brother Charles who had fallen away from Christian faith during his adolescence. Newman concluded that it was useless to argue when there is a 'secret antipathy for the doctrines of Christianity, which is quite out of the reach of argument'.[9] Secondly, Newman identifies a *process* from reason to faith, with 'Reason warranting, on the ground of evidence ... and *then* Faith embracing it'.[10]

Implicit and Explicit Reason

According to Newman, then, 'Reason is a faculty of proceeding from things that are perceived to things which are not ...'[11] To this very basic definition of reason, he later made a significant refinement in Sermon XIII, by drawing out the distinction between reasoning 'by an inward faculty' and reasoning 'by rule'. The difference is between 'living spontaneous energy' and 'art', or between 'implicit' and 'explicit' reason. Newman gives us an analogy to illustrate what he means by implicit reasoning in saying that the mind

> makes progress not unlike a clamberer on a steep cliff, who, by quick eye, prompt hand, and firm foot, ascends how he knows not himself, by personal endowments and by practice, rather than by rule, leaving no track behind him, and unable to teach another.[12]

Reasoning is therefore something that we do without necessarily being conscious of how we are doing it. It is often the case that we try to give an account of how we have arrived at a conclusion only after we have reached it. Faith, says Newman, is that kind of reasoning. Newman calls it 'the reasoning of a religious mind, or of what Scripture calls a right or renewed heart, which acts upon presumptions rather than evidence'.[13] This is therefore not explicit and formal reasoning, but rather the 'inward faculty' and 'living spontaneous energy' which explicit reasoning tries, but must fail, to capture and represent. Therefore, while believers must have reasons for believing, they may not be able to give an explicit account of those reasons.

Demonstrating our Reasons

Newman argues in Sermon XI that men frequently disagree among themselves about the interpretation of facts, yet do not ascribe such diversity to deficiency of reasoning, since 'the experience of life contains abundant evidence that in practical matters, when their minds are really roused, men commonly are not bad reasoners',[14] and instinctively know how to act in their own best interests. For this reason, it is possible to say that although men 'may argue badly ... they reason well', advancing 'on grounds which they do not, or cannot produce, or if they could, yet could not prove to be true, on latent or antecedent grounds which they take for granted'.[15]

Moreover, however exhaustive our analysis of reasons may be, 'there must ever be something assumed ultimately which is incapable of proof'.[16] He points out that we continue to trust our sense, memory and reason, despite the fact that they often deceive us. Since they cannot vindicate themselves, we trust them instinctively and take their evidence for granted. Hence, says Newman, those who do not have an 'instinctive apprehension' of God's omnipotence and providence, 'must not be surprised that the evidence of Christianity does not perform an office which was never intended for it',[17] for quite generally, 'we must assume something to prove anything, and can gain nothing without a venture'. Only when we have taken that step can we attain knowledge, for 'according to its desirableness, whether in point of excellence, or range, or intricacy, so is the subtlety of the evidence on which it is received'.[18]

Therefore, he says that it is not surprising that 'Divine Truth should be attained by so subtle and indirect a method, a method less tangible than others, less open to analysis, reducible but partly to the forms of Reason ...'[19] He defends this assertion by pointing out that 'the most remarkable victories of genius' have come through 'recondite and intricate' ways of thought; for example, in mathematics, metaphysics, or 'the preternatural sagacity of a great general', so that 'the act of mind, for instance, by which an unlearned person savingly believes the Gospel, on the word of his teacher, may be analogous to the exercise of sagacity in a great statesman or general, supernatural grace doing for the uncultivated reason what genius does for them'.[20]

Belief and Unbelief

Newman's argument is ultimately polemical, as emerges clearly in Sermon XII: 'Unbelief, indeed, considers itself especially rational, or critical of evidence; but it criticises the evidence of Religion, only because it does not like it, and really goes upon presumption and prejudices as much as Faith does, only presumptions of an opposite nature ... [as if] presumptions on the side of Faith could not have, and presumptions on the side of unbelief might have, the nature of proof.'[21]

Moreover, faith not only has its own ways of proceeding, as different subjects tend to have their own particular kinds of reasoning, but it is also the case that every person will exercise it in an individual way. Different kinds of evidence will be brought out by different persons in giving an account of their reasons, and these same evidences may often have a different weight or come in a different order in another person's judgement.

Newman provides us with a number of explanations of the various kinds of reasons which underpin faith. For example, he says that 'Faith is influenced by previous notices, prepossessions, and (in a good sense of the word) prejudices ... the mind that believes is acted upon by its own hopes, fears and existing opinions ...'[22] Newman says that what a man hopes for and what he desires are shaped not just affectively, but as reasonable *anticipations* originating in his understanding of the world.

Newman argues that one of the major difficulties experienced by believers in discussing faith with non-believers is the absence of common ground in what is meant both by reasoning and by its subject matter. 'When we come to what is called Evidence, or, in popular language, exercise of Reason,' he says, ' ... Nothing can be urged ... but what all feel, all comprehend ... only such conclusions can be drawn as can produce their reasons; only such reasons are in point as can be exhibited in simple propositions ...' Newman says that the antecedents of Faith are 'not so much ... facts, as ... probabilities', which are indeterminate and depend on 'moral temperament', and that 'A good and a bad man will think very different things probable'.[23]

Newman anticipates the analytic 'philosophy of religion' of the contemporary university: 'those who profess themselves [religion's] champions allow themselves to stand on the same ground as philosophers of the world, admit the same principles, and only aim at drawing different conclusions'.[24] But this will never succeed since

> Faith is a process of the Reason, in which so much of the grounds of inference cannot be exhibited, so much lies in the character of the mind itself, in its general view of things, its estimate of the probable and the improbable, its impressions concerning God's will, and its anticipations derived from its own inbred wishes, that it will ever seem to the world irrational and despicable ...[25]

This describes the particular character of the antecedents of religious faith, and also the distinguishing sense in which religious faith is reasonable. For since 'in the judgement of a rightly disposed mind, objects are desirable and attainable which irreligious men will consider to be but fancies', here we have *no common and agreed basis* for estimating the evidential value of phenomena which are 'the very medium in which the argument for Christianity has its constraining force'.[26]

Conscience, Truth and Love

But there is another element in Newman's analysis of the reasons by which a person comes to have faith: *conscience*. Obedience to conscience helps one *to come to know* the world in ways that remain closed to the disobedient. Newman develops this in Sermon II:

Conscience is the essential principle and sanction of Religion in the mind. Conscience implies a relation between the soul and a something exterior and ... superior to itself; a relation to an excellence which it does not possess, and to a tribunal over which it has no power. And since the more clearly this inward monitor is respected and followed, the clearer, the more exalted and the more varied its dictates become ... a moral conviction is thus obtained of the unapproachable nature as well as the supreme authority of That, whatever it is, which is the object of the mind's contemplation. Here then, at once, we have the elements of a religious system; for what is Religion but the system of relations existing between us and a Supreme Power, claiming our habitual obedience?[27]

Fidelity to conscience gives birth to 'further hopes and desires' which remain inchoate and unfulfilled until faith alone provides the form that answers them. Faith, as Newman understands it, is inseparable from the revelation of the God to whose authority our conscience bears witness. Before that revelation was made in the Incarnation of Christ, natural religion and paganism could not supply what fidelity to conscience seemed to offer. Newman explains in Sermon II:

The God of philosophy was infinitely great, but an abstraction; the God of paganism was intelligible, but degraded by human conceptions ... it was left for an express Revelation to propose the Object in which they should both be reconciled, *and to satisfy the desires of both* in a real and manifested incarnation of the Deity[28]

Therefore, Newman argues, the fact of God's self-revelation in Christ both gives explicit form to a desire for God already present in the human soul and mind, and furnishes the only adequate means of fulfilling that desire, through a personal act of faith.

Newman accounts for the distinctiveness of faith by saying that it is not natural to man, and comes only of supernatural grace.[29] For Newman, faith's 'inward principle' is both a kind of rationality or reasonableness, and also 'a supernatural principle'. Ultimately, faith is inseparable from love of the God whom faith discloses to us. Newman expounds this theme in Sermon XII as he asks: 'Does a child trust his parents because he has proved to himself that they are such, and that they are able and desirous to do him good, or from the instinct of affection? We *believe*, because we *love*.'[30] In short: the distinctiveness of faith lies in its being a kind of implicit reasoning that requires God's grace.

A Grammar of Assent

Newman returned to the area of faith and reason in his last great work, *An Essay in Aid of a Grammar of Assent* (*Grammar*), published in 1870. This was virtually the only book which Newman ever wrote out of his own personal interest, since he usually wrote in response to some external stimulus or occasion. The *Grammar* was over thirty years in gestation. Newman had continued to ponder the issues he had tackled in the university sermons throughout the intervening years, and prepared for the writing of the book by keeping a philosophical notebook. He wanted to avoid reading other writers in order not to be influenced by their arguments and categories.[31] Indeed, his definitions are his own and not directly derived from any philosophical school. The first part of the *Grammar* deals with the relation between assent and apprehension, while the second part explores the question of belief in what cannot be proved.

Newman argues that human beings do not think mechanically in matters of faith and that there are really only two positions – belief or disbelief. In short, Newman is saying that a religious person is committed to the reality of God before knowing what God is. However, this does not justify unreasoned and unfounded beliefs about God, for a person's commitment to the reality of God seeks whatever evidence can come from experience and intelligence about the nature of God.

Reason and Certitude

Some would suggest that in reaching this conclusion Newman shows himself to be an irrationalist. On the contrary, Newman was opposed to a narrow rationalism which 'does not square with the way in which people actually, and legitimately, think and reason in concrete issues'.[32] While Newman successfully added to the philosophical lexicon a series of many complex distinctions from the *Grammar* which are important for a philosophical account of belief, they are nevertheless not without their critics.[33] However, Frederick Copleston observes that 'those who take an interest in his philosophical reflections tend to look on them as a source of stimulus and inspiration rather than as a rigid, systematic doctrine, which, of course, Newman himself never intended them to be'.[34] Newman raises many questions in the philosophy of belief in the *Grammar*. He was, as Avery Dulles says, 'quite conscious that his positions seemed to invite a kind of subjectivism with regard to the truth'.[35]

Assent and Apprehension

An assent, as Newman uses the term, is the unconditional mental assertion of a proposition as true. Newman therefore begins by exploring propositions and our apprehension of them. There are two kinds of propositions: either abstract and general, such as 'a line is length without breadth', or concrete and particular, such as 'the earth goes round the sun'. We apprehend abstract propositions in what Newman calls a notional way, and concrete propositions in a real way. Of these two modes of apprehension, the real is the stronger, or more vivid, 'for intellectual ideas cannot compete in effectiveness with the experience of concrete facts'.[36] It is, of course, possible for a proposition to be notional for one person and real for another, depending, for instance, on differing personal experiences. Apprehension implies our interpretation of the terms of a proposition. We can assert without assenting, for assent is more than assertion, it is the apprehension of the matter asserted.

Frederick Copleston explains how the concepts of notional and real assent apply to religious belief: 'it is obvious that the belief in God with which [Newman] is primarily concerned as a Christian apologist is a real assent to God as a present reality, and an assent which influences life or conduct, not simply a notional assent to a proposition about the idea of God ... from this it follows that Newman is not, and cannot be, primarily interested in a formal demonstrative inference to God's existence'.[37] We can therefore assent to a proposition concerning

God or religion either *notionally*, which is merely intellectual assent, or *really*, which is an assent of the imagination as well as of the intellect. Now it is easy to understand what is meant by a notional assent to a proposition about God, in that God is beyond our direct personal experience. Newman therefore asks *how* it is possible for an assent to God to be more than intellectual. How can we have a 'more vivid assent to the Being of a God' than a merely intellectual idea can give us?[38]

He conceives that a real assent *is* possible, even though we cannot see God. He argues that the evidence we have of the world around us comes to us in the form of sense phenomena, and it is by instinct that we take these phenomena as true evidence.[39] In other words, we do not have direct experience of those things which we know only through our sense-perception, but we believe the evidence of our senses. In an analogous way, says Newman, just as we accept the evidence of our senses with regard to the natural world, we exercise the same trust indirectly towards the phenomena within our minds which refer to God. In Newman's words, 'the office which the senses directly fulfil as regards the external world, that office devolves indirectly on certain of our mental phenomena as regards its Maker. These phenomena are found in the sense of moral obligation.'[40]

Conscience and Real Assent

Newman does not propose actually to prove 'the Being of a God', but he says that it is through the evidence of God's impression upon our minds in the *conscience* that he would 'look for the proof'. Conscience is 'a moral sense, and a sense of duty; a judgement of the reason and a magisterial dictate'. It is 'a voice, imperative and constraining, like no other dictate in the whole of our experience'.[41] It is these 'phenomena of Conscience [which] avail to impress the imagination with the picture of a Supreme Governor, a Judge, holy, just, powerful, all-seeing, retributive, and is the creative principle of religion ... '[42] Newman appeals to an experience which is universal, while recognizing that not everyone draws the same inference from it as he does. All who recognize conscience do not necessarily agree on its meaning or implications. Yet, Newman argues, if assent is given to God from this 'imagination', it is not only real, but can be helped to grow in reality by education and devotion, for 'knowledge must ever precede the exercise of the affections'.[43] Hence Newman argues for the necessity of knowing the propositions of the creed and catechism in order to strengthen the reality of our assent to faith. Just as 'we love our parents, as our parents, when we know them to be our parents; we must know of God, before we can feel love, fear, hope, or trust towards Him'.[44]

Newman goes on to investigate how faith in what one cannot prove can be justified. He takes the idea of assent which he has already explored and applies it to more complex kinds of reasoning. Since assent is given to propositions as being true (or else it cannot be assent), Newman asks what kind of reasoning can lead one to make an assent. What makes for certainty that an assent is, in fact, true? He is not claiming that certainty is infallible, but he argues that we often do have reasons for being certain in matters that are incapable of logical demonstration. Granted that there is always a possibility of being in error, what is it about our way of reasoning that allows us so often to make assents which are true, and which we safely rely upon?

The Illative Sense

Newman defines the 'inward faculty' which brings the mind to make an act of assent as the 'illative sense'. It is a faculty of reason that can give rise to certitude by drawing together several different strands of argument or it can be seen as the ability to make conclusions based on inference, as opposed to hard facts and proof. Nichols describes the process as 'the heaping together of tiny indications, none of which by itself is conclusive, [which] produces certitude in ordinary human affairs. At some point there is a qualitative change in the quantitative amassment of evidence. Spread out the pieces of a jigsaw puzzle on a table, and it may be only probable that they are more than an accidental collocation. Fit them together and there will be no doubt.'[45] The illative sense can be defined as the power to judge and conclude from many interacting pathways, which is why Newman called it 'a grand word for a common thing'.[46] It is simply a process of practical reasoning which gives us a sense that allows us to 'connect the dots'.

While the illative sense originates in nature it is formed and matured by practice and experience, and it has an elastic character which is both highly personal and at the same time rational in an informal way. It involves the reasoning of the whole person, not just intellectually, but morally, emotionally, religiously, imaginatively, and so forth. The illative sense is not the possession of the privileged few since all have a claim to possess it. Newman characterizes the illative sense as the skill to discern truth from this accumulation of probabilities. While Newman was chiefly concerned with clarifying and justifying religious faith in the *Grammar* he claims that the same process of the accumulation of probabilities leading to assent applies in other areas, including the sciences. Newman maintains that all knowledge is one and that notions of secular truth cannot contradict religious truth.

While the illative sense is the product of intuition, instinct, and imagination coupled with long experience, it also needs to be strengthened through an appropriate education. Since the processes by which it is reached can lead to error, it is not infallible in any person. Newman believed that education should guide its development and that authority could correct the illative sense that erred, and by this authority he meant the teaching of the Church. Newman's aim was that education should assist a person to integrate notional and real assent to the truths of the faith. As Mary Katherine Tillman says:

> Assent that is only notional remains exclusively conceptual and content-oriented with no living faith in a personal God; assent that is exclusively imaginative tends towards excesses of emotion, even superstition, and has no interest in doctrine or dogma. Newman's intention was to describe the necessary synthesis and integration of notional and real assent in the mature and plenary act of religious faith.[47]

Theology and Education

Newman did not deliberately set out to elaborate a theory of education, if by that we mean a comprehensive statement of principles intended as a guide to educational practice. Since he was not a systematic thinker his terminology may often appear imprecise and inconsistent. Moreover, as we have seen, he does not provide a comprehensive epistemological framework that can be applied to education per se. He was clearly an individualistic thinker who opened up new avenues of enquiry. He sets out a series of principles based on his view of the mind's limitations and weaknesses that may act as guides to particular aspects of educational practice. Yet he never organized these within a comprehensive framework of categories.

Since he was involved in education as a churchman throughout his life, it is understandable that Newman was principally interested in its religious dimension. For Newman, of course, education as seen from a religious viewpoint is not solely about the formation of the human mind, but is properly a process directed to the formation of the whole human person. Religious education is therefore not simply to be identified with the imparting of religious knowledge, however important such knowledge may be, but is rather an essential requirement for the proper shaping of the human person to fulfil his or her role and destiny. Given this view of human nature and the role of religion in forming it, it might be readily assumed that Newman's argument was based upon an *a priori* assumption of the truth of the Christian religion. Newman, however, did not argue thus.

As we have seen, Newman's theories were always based on keen observation of reality. Both as an Anglican and as a Catholic Newman was involved in educational institutions of many different kinds and levels: Sunday schools, parish or mission schools, a grammar school and a public school, two universities, and the teaching of adults. Through all these endeavours Newman came to a mature and comprehensive understanding of the nature and importance of education at all stages of life and for all conditions of persons. For Newman, just as all knowledge is one and leads to God, so too all education is ultimately religious in its aim. However, although knowledge and truth are one, education needs to take into account the individual gifts and circumstances of each human person.

The Place of Theology in Education

Newman gave his most thorough exposition of his principles of education in *The Idea of a University* in which he collected the various discourses he had written for the nascent Catholic University he founded in Dublin in 1852. Newman had been invited by the Pope and Irish bishops to set up the Catholic University in opposition to the 'Queen's Colleges' established in Ireland by Sir Robert Peel's government. It was hoped that by excluding all confessional religion from their curricula, these would attract Catholics who could not attend the Anglican Trinity College in Dublin. By contrast with the Queen's Colleges, the *Idea* makes it clear that education must be founded on religious principle. Newman takes this stand at a time when many others, like Peel, had already adopted liberal and sceptical views dismissive of the need for Christian theology in education. As we have already seen in Chapter 1, Peel had dismissed Christian doctrine at the opening of the Tamworth Reading Room in 1841 as 'controversial divinity', and had excluded its study from the range of reading by which he judged that people would find instruction and virtue. For Newman doctrine is not 'controversial divinity' but 'Christian knowledge'. Without Christian knowledge, or theology, faith is empty of all but the vaguest content. Nevertheless, Newman realized that he must first defend his claim for the place that religion and theology are to play in his university. The first part of *The Idea of a University* is devoted to the relationship between theology and other branches of knowledge. In Discourse 1 he states that the principles on which he is going conduct his enquiry do not come from theology as such, but are attainable by human prudence and wisdom reflecting on the mere experience of life.[48]

The Ends of Education

Newman distinguishes carefully between the ends or purposes of education, and the ends of those institutions in which education is conducted. The end of education, considered simply as such in its most comprehensive sense, is the formation of the human person. But the instruments of education can have their own closely defined ends within the context of education as a whole. Thus, for instance, Newman held that the end of a university education is not moral or even religious but simply intellectual. In the *Idea* he explains that a university fulfils its purpose by cultivating the intellect for its own sake. In this it is analogous to a hospital, whose end is the healing of the sick or wounded, or an almshouse whose end is aiding or solacing the old, or a penitentiary whose end is restoring the guilty.[49] Now although the persons who are served by such institutions have ends over and above those fulfilled by those institutions, the institutions can fulfil their own particular ends without having to serve all the ends of those who benefit from them. According to Newman, it is exactly the same with an educational institution such as a university. It may perhaps be said to have more than one kind of end: an immediate end which is the formation of the intellect, and an ultimate end, which is the formation of the person. But what is interesting about Newman's view of the end of a university is that he held it to be true for *all* universities, whether Catholic or non-Catholic.

Although the end of a university considered in the abstract was the formation of the intellect, that is teaching and learning, in reality a university would, for all practical purposes, embrace other ends, including research. Newman himself encouraged research among his faculty, founding the journal *Atlantis* to carry learned papers and addresses given by them in the university, a theme to which we will return in Chapter 5.[50] A Catholic university would necessarily have a Catholic way of life, and would endeavour to inculcate its values in its subjects. This ultimate end, the Catholic formation of the students of his university would, as he says, require disciplinary structures to protect and foster its specifically Catholic identity and that of its faculties and students.

For Newman, then, a university was a very specific kind of entity whose end is the formation of the intellect through teaching *de omni scibili*, that is, of all subjects considered 'knowable'. This end sets a university apart from any other kind of institute of higher education, such as a seminary or technical college, whose end is more restricted, being the imparting of a certain branch of knowledge or range of technical skills. Apart from the Queen's Colleges in Ireland, other university foundations were being made which did not accord with the principles explained in the *Idea*. As we have noted, Newman was aware of them and critical of them. The same views espoused by Peel in the establishment of the Tamworth Reading Room were enshrined in some of those other recently founded universities. As Peel had avoided 'controversial divinity' in setting up his Reading Room, so too did some other recently founded institutes of higher education.

Theology as a True Branch of Knowledge

The University College in London from its foundation excluded all theology from its curriculum, not only on the grounds of religious neutrality, as did the Irish Queen's Colleges, but also on the grounds that theology was not true knowledge. Herein Newman saw an even greater challenge to the identity of a university than that posed by the Irish non-denominational colleges. In the *Idea* Newman challenged the exclusion of all theology from any university curriculum as 'an intellectual absurdity'. He argues in the form of a syllogism that a university

> by its very name professes to teach universal knowledge: Theology is surely a branch of knowledge: how then is it possible for it to profess all branches of knowledge, and yet to exclude from the subjects of its teaching one which, to say the least, is as important and as large as any of them?[51]

Although Newman admits that the derivation of the word 'university' is uncertain, he explains that it first appears in the Middle Ages exclusively in connection with institutions which claimed to teach all branches of knowledge, as, for instance, Paris. Other medieval institutions may have been larger, or more famous in some particular art or science, but what distinguishes a university as such is its claim to teach *universal* knowledge. Newman returned to the question 'What is a University?' in Chapter 2 of 'The Rise and Progress of Universities'. From the designation 'School of Universal Learning' he argues: 'this implies the assemblage of strangers from all parts in one spot', rather than implying the teaching of 'universal knowledge' as in the *Idea*. According to Newman, then, if a university is to merit the name, it need not profess to teach everything that is counted as knowledge, but it definitely may not deliberately exclude any such thing. Therefore, he argues, if the subject of religion is excluded from a university, then one of two conclusions is inevitable: either the province of religion is barren of real knowledge, or else in such a university one special and important branch of knowledge is omitted.

Newman quotes Brougham:

> the great truth has finally gone forth to all the ends of the earth [and (says Newman) he prints it in capital letters], that man shall no more render account to man for his belief, over which he has himself no control. Henceforward, nothing shall prevail upon us to praise or blame any one for that which he can no more change than the hue of his skin or the height of his stature.[52]

Hence Newman understands Brougham to hold that 'religious ideas are just as far from being real … are as truly peculiarities, idiosyncrasies, accidents of the individual, as his having the stature of a Patagonian …' If a man's belief is that 'over which he has himself no control', then it cannot be taught. It can have no objective foundation in fact. What role, then, is left to religious belief under such conditions? Newman moves from Brougham to a contemporary Parliamentary Report which places the teaching of religion in schools along with poetry and music in the category of 'the inculcation of sentiment'. Newman observes that such a view arises precisely where religion is no longer understood to be true knowledge, but only refined feeling. No matter how much respect is shown to religion, and even though it is still taught in schools, it is clear to Newman that once religion is treated in this way it cannot be understood to be knowledge or to have anything to do with knowledge. Therefore the exclusion of the study of religion from a university course of instruction need not result from political or social obstacles, but simply cannot be helped, 'because it has no business there at all, being considered "taste, sentiment, opinion, and nothing more"'.[53]

Historically, Newman sees the Reformation as the origin of the sundering of theology from all other branches of knowledge. It was at the hands of the Protestant reformers that religion began to be treated as a matter of subjective sentiment rather than of objective science, and thence by logical development came the Enlightenment and rationalism.[54] Newman, on the other hand, maintains that theology is certainly among the subjects that not only can, but definitely should, be taught in a university. In the first place, as we have already seen, he argues that the existence of God is a truth in the natural order as well as in the supernatural, and is known by various ways, which he enumerates: 'Is not the being of a God reported to us by testimony, handed down by history, inferred by an inductive process, brought home to us by metaphysical necessity, urged on us by the suggestions of our conscience?' Newman therefore argues not merely for the admissibility of theology, but for its absolute necessity on the grounds that once you admit the existence of God, then you allow, by definition, 'a fact encompassing every other fact conceivable'. Once you admit the definition of God as creator, he says, then it follows that the existence of such a being has implications for all other facts and their study. The idea of God is itself 'at once a whole dogmatic system'.[55] Newman is arguing against deism, which held that God's existence is likely, but ultimately of little consequence for the actual order of the world and knowledge about it. If God exists, Newman maintains, then his existence is not only a fact, but it must be a fact that has implications for all other facts and our knowledge about them. He is also effectively turning the tables on the sceptics and rationalists who claim that belief in God is at best a matter of 'sentiment' rather than reality, by claiming that it is the rationalists who are being irrational in excluding from the body of human knowledge a fact that is knowable.

Theology and the Circle of Knowledge

Newman argues that the omission of theology from the curriculum is not merely an error in itself, but generates a further distortion in the understanding of what 'universal knowledge' consists. 'How can we investigate any part of any order of Knowledge,' he asks, 'and stop short of that which enters into every order?'[56] Here he argues that theology is not even just another branch of universal knowledge, but one which has connections with, and implications for, all other branches. The interconnection of all truth is for Newman an essential principle of knowledge and of the foundation of a university's claim to teach all that is knowable. It is not simply a question of exhaustiveness of content, but of the interrelation of the subject matter. All this follows from the conviction that all truth is one, whether it is divine or secular. If all knowledge is ultimately a unity, then no part of it can contradict another. Truth cannot contradict truth. Newman follows an older tradition of nomenclature when he refers here to 'the circle of knowledge'. The term 'encyclopaedia' originally designated what Bacon had called 'circle learning', meaning the whole of common knowledge in general circulation. Newman comments on this:

> It is curious how negligent English writers seem to be just now of the necessity of comprehensiveness and harmony of view, in their pursuit of truth in every detail. The very word Encyclopaedia ought to suggest it to them; but the alphabetical order has assimilated the great undertaking so designated to a sort of Dictionary of portions and departments of knowledge.[57]

The method of arrangement of facts and subjects in the newer kind of 'encyclopaedia' represented by the Britannica indicated a fundamental departure from this idea of organic unity and interrelationship. Newman comments: 'A philosophical comprehensiveness, an elastic constructiveness, men have lost them, and cannot make out why. This is why: because they have lost the idea of unity.'[58]

Newman illustrates his understanding of the concept of the 'circle of sciences' in Discourse 3. The sciences need each other for completeness insofar as they treat the same subject matter under different aspects. Each on its own would be incomplete. So, for instance, 'Man' is an object of study from many different viewpoints or relations – as, for instance, in the sciences of physiology, moral philosophy, economics, politics, and theology. What each of those disciplines has to say about man may be true, but as a description each will be incomplete without all the others. Moreover, each of the sciences corrects another. Nor can any one science dogmatize without the other, except hypothetically and upon its own abstract principles. The same applies to other scientific theories: Newton's physics requires the admission of certain metaphysical postulates, as, for instance, that matter exists, that our senses are trustworthy, and that what happened yesterday will happen tomorrow.[59] As all the sciences belong to one and the same circle of objects, they are one and all connected together. If any one science is systematically omitted from the catalogue, then our knowledge will be falsified, leading to what Newman calls an 'unreal idea'. 'Were I a mere chemist', he says, 'I should deny the influence of mind on bodily health.'[60] This kind of distortion is possible, Newman claims, because each of the sciences is *complete in its own idea*. Any single discipline may not only be studied independently of others, but may be exhaustive in its own particular limits. Each discipline requires other disciplines to comment on, and where necessary, correct it. The danger Newman perceives of concentrating exclusively on one science to the detriment of the others is that 'the devotees of any science ... necessarily become bigots and quacks, scorning all facts which do not belong to their own pursuit, and thinking to effect everything without aid from any other quarter'.[61] This principle would seem to command acceptance in contemporary higher education circles since, as sciences become ever more detailed and remote from each other, there is an increasing emphasis on the need for interdisciplinary studies and research.

Moreover, the harm done by such an imbalance of view will be proportional to the importance of the science (discipline) omitted. Theology, according to Newman, not only has a rightful place among the sciences, but is the very one whose omission from the circle is proportionally all the more harmful. This is because the unity of the circle of sciences, so necessary for the mutual correction of different branches of knowledge, is grounded in the origin of all things in the Creator. Newman says that 'we cannot truly or fully contemplate [creation] without in some main aspects contemplating [the Creator]'. Now since there is such a bond of unity between all things, then, Newman argues, there is a science corresponding to this bond of unity which unifies all the other sciences, while remaining distinct from all of them. This he calls 'Philosophy', or 'the Science of sciences'. We must be careful to note that he uses the word philosophy here not to designate what is generally known as philosophy, but a faculty of the intellect, or 'habit of mind', which is capable of grasping how things stand in relation to each other.[62]

In order to illustrate what he means by philosophy, or rather, by the lack of it, Newman asks us to suppose that there are such extreme disagreements among academics about the nature of necessity, responsibility, morality and virtue that, in order to avoid constant quarrelling it is decided to have no university studies or professors in ethics and psychology. Those subjects will therefore be treated as matters of private judgement, while other sciences such as astronomy, optics, pure mathematics, geology, botany etc., are studied. Newman comments that, by omitting all study of the mind and its powers, 'henceforth man is to be as if he were not, in the general course of education'.[63] Newman does not imagine that such a mutilation of humanities would actually occur in fact, but considering it in the abstract, he refuses to allow that any such institution should be able to call itself a university.

He goes on to make the further remark that, allowing this imaginary state of affairs to be set up, although

> common sense and public opinion [would] set bounds at first to so intolerable a licence; yet, as time goes on, an omission which was originally but a matter of expedience, commends itself to the reason; and at length a professor is found ... who takes on him to deny psychology *in toto*, to pronounce the influence of the mind in the visible world a superstition, and to account for every effect which is found in the world by the operation of physical causes.[64]

Newman speculates that such an assertion, at first made simply, would then be elaborated into a regular system to account for everything which had previously been ascribed to the agency of the human mind. To deny the motive power of the soul would thus make impossible a true account of the difference between the physical movements of a living person on the one hand and, say, a scarecrow on the other. But Newman is careful not to deny that such an account, although unreal, could still be quite logically sound on its own internal criteria. Thus, 'to assert that the motive cause *is* physical, this is an assumption in a case, when our question is about a matter of fact, not about the logical consequences of an assumed premiss'.[65]

Even though this kind of development is clearly contrary to the truth, Newman claims, it is still possible to imagine how such a state

of affairs might come about. He then takes this extreme example of
the effect of denying human causality in the world:

> If a people prays, and the wind changes, the rain ceases, the sun
> shines, and the harvest is safely housed, when no one expected it,
> our Professor may, if he will, consult the barometer, discourse about
> the atmosphere, and throw what has happened into an equation,
> ingenious, even though it be not true.[66]

He now applies it to the more familiar possibility of denying *divine*
causality in the world:

> If the creature is ever setting in motion an endless series of physical
> causes and effects, much more is the Creator; and as our excluding
> volition from our range of ideas is a denial of the soul, so our
> ignoring Divine Agency is a virtual denial of God.[67]

In all this the fictional professor may be assigning causes entirely from
within the narrow range of his own expertise, and then applying them
to the whole. Thus, Newman identifies two great dangers in ignor-
ing the 'Science of sciences': first, that the fundamental existence
of divine causality may initially simply be ignored, then ultimately
rejected; secondly, that in the absence of the 'Science of sciences',
each of the remaining sciences may soon claim as its own what belongs
to others by rights.

Newman identifies the role of theology as providing the *equilibrium*
for the whole system of knowledge. He defines theology as 'the Science of God, or the truths we know about God put into system'.[68] It is
important to understand that, contrary to most expectations, he does
not rely on the claims of Divine Revelation or Catholic doctrine in
explaining this central place for theology. Newman here relies instead
on 'natural theology', that is what human reason itself can deduce
about God from the *idea* conveyed by the term. If there is such a being
as God, Newman argues, He must be of a very specific nature. Just as
there is a living principle acting upon the human frame by means of
volition, so too there is an invisible and intelligent Being acting on the
visible universe, as and when He will. In brief, Newman explains that
theology teaches that this being must be without beginning, must be

uniquely self-dependent and must possess all perfections in fullness, must be the source of all things He has created, seeing and knowing them intimately at all times and providing lovingly for their particular needs and natures. Most particularly, theology teaches that God manifests 'Himself to each according to its needs; and has on rational beings imprinted the moral law and given them the power to obey it ... putting before them a present trial and a judgment to come.'[69] Therefore, says Newman, to God belongs

> the substance, and the operation, and the results of that system of physical nature into which we are born. His too are ... the laws of the universe, the principles of truth, the relation of one thing to another ... the order and harmony of the whole ... and if evil is not from Him, as assuredly it is not, this is because evil has no substance of its own, but is only the defect, excess, perversion, or corruption of that which has substance.[70]

Moreover, says Newman, not only the laws of the physical universe can be ascribed to this being, but every aspect of man: his intellectual, moral, social and political world.

Therefore, supposing this to be true, how can this teaching fail to exert a powerful influence on philosophy, literature, and every intellectual creation or discovery whatever? Given, then, the magnitude of what theology has to say about God, Newman cannot understand 'how it is possible, as the phrase goes, to blink the question of its truth or falsehood?' If you admit the truth of theology, and recognize that it is a precise and consistent intellectual system, then all follows as Newman has described. If, therefore, you omit theology from the circle of knowledge, then you must deny that it is a science at all.[71] While the interdependence of all the sciences is emphasized, theology is not seen by Newman as simply equal with the other sciences, since theology 'impinges upon' them all. It is here that Newman sees that the Church must keep a check on the university for, left to their own devices, the sciences would dispense with God and substitute a secular philosophy. While the Church must therefore set the boundaries for the university, Newman insists that these must not be so narrowly defined as to harm the university or Church. The university must be independent of clerical control, but the Church must be the animating principle behind its intellectual and social life. By this argument Newman was seeking to achieve equilibrium among competing claims of science and theology in his university.

Seen thus, Newman says that theology cannot be dismissed as something particular or private, or merely fashionable. Even outside Christendom monotheistic natural theology is found throughout the ancient and modern world. Atheism and pantheism have never attained a comparable formation or completeness as systems of thought. To withdraw theology from university studies is therefore not simply likely to impair the completeness of them, but 'to invalidate the trustworthiness of all that is actually taught in them'. And so, Newman concludes, it is according to the Greek proverb, to take the spring from out of the year, or to play *Hamlet* without the Prince.[72]

Newman the Teacher

The Tractarian Battle for the Control of Parish Schools

Newman and the other Tractarians in the 1830s saw themselves as belonging to a Christian nation in a public and collective sense. The Church of England was a major public institution and played an important role in public life, particularly in the direction and provision of schooling. The battle for control of schooling came to a head with the appearance of Lord Brougham's Bill to establish a Ministry of Education which would allow the state to provide education for the masses as well as training the teachers for these proposed elementary schools. The Tractarians recognized that by means of this Bill Brougham and the enlightened liberals were launching an attack upon the central place of Christian teaching in schools. They believed that any concessions would open the doors of the Church to unbelief. Because of their fear of liberalism in theology and education, they responded with a campaign, supported by Newman, to have all education come under the influence of the Church of England, particularly along what they understood to be Catholic lines. They first sought to disqualify the proposals for a non-denominational system of schooling and, secondly, disputed the grounds for the state's claims to greater control of education. They also campaigned, with some success, to ensure that only Tractarians were appointed principals of Church of England teacher training colleges. By the time that Newman had left the Church of England, however, the early success of the Tractarian campaign against the state had been reversed and it is unclear how Newman would have reacted to the changed situation for religious teaching in state schools had he remained an Anglican.

Parochial Teaching

Newman was not only involved at the political level, but at the practical. As we saw in Chapter 1, Newman strove to provide basic religious education for his parishioners both in his regular Sunday preaching and in the Sunday school he established at St Clement's. After this he had no direct involvement with schools until he moved out to Littlemore in 1841. There he became more directly involved in general school teaching. As far as he was concerned, the clergy should be positively active in all aspects of education, not just religious. In 1827 he had said that: 'it seems indeed to be a fundamental mistake ... when the instructors of youth in general knowledge are not also their religious instructors'.[73] His dedication to this duty can be judged from his subscription to the *English Journal of Education* which was launched in 1843.[74] Newman clearly did not discharge his office as teacher simply by imparting information to the children, but by both inspiring and directing them.

Newman certainly did not believe in what might be termed 'value-free' teaching. In his 1826 sermon 'On some popular mistakes as to the object of education',[75] Newman declared that even simply teaching children to read was not a neutral act, for 'everything depends on the way we use it'. The imparting of skill in reading is the beginning, not the end, of education, since the skill is for the sake of what children may then be able to read. Using a favourite analogy he says that

we should never suspect that a person called in a physician merely in order that he might take medicine – as if taking medicine was in itself a desirable object – whereas it is taken *in order to* gain health – and in like manner a child learns to read, not as if that were all, but that *through reading* he may be introduced to the revealed word, the gospel of his salvation.[76]

Newman's whole approach to schooling is based on the principle that man has a religious nature and a destiny for which this life must prepare him. Within this picture, education is a lifelong process. Whatever a child achieves in school is therefore only part of his or her preparation for adult life and beyond.

The Oratory School

After his ordination as a Catholic priest Newman had been involved in mission schools in the poorest districts of Digbeth, Smethwick and Edgbaston, in and around Birmingham. By the time he set up the Oratory School in 1859, therefore, Newman had had a very varied experience of teaching schoolchildren, and not only teaching them their faith. But whereas his earlier experience both as an Anglican and a Catholic had been in running and teaching in parish schools, this new school was set up at the request, and with the cooperation, of Newman's fellow converts. There was a long period of preparation and discussion of terms and conditions with prospective parents before Newman finally opened the school. This was because, in accordance with his principle that teachers acted *in loco parentis*, Newman was unwilling to found and run a school without the full participation and cooperation of those parents. Shrimpton contrasts this attitude with that of a contemporary Anglican founder of schools, Nathaniel Woodard, who 'aimed to substitute the degradation of family life with the moral and religious atmosphere of school, and therefore, unlike Newman, brooked no interference in school affairs by parents or others'.[77]

This conviction of the quasi-parental character of the Oratory School was also shown in Newman's determination that there should be a female as well as a male authority over the boys in his school. He was, perhaps to a degree unusual for his time, aware of the importance of maternal choice and care for their sons in the choice of a school, as he wrote that 'it is a tremendous thing to be intrusted [*sic*] with the hopes and loves of so many mamas'. Newman asked the widow of an old friend, Mrs Wootten, to take on this role. It was Newman's conception of the complementarity of male and female roles in the lives of the boys at school that had largely underlain the almost catastrophic quarrel between him and the then headmaster of the school, Fr Nicholas Darnell, in 1861.

From its inception, Newman as president had given authority in school to Darnell as headmaster, while care of the boys' welfare outside school hours was entrusted to the widow of one of Newman's friends, Frances Wootten. Although there were matrons and dames in other public schools, notably Eton, Newman envisaged Mrs Wootten's role as being more than a sympathetic mother-substitute. Newman saw her as 'in some respects on a par with the Oratorians', and believed that 'but for the presence of Matrons of a high class and of spiritual directors' the school would slip into 'subordinating religion to secular interests and principles'.[78] Thus Newman saw the role of the matrons in his school as promoters of religious devotion among the boys, over and above caring for their physical and moral welfare. Such was the importance Newman accorded her, that when Darnell eventually led a rebellion of his staff against Mrs Wootten's parallel authority, Newman supported her. Darnell and his supporters resigned and Darnell left the Oratorian community for good. Newman was forced to become much more closely involved in the running of the school. He replaced the headmaster and most of the staff almost instantaneously, but though he regretted the departure of such a gifted teacher and head as Darnell, he felt that too much was at stake in losing all that Mrs Wootten stood for and did for the boys in the school.

Newman even consulted Mrs Wootten about important matters not usually discussed with women, such as the spiritual welfare of the boys. For instance, since he was particularly sensitive to the inclination of certain young boys to the possibility of a priestly vocation, Newman would not encourage their separation from the world as was customary in other Catholic schools and seminaries. In one noteworthy instance, when his friend Bellasis asked Newman's advice about sending his younger son who had expressed an interest in the priest-hood either to a seminary, or to join his older brother at Newman's school, Newman delayed replying until he had consulted Mrs Woot-ten, then answering the enquiry by saying that it was better for such boys not to be hidden away from the world until they discover after ordination 'with the most solemn vows upon them that the world is not a seminary'.[79] As if to prove Newman's point, the younger son eventually became a lawyer, while his older brother, who had initially shown no interest in the priesthood, became an Oratorian priest.

After this, Newman took on more of the day-to-day direction of the school. This enabled him to work out in practice the kind of reli-gious education that he judged was most suitable for boys destined for secular careers rather than for the priesthood, as in other Catholic boarding schools. An essential part of the religious education that Newman provided was training in regular prayer and devotion. He insisted that the boys should rise punctually in order to devote the first part of the day to private prayer followed by attendance at Mass. At the end of the day they were to listen to a reading from a spiri-tual classic, such as the popular Catholic anthology *Garden of the Soul* before reflecting privately on what they had heard for a few minutes before going to bed.

But although such cardinal points as the beginning and end of the day were fixed in routine, Newman also encouraged the boys to develop a certain sense of freedom and responsibility for their own religious practice, for instance, by making attendance at daily Rosary optional. Some of the boys tried to push this freedom further when they complained about the length of the chapel services and asked for *them* to be made voluntary. As Paul Shrimpton observes, it is not surprising that, although Newman was very much inclined to listen to boys' complaints and suggestions, and even act on some of them, he turned a very deaf ear to such complaints as these.[80] The rhythms of the Church year also were marked by their special character and observance: during Holy Week the boys made a three-day retreat, a time devoted entirely to sermons and reflection on the meaning of the time. Moreover, these retreats were often attended also by the masters.[81]

Newman was convinced of the importance of the senses in learning. He wrote to Bellasis that 'children and boys take in religion principally through the eye'[82] and resolved to enhance the beauty of the economically built Oratory church accordingly, so that it might be 'one main instrument of religious and moral training'.[83] Similarly, he encouraged the development of those devotions which would engage the boys both physically and imaginatively, such as the Stations of the Cross during Lent, in which the boys would walk around the church to contemplate images of the Passion and Death of Christ and listen to meditations on them. In spring and summer the joyful aspects of the Catholic faith were observed with great panoply in processions around the school grounds, such as the Blessed Sacrament Procession, celebrating the Feast of Corpus Christi, which was accompanied by a band.

The celebration of the school's patron saint, St Philip Neri, which fell at the end of May, was also made an occasion of much splendour in accordance with the joyful character of the saint himself. In sixteenth-century Rome, Philip Neri was not only a lover of music, but had also appreciated its power of influencing the religious imagination. After his example, Newman organized for the boys special events of a musical and religious character, interspersing sung and instrumental music with readings and short sermons which were rather devotional than didactic in tone. Newman's devotional regime was clearly designed to provide what he had identified as the need that youth have for a 'masculine religion',[84] involving plenty of stimulating and enjoyable activity to engage the imagination. Yet just as he had recognized the boys' need of a maternal influence in his defence of Mrs Wootten's role in the school, so too did he believe that a masculine religion positively required devotion to the Mother of God. Throughout the month of May, in accordance with Catholic custom, the boys were encouraged to take part in short daily services honouring Our Lady.

Newman improved the religious education in several ways. The younger boys were not allowed to recite prayers carelessly and mechanically, but had to pay attention to their meaning and demonstrate their understanding of them. They also learned the standard catechism questions and answers about the faith, and were

encouraged to test each other in pairs, in a manner that recalls Newman's own practice with his friend Bowden in their undergraduate
days. For the older boys, whose age and intellectual development
required a more stimulating and advanced treatment of the catechism, Newman himself gave catechetical lessons and, to ensure that
the subjects on which he had lectured had been properly understood and assimilated, he set the boys essays which he then marked
and carefully annotated for them.[85] It was typical of his outlook that
Catholic laity needed such kinds of preparation for survival in a non-
Catholic world, where they would have to be able to hold their own
in discussion and controversy.

Despite his already enormous workload, Newman clearly found this
commitment to the religious direction and running of the school very
fulfilling. In 1864 he wrote that 'if I could believe it to be God's will,
[I] would turn away my thoughts from writing any thing, and should
see, in the superintendence of these boys, the nearest return to my
Oxford life'.[86]

The Catholic University

When Newman was charged with the task of setting up a Catholic
university in Dublin, the question of establishing and protecting its
religious character exercised his mind a great deal. It was founded
in the very real sense of character of an institution, which he calls its
genius loci.[87] This character is usually the product of tradition and is
embodied in the patterns of life and the common aims and values of
the members. Yet it is also capable of being influenced, if not transformed, by the actions and characters of its members. For instance,
Newman recognized that the genius loci of Oxford had been built
up over many centuries and was embodied in such aspects as its collegiate life, its clerical associations, the courses of studies followed. But
in the case of Dublin, the university was completely new and so had
no established character of this kind. Yet Newman realized that it was
important to form it, and to do so as quickly as possible. Hence some
of the references to Oxford that Newman made in his early years at
Dublin. It is not so much the case that he naively tried to transplant
Oxford into Dublin, as that he sought to create in Dublin the kind of

fundamental stability of character that is represented by the idea of a genius loci.

It was, perhaps, inevitable that Newman would turn in the first instance, or in the absence of other suitable candidates, to men he had known at Oxford in order to set up the university. It was also to a certain extent a matter of policy. After all, Newman wanted to gather round himself men who would share his vision in the governance and teaching work of the university. Especially he wanted men who would be tutors after the model he had abortively attempted to establish at Oriel. Thus he appealed for 'young men, for the most part unmarried [who] would be in the position of private Tutors and Junior Fellows at Oxford ... friends of my own, so that they, with me, would be the nucleus of a tradition or genius loci'.[88] Yet there was more to this matter of establishing the genius loci than finding congenial men to help him run the University. The essential thing was the centrality of the Catholic Faith. As he wrote in *My Campaign in Ireland*, Newman did not believe it possible for a university to have a *genius loci* while it had professors of different religions[89].

In religious terms he sought to mould the university's Catholic spirit around the presiding physical presence of a university church which would, in a sense, be to Dublin what St Mary's in Oxford had been in his time there as vicar. Hence the importance which Newman invested in the design and decoration of his church, and of the arrangement of its preaching and services. His aim was for the church to 'give a unity to the various academical foundations' and to 'maintain and symbolize that great principle in which we glory as our characteristic, the union of Science with Religion'.[90] He commissioned his friend and fellow-convert, John Hungerford Pollen, to design the church after the pattern of a Roman basilica and he was extremely proud of it, saying that it was 'to my taste ... the most beautiful one in the three kingdoms'.[91]

The Role of General Religious Knowledge in University Studies

Newman was aware that students need a broad range of general knowledge beside those studies which comprise their degree. In the second part of the *Idea,* Newman collected a variety of his occasional lectures and papers on 'University Subjects'. In the fourth chapter entitled 'Elementary Studies' he deals with the need for general religious knowledge together with basic grounding in grammar, composition and style or expression through the medium of Latin writing. Newman introduces the need for such elementary studies by describing the way that a baby, confronted by a vast array of sense-perception,

> gradually learns the connexion of part with part, separates what is moving from what is stationary, watches the coming and going of figures, masters the idea of shape and of perspective, calls in the information conveyed through the other senses to assist him in his mental process, and thus gradually converts a calidoscope [*sic*] into a picture.[92]

Newman says that the education of our intellect is to a certain extent analogous with this process. One of the labours of both school and university is

> to remove the original dimness of the mind's eye; to strengthen and perfect its vision; to enable it to look out into the world right forward, steadily and truly; to give the mind clearness, accuracy, precision; to enable it to use words aright, to understand what it says, to conceive justly what it thinks about, to abstract, compare, analyse, divide, define, and reason, correctly.[93]

This process is summed up as 'discipline in accuracy of mind'. Newman recognizes that such discipline is not only necessary for the successful prosecution of study, but also as a preparation for 'the general duties of secular life'.[94] Observing that English universities of his day customarily introduced religious instruction into the School of Arts, he agrees that such is indeed 'a very right custom' which he intends to follow. Nonetheless, he recognizes that this practice 'is not without its difficulty', and that he hopes to identify 'some intelligible principle' to justify its inclusion in a secular faculty without its becoming an 'intrusion'. Whereas some of Newman's contemporaries might wish to make over the subject of religion to the theologian exclusively, others might wish to go to the opposite extreme, both replacing classical literature with scripture, and teaching theology proper to all university honours students. Newman will have neither of these. Instead he maintains that it is simply 'congruous' that a Catholic university should prepare its students for the duties of secular life by sending them out with some knowledge of their religion. Indeed, it would be a scandal if such an institution failed to do just that. The question, of course, is how much knowledge of this kind the graduate who enters the secular professions is likely to need.

In the first place, there is a positive danger in not providing any religious education at all for the student whose mental powers are sharpened and refined by study; namely the chance of its exercising those powers wrongly. A mind whose critical powers are strengthened but which has not acquired a suitable basic knowledge of religious matters may well fall into error. The greater the powers of mind and the less the general level of religious knowledge, the greater the danger. Moreover, Newman recognizes that the intellect gains an appetite for knowledge when it is properly developed. It is therefore necessary for the correct balance of that development that the intellect should be fed 'with divine truth' as well as with other areas of knowledge. Newman acknowledges that in the area of general religious education at this level there is a danger to be avoided; namely the possibility that 'A little learning is a dangerous thing'. It is all too easy for a person who has acquired a superficial knowledge of a subject to imagine that he or she has grasped all the necessary principles for further unguided speculation. In dealing with the Catholic religion, one is dealing with divinely revealed truth whose origin is not human reason. Human reason has its proper role in deepening its understanding of that revealed truth, but part of the role of human reason in this matter is precisely to recognize its own limits as well as its powers.

Secondly, a student necessarily encounters many other well-educated, but by no means sympathetic, persons with religious views and beliefs opposed to those of the Catholic Church. Newman says that it is desirable that a Catholic should be on a par with such other persons and be able to keep up a conversation with them, being equally conversant 'with the outlines and the characteristics of sacred and ecclesiastical history as well as of profane'.[95] This means that one who has been educated at such a university as Newman's should know, as well as non-Catholics are presumed to know, the history of the basic divisions of Christianity, and of its spreading through the world; the major Christian writers, as regards both their influence and their historical circumstances; heresies and other opposition to Catholic teaching; religious orders; how the Church has contributed to science and learning; scripture and the development of the biblical canon – in short, areas of fact that are likely to be controversial, and in which Catholics might find their religion unjustly attacked or mis-understood. Moreover, says Newman, no harm can come to students from a certain superficiality in this area of general knowledge.

Yet when it comes to theology itself, Newman is more cautious about the danger of superficiality. He would only have students 'apply their minds to such religious topics as laymen actually do treat' and 'content myself with enforcing a broad knowledge of doctrinal subjects as is contained in the catechisms of the Church'.[96] Just as ecclesiastics who meddle with law, or medicine or finance, are likely to succeed ill, so too are lawyers, physicians or merchants who set about discussing theological points solely from their own discipline's perspective.

The principle which governs Newman's approach to general reli-gious education is that of usefulness to the student in his secular life. He wishes to inculcate an 'intelligent apprehension' of those matters which are commonly controverted in society. 'Half the controversies which go on in the world,' he says, 'arise from ignorance of the facts of the case; half the prejudices against Catholicity lie in the misinforma-tion of the prejudiced parties.' Newman shows that he is not aiming at a fully professional knowledge of theology for the student when he indicates the end or purpose of his programme for general religious instruction: 'Candid persons are set right, and enemies silenced, by the mere statement of what it is that we believe.' He illustrates this point by recalling the effect upon several Anglican clergymen of ques-tioning a young Irish country boy about his religion; 'one of them confessed to me that that poor child put them all to silence. How? Not, of course, by any train of arguments, or refined theological dis-quisition, but merely by knowing and understanding the answers in his catechism.'[97]

Adult Education

As an Anglican Newman had recognized the danger to the faith that was posed by ignorance of the ordinary people and the apostasy of the intelligentsia. There were plenty of educational institutions run by the Established Church, but few of them were being used effectively to guide people into a fuller understanding and practice of the Christian faith. As a Catholic Newman recognized that ignorance was also a danger to the English Catholic body, but of a different kind. There were simply too few educational institutions, and none of them was, in his view, really adequate to 'the great infidel questions of the day'.[98] Although this state of affairs was hardly the fault of the Catholics, who had been persecuted and excluded from most educational institutions and professions for centuries, nonetheless it had left them not only behind their Protestant neighbours in educational attainment, but even unaware that this was the case. It was in this situation that Newman aimed 'at improving the condition ... of the Catholic body ... by giving them juster views, by enlarging and refining their minds, in one word by education'. His practice both in Dublin and in Edgbaston illustrate what he was aiming at when he said in 1851 that

> I want a laity, not arrogant, not rash in speech, not disputatious, but men who know their religion, who enter into it, who know just where they stand, who know what they hold, and what they do not, who know their creed so well, that they can give an account of it, who know so much of history that they can defend it.[99]

He saw that Catholics in England, only twenty years after Emancipation, were gradually trying to raise their profile, but mistakenly, he judged, through the 'showy' architecture of Pugin and his disciples rather than through education. But many Catholics resented the famous Oxford convert coming among them and criticizing their level of learning. Newman's reaction was to comment that education 'is (in [the Catholics'] view) more than a superfluity or a hobby, it is an insult'.[100]

One of the principal motives for Newman's original attraction to the Oratorian way of life had been its openness to all kinds of educational work without being restricted to running schools. As Oratorians, he said that he and his companions were '*called* to education'.[101] The Papal Brief by which the Oratory was set up in England under Newman's leadership specified as their preferred work 'to aim at doing whatever they think will best promote the cause of religion in the bigger cities, and among those in the higher ranks, the more learned and generally among the more educated'.[102] The Pope conferred with Newman about the contents of the Brief and accordingly decreed that the Oratory should be set up in Birmingham, where Newman's ecclesiastical superior resided. The essential part of this choice is the fact that an Oratory is located in a large town or city because its nature is to be a presence among urban rather than rural people, because of the more varied nature of their interests, occupations and contacts.

Moreover, the Fathers of an Oratory both live and work in the same place. They do not take on work as missionaries to outposts beyond their immediate locality. This was crucial to Newman's conception of his future work as an Oratorian priest: that he would live and work in the midst of a large population where he would provide for their sacramental life in church, and for their education in the faith. Where the Pope had mentioned 'the higher ranks' of society, some of Newman's companions complained that Birmingham was hardly the place to find such people. But Newman was adamant. The Pope had not meant to tie his hands by using that phrase, but had assumed that any city would have something corresponding to its own 'higher order'.

Newman had explained to the Pope that the 'ordo doctior, honestior [i.e. the higher and more educated ranks] was in *great measure* synonymous with the classes I had specified – so that *if there* be a class in Birmingham of sharp intellects, who are the recipients of political power, and who can be made Catholics, I think we are fulfilling the Brief'.[103] In other words, where Faber concluded that Birmingham was a far less suitable location for an Oratorian foundation than London, Newman understood 'higher order' to apply to people of any social class who were capable of, and in need of, sound general religious education. It was to this work that Newman henceforth dedicated himself. Nor did he ever regret this choice. It was Faber, not Newman, who set up the Oratory in London, although Newman was a native of the city. During the years of his rectorship in Dublin Newman never severed links with Birmingham, even though he was obliged frequently to travel back and forth across the Irish sea and delegate much of the day-to-day work both in Birmingham and in Dublin. In fact he retained a fairly close interest in much of the detail of what was being planned and done. Once he had returned from Dublin for good, Newman very rarely left Birmingham again, preferring to remain quietly at a home which allowed him 'time for study, [and] missionary work of the most intimate kind'.[104] He used the institution of the 'Little Oratory', a confraternity of laymen, to further his aim of instructing adult lay Catholics in Birmingham. His addresses *On the Present Position of Catholics in England* were delivered in 1851 to the men of the Oratory congregation and are the best-known product of this aspect of his work, designed to educate, inform, entertain and encourage laymen to live and understand their faith in a hostile environment. It was in the course of these lectures that he expressed his desire that

> I want an intelligent, well-instructed laity ... I wish you to enlarge your knowledge, to cultivate your reason, to get an insight into the relation of truth to truth, to learn to view things as they are, to understand how faith and reason stand to each other, what are the bases and principles of Catholicism, and where lie the main inconsistencies and absurdities of the Protestant theory.[105]

From his first days as an Anglican curate to his old age as a Roman cardinal, Newman's conviction that the Church had a solemn duty to educate the baptized laity remained at the heart of his mission, and in the midst of so many and varied activities, as he himself said, 'from first to last education ... has been my line'.[106]

Chapter 3

The Moral Purpose of Education

Introduction

Newman's view of moral education belongs firmly within the tradition of the Graeco-Roman tradition of moral philosophy as it had been adopted and reformulated by Judaeo-Christian philosophy and theology. Yet Newman's approach to moral education contains distinctive elements which arise from his own personal experience and from his reflection upon developments in moral theory from the Enlightenment period that contrasted significantly with the tradition, and even opposed it. We consider this backdrop to Newman's thought and action.

Classical Greek Ideas of Morality

Newman was, of course, deeply influenced by classical Greek thought. Plato, in the first work on the philosophy of education, the *Republic*, considered morality from the point of view both of the individual and of society. He argued that an essential prerequisite to becoming fully human and to the creation of a just society, was the formation of a good character. But what does it mean to have a good character? A good character is one which embodies the quality of *aretē*, 'moral excellence', which is often rendered 'virtue'. But in what does moral excellence or virtue consist? Socrates, Plato's tutor, had taught that virtue is *knowledge of the good*. He asked whether a child who has no knowledge of moral principles can therefore truly *be* good. In the *Republic* Plato answered that although only a philosopher who knows the good can truly be a good man, there is a lesser kind of goodness which can begin with the right training and which can lead towards the fullness of knowledge of the good. Moral education in Plato is directed towards a fully intellectual apprehension of what the good is. A truly good character will be one that understands the Good and therefore does what is good. Plato held that a person who knows what is good will therefore do it. He did not think that anyone willingly acted immorally, and explained that if they did so act then it could only be through ignorance of the good.

Plato's pupil, Aristotle, took a different view in his *Nicomachean Ethics* and *Politics*. Where Plato had taught that a prior intellectual understanding of the good alone makes moral excellence attainable, Aristotle argued rather that a person becomes good by learning first what it is to do good. He also recognized, in contrast to Plato, that a person may have the ability to think about the good without having the disposition to implement it. Nevertheless, both agreed that the teaching of virtue was ultimately concerned with the formation of character, which must be actively cultivated in the young, so that they might eventually be virtuous persons and not merely perform virtuous actions.

Since Plato and Aristotle were teachers of aristocratic young men who had already been trained to exercise self-control and had attained a certain maturity, they were aiming to perfect in these young men the final stages of the process of their moral education: a philosophical understanding of the virtues and of what constitutes 'the good'. On the one hand, Plato tended to argue from the assumption that intellectual and moral excellence was the preserve of the aristocratic minority, whose political duty it was either to persuade or coerce the majority of citizens to act in particular ways. On the other hand, although Aristotle recognized that the freedom to think and act virtuously was to some extent greater for the aristocracy, he taught nonetheless that every person acts morally, and requires some knowledge of the virtues.

Aristotle therefore gave more specific attention to the whole process of moral education in children than did Plato. He posited three educational stages: first, the training of the body; secondly, the training of character; and finally, the training of the intellect. He observed that intellect appears later in the child. Only after children have built certain good habits within the second stage can they reasonably move to the stage of comprehension. In the words of Gerard Hughes,

Aristotle offered 'the theoretical backing to a process of moral training which had already been largely completed'.[107] Students already deemed to have developed virtuous characters are to be taught subsequently how to think about moral decisions. Yet, paradoxically, Aristotle says that unless one already has the skills necessary to think correctly about moral decisions one cannot be virtuous. This is because Aristotle defines virtue as 'a deliberated and permanent disposition, based on a standard applied to ourselves and defined by the reason displayed by the man of good sense'.[108] Virtue is based on reason which is conducive to the good and which engenders the human capacity deliberately to seek the good. For Aristotle, rationality is an essential element in moral choice. Reason is therefore an element in the educational process by which virtue is formed. A person achieves freedom in deciding how to act by learning gradually how to use reason in making moral decisions. This freedom is self-mastery or self-control.

Newman was well acquainted with these ideas and arguments concerning morality. He believed, like Aristotle, that young children are not capable of moral judgements, but have the capacity to arrive at moral maturity through appropriate education and training; first in moral habits, then by skills in reasoning. Newman accepted that children need to be brought up in a way that disposed them towards the good and that this required them to be active in doing 'good acts'. He believed that all individuals have the natural potential to do good acts and that in so doing they effectively fix 'goodness' within their own character. The formation of good habits is an essential part of the process of growth towards maturity and self-control. In his *Autobiographical Writings* he said that 'he had from the first made much of [Greek and Latin authors], as the Holy Fathers did, as being in a certain sense inspired moralists, and prophets of truths greater than they knew'.[109]

Christian Patristic Morality: the Image of Christ

In formulating moral philosophy, the Greek Fathers of the Christian Church carried over much of the language and structure of virtue and *paideia* from Plato and Aristotle, but they did not regard it as the last word. For the Fathers, the ultimate truth about all human existence was to be found in divine revelation. The central fact of Christian faith is the person of Christ the Son of God and Redeemer of mankind whom St Paul proposes as the model of the 'perfect man', to whose standard of perfection all are called to aspire.[110] Thus Christian moral perfection is founded not in the abstract ideas of the virtues but in the goodness and love of God incarnate in Christ. This perfection, however, would be impossible to attain by human learning and effort without a special assistance from Christ Himself in the form of the power of divine grace (*charis*).

Complete and perfect self-mastery is actually beyond any human person's reach on account of a serious flaw in man's moral nature, a flaw called 'original sin'. This doctrine expresses the rupture of the original relationship between God and man; a relationship of mutual love grounded in the authority of the Creator and the obedience of the creature. The rebellion against the authority of God, the Fall, which is described in Chapter 3 of the book of Genesis, results in man's loss of his properly ordered faculty of reasoning in moral matters. Man's original moral integrity has been destroyed. Since the Fall man is subject to the vagaries of passions which subdue his reason in moral judgements. Paul describes the moral state of fallen man thus: 'That which I do, I do not understand. For the good that I wish to do, I do not; rather, it is the evil which I hate that I do.'[111] If this analysis, coupled with the command to imitate Christ in his moral perfection, were all that Christian morality had to offer, it would indeed be a counsel of despair. But Paul teaches that Christ is not only the model for human perfection, he is also the *means* whereby it can be attained. This is achieved by 'spiritual adoption'.[112] This adoption means that God accepts fallen man as he accepts Christ his own Son. This is the effect of the redemption of man achieved by Christ's death and resurrection. Fallen Man is thus transformed by the action of God's free gift of grace and he is given the means to grow into moral maturity. The innate human capacity for moral maturity and self-control, lost by sin, is thus made possible once more by grace. The moral life is therefore not simply a matter of attaining self-mastery, but of growing into the 'image of Christ', who, being sinless Himself, is alone capable of being both the model and the means of attaining true human perfection.

The Greek Fathers articulated a unique kind of pedagogy, or *paideia:* a much broader term than 'moral education'. *Paideia* implies more than a purely intellectual grasp of morality, by including a thorough training in its practice. Although it is a word that has been lost to modern educational vocabulary, *paideia* was central to Newman's thought, embracing the total development of the human person: body, mind, heart, will, senses, passions, judgements and instincts, aiming at *aretē*, excellence in living. It is this concept of *paideia* that Newman took from the classical philosophers and Greek Fathers of the early Church and it runs through all his works. In the Fathers Newman found articulated the view he already held about the true value of education and learning.

Newman was greatly influenced by patristic thought which aimed at the formation of the *imago Christi* in the *anima christiana* – the likeness of Christ in the individual Christian soul, and he was to articulate more clearly his understanding of the proper relationship of education to Christian virtue particularly after he began to study the Greek Fathers of the Church. It is Newman's achievement to have combined the humane tradition of the Ancient Greeks with the religious traditions of the Greek and Latin Fathers, particularly St Augustine.

Aquinas

Later in the Christian tradition, Aquinas laid special emphasis upon the role of reason in making moral choices, and developed a language of natural law as common to men even before they were under the influence of grace. Newman accepted this emphasis. Aristotle had taught that becoming virtuous involved using one's powers of reasoning to shape virtues that are innate in each individual, and that it was this inherent condition or potential that produced a natural impulse to desire the good. Aquinas combined this natural impulse with the power of rational thought and claimed that together they allow human beings to reach an understanding of what is morally right. In other words, this led Aquinas to develop a more sophisticated sense of the natural law which, he says, allows us to grasp God's moral laws through our own reasoning powers. Aquinas taught that reason and faith are mutually interdependent in the formation and operation of moral character. In making right moral judgements, man's natural powers must necessarily be assisted by the action of God's grace. Grace does not do violence to nature, but builds on it. Thus, in Aquinas's understanding, reason (which is natural) and faith (which is supernatural) sustain each other as do nature and grace.

The Enlightenment

By Newman's time the Christian tradition had not only experienced the sundering of the Reformation, but also the effects of the Enlightenment and post-Christian rationalism. Newman was aware of various objections to an objectivist account of morality made by David Hume in his *Treatise of Human Nature* (1740). Hume had written that no observed facts reveal or entail any values so that there can be no way of reading off values from the external world. Hume had observed that there is a gap between fact (descriptive) and values (prescriptive), which meant that attitudes and sentiments largely determined moral judgements – not facts themselves. Values could therefore be subjective and Hume's ideas came to be regarded by his contemporaries and succeeding generations as having destroyed the possibility of any kind of ethical objectivism.

Newman was aware that an emphasis on individual freedom, on innovation, subjectivity and instrumentality would lead eventually to relativism in moral judgement. He saw the implications for Christianity and particularly Christian moral teaching of growing scepticism among the followers of Hume and Kant. Private judgement would more likely lead to competitive self-interest than to common moral efforts. Therefore Newman, believing that moral character was rooted in intellectual insight and rational judgement, emphasized rational enquiry. He saw moral education as the preparation of the individual for eternal life and therefore insisted that the natural law, the belief in an 'objective moral order', was inextricably linked to Judeo-Christian theism.

Foundations of Moral Conscience in Newman

1   *The Priority of the Unseen World*

Newman was convinced of the primacy of the 'unseen world' over the visible world. He believed that man's spiritual faculties are the most important in his nature, and are central to understanding his origin, his calling and his destiny. Therefore the invisible world of the spirit, the realm of God and His hidden work in the world and in men's hearts; the world of the angels and of Satan the great adversary of God and man – this world was the one which had priority over the material world of sense, and influenced its workings in hidden ways. For Newman, the invisible and visible worlds are inextricably linked by what he called the 'sacramental principle', by which the mind considers physical reality as a sign or symbol of a higher order of reality. It sees the world as not only governed by physical laws or uncovered by scientific hypotheses and experimentation but also as governed by Divine Providence. The recognition of Providence requires faith. It was in order to justify this action of faith upon reason that Newman wrote his last great work, *An Essay in Aid of a Grammar of Assent*.

2   *Opposition to Scepticism*

Newman addressed himself to a generation who considered themselves Christians while increasingly failing to practise the discipline taught by revelation. Then again, Newman's understanding of conscience contrasted with an increasingly common view of morality as either social convention or 'good taste', which was devoid of any sense of duty to obey God who had authority over them, and who cared about every aspect of their lives. Also as he understood the priority of the unseen over the visible world, Newman was out of step with the spirit of the age of enlightenment and materialism which considered the idea of God to be superfluous in any account of man and the world. His awareness of the presence of God in the individual person contrasted with a growing scepticism about God's existence in the nineteenth century, not only among intellectuals, but also practically among ordinary men and women.

3   Conscience

Newman's understanding of morality is founded in the relationship between the Creator and man as a rational creature. We have already stated that Newman held that man has a natural capacity to know God. This capacity is founded in man's rational nature, which is his power both to reason in order to understand, and to act on what is reasoned about. Such a capacity, by definition, needs to be properly activated in order to function effectively. Like the power of reasoning and intelligence itself, the capacity to know God must be guided aright if it is to serve man's needs and his purpose in life. For Newman, the guidance to maturity of this capacity is the most important aim of education: 'It can never be too often repeated that the object of education is to *write the divine law upon the heart*'.[113] At the heart of all human morality is God's law for man, which is designed to help man find his true fulfilment in perfect union with his Creator. This search for fulfilment is arduous, because it requires the training of the mind and will both to understand God's law and to choose it against the prevailing tenor of the will. Although created to work together in harmony to bring man to fulfilment in God, the human mind and will are no longer orientated naturally towards God as Creator and Last End because, although the power of the intellect and will were not actually destroyed through original sin, yet their original integrity and harmony were lost. Even so, Newman argues, man still has a most important faculty of the mind and will which, when properly guided and used, remains within him to assist his recovery from the confusing effects of the fall. This faculty he identifies as *conscience*.

4   Divine Origin of Conscience

In order to understand Newman's detailed and highly original account of the nature and role of conscience in the individual person, it is important to begin with his own experience. Newman recognized the central importance of conscience as a witness, personal in nature, to the relationship between each individual person and God. His conversion had left him with a lasting sense of the abiding presence of God in his soul. In the *Apologia* he tells how he became aware of 'two, and two only absolute and luminously self-evident beings, myself and my Creator'.[114] Not only was Newman aware of God's presence within him, but also of God's authority, which Newman describes as an inner 'voice' which commanded certain things and forbade others, and spoke of judgement, punishment and reward.[115] Newman recognized that this sense of authority was implicit in the relationship of the creature to his Creator. It meant that the creature owed God not only thanks and respect, but also obedience. For Newman, therefore, conscience is the most important guide to morality and its foundation, which he describes as the 'voice of God' and the 'aboriginal vicar of Christ' in the individual human soul.[116]

Newman's lively sense of the centrality of the relationship between the individual person and God as 'two self-evident beings' not only does not preclude other human relationships, but rather underlies them and gives them their form and meaning. From this principle it follows that for Newman all human relationships, and the morality which governs them, depend upon our primary relationship with God our Creator. But though conscience is planted in every soul by virtue of our being God's creatures, nevertheless we need to learn to hear and respect it, and above all, obey it. This seems at first contradictory: that conscience is a faculty with which each person is endowed from birth, and yet that it should need guidance and training. That is resolved when we realize that Newman is saying that conscience has two distinct aspects: it has both a critical and a judicial function.[117] The knowledge that conscience gives is of a 'general' nature: to do good and avoid evil. This general knowledge has, however, to be applied to particular situations which call for moral action. A person has the freedom to reject or ignore the judgement of conscience, but not its critical voice. This twofold act of conscience, for Newman, operates through intellect and feeling. The former he calls the moral sense, meaning one's own inner knowledge of right and wrong; while the latter he characterizes as the feeling of being judged, commanded and sanctioned by someone external to oneself. The intellectual aspect would be the 'critical voice', and the feeling of a good or bad conscience, of being commanded and judged, would be the 'sanction', a result of 'the judgement of conscience'. What Newman realized is that action or behaviour contrary to the dictates of conscience can seriously impair, although never quite destroy, that faculty. We will return to this theme when we consider Newman's *paideia*, and particularly his attitude to the forming of moral judgement in the young.

5   Personal Nature of Conscience

Newman also recognized the distinctively personal aspect of the presence and working of conscience. It is the law of God 'apprehended in the minds of individual men'.[118] Each person receives the promptings of conscience according to his own characteristic 'intellectual medium'. In the *Grammar* Newman explains that a person's powers of reasoning are coloured and, to an extent, formed by his previous experiences and training. So, too, the working of conscience within a person is distinctively individual in its mode of operation. Nevertheless, conscience is not purely subjective. Because it originates not in man, but in Christ, who is 'Priest, Prophet and King', it is still 'a prophet in its informations, a monarch in its peremptoriness, a priest in its blessings and anathemas'.[119] Yet the conscience is not only an authoritative voice, bidding us do certain things and avoid others, it is also a *judgement of the reason* that certain acts are good and others wicked.[120] Although this faculty cannot be entirely destroyed, its power of discrimination can be misled by pride or by bad guidance. The formation of conscience was therefore a fundamental requirement for Newman, since, as he states, 'it admits of being strengthened and improved'. 'The end of education', he said, 'is to affect the heart.'[121] For this reason, the development and use of conscience can and must be assisted and sustained by careful guidance. Newman saw this to be his special responsibility as a pastor, both in his preaching and in his teaching.

6   False Accounts of Conscience

Conscience, as Newman understood it, is a 'given'. Yet even though it does not depend on us for its existence or operation, it can be damaged through our ignorance or disobedience. It is also capable of being from the outset falsely understood or wilfully misinterpreted. Newman condemned the abuse of conscience as a synonym for self-will, which can so successfully masquerade as a 'counterfeit' of the real thing that 'it is the very right and freedom of conscience to dispense with conscience'.[122] A true evidence of conscience as opposed to mere self-will is, according to Newman, its dependence on 'serious thought, prayer and all available means of arriving at a right judgement on the matter in question'.[123]

Thus, as a Catholic priest, Newman continued to champion the sovereignty of conscience, famously stating that 'I shall drink – to the Pope, if you please – still, to Conscience first, and to the Pope afterwards'. Only if we ignore Newman's lifelong consistency in teaching the divine origin of the awesome voice of conscience can we misread this as Newman's support for self-will against Church authority. Since truth cannot contradict truth, and because Christ has endowed His Church with the guidance of the Holy Spirit through His chosen channels of authority on earth, Newman saw that it is impossible that God's inner voice in any individual soul should contradict God's prophetic teaching voice in the visible organs of Church authority appointed by Christ. Therefore, he says that no man can claim the authority of his conscience to overrule the authority of the Church unless he can 'say to himself, as in the Presence of God, that he must not, and dare not, act upon the Papal injunction'.[124] For Newman, then, conscience is never anything less than a commanding voice of authority, which although intimately internal, comes originally from without, that is from the Creator.

Newman also recognizes that conscience can be mistakenly thought of as a human construct. In the *Idea* he refers to the tendency common in his time, to interpret morality as a matter of 'taste': 'Knowledge, the discipline by which it is gained, and the tastes which it forms, have a natural tendency to refine the mind.'[125] Allowing that, Newman points to the radical difference between 'mental refinement and genuine religion'. He agrees that a sharpening of moral perceptions and tastes can follow after refinement of the mind. A refined and cultivated mind can feel 'scorn and hatred ... for some kinds of vice, and utter disgust and profound humiliation ... if it should happen in any degree to be betrayed into them'.[126] This sense of disgust and humiliation may come from the judgement of conscience, but equally it may not; 'there is nothing really religious in it, considered by itself'. He expands this: 'when the mind is simply angry with itself and nothing more, surely the true import of the voice of nature and the depth of its intimations have been forgotten, and a false philosophy has misinterpreted emotions which ought to lead to God'.[127] This danger he identifies as a 'spurious' religion, characterized by taste. The anger that such a conscience feels may only be the effect of wounded pride in a cultivated person who despises himself for a moral failing. Conscience considered exclusively as 'taste', that is, as an intellectual evaluation or critical judgement or refined sensibility, results from the denial of the second aspect of conscience, the strong sense of feeling of duty commanded and sanctioned from outside the self.

Unfashionably and uncomfortably both for his own time and ours, Newman identifies fear as the element whose absence warps the developing conscience, being all too often replaced with shame. 'Fear takes us out of ourselves whereas shame may act upon us only within the round of our own thoughts.' Now whereas shame implies that the mind is simply angry with itself, fear implies the transgression of a law, and a law implies a lawgiver and a judge.[128] The danger for a civilized and intellectually developed age such as Newman's was, he said, that 'conscience tends to become what is called a moral sense . . . sin is not an offence against God, but against human nature'.[129] Newman objects to such a view of conscience as a 'moral sense' because it does not correspond to what people understand the conscience to be. The 'moral sense' by itself means only the intellectual or knowing aspect of conscience, whereas having a 'good or bad conscience' means feeling judged or sanctioned because of obeying or failing a 'command'. 'Half the world would be puzzled to know what was meant by the moral sense; but every one knows what is meant by a good or bad conscience.'[130]

Yet Newman was far from saying that the reduction of conscience to a mere 'moral sense' was a purely contemporary phenomenon. Any society which valued learning and intellectual attainments could be vulnerable to it. He identified the Roman Emperor Julian from the fourth century as an example of a 'near-perfect' man endowed with many human virtues and great intelligence who had knowingly rejected the commanding voice of conscience. Newman ponders the approving tone of Gibbon's account of Julian's death, as he lay in his tent, fatally wounded in battle, discussing the nature of the soul with two philosophers and reasoning about his impending glorious departure from the world without any sense of approaching judgement. Newman comments: 'in the insensibility of conscience, in the ignorance of the very idea of sin, in the contemplation of his own moral consistency, in the cloudless self-confidence, in the serene self-possession, in the cold self-satisfaction, we recognise the mere Philosopher'.[131]

Newman was well aware that in this interpretation of conscience he was opposing the cultural and intellectual tide of his day. The idea of moral perfection as a form of aestheticism was gaining ground precisely where the rights and presence of God were being ignored and replaced by the philosophy of taste. It was not simply that Newman's view of conscience was regarded as old-fashioned by contemporary progressives, but that it was regarded as inimical to human freedom and progress. He identifies Gibbon as exemplifying this tendency: 'he says that Christianity is the enemy of moral virtue, as influencing the mind by fear of God, not by love of the good'.[132] But Newman objects to this reductivist view of the nature of conscience to a mere 'taste' or aesthetic judgement by pointing out that conscience is 'a voice, or the echo of a voice, imperative and constraining, like no other dictate in the whole of our experience'.[133] In other words, no merely aesthetic account of conscience can adequately account for all the phenomena or characteristic experiences of conscience.

7   Knowledge and Virtue

Just as Newman recognized the falsity and danger of reducing moral sense to mere good taste, so too did he clearly identify the tendency to conflate knowledge and virtue. We noted earlier that he held that 'knowledge, the discipline by which it is gained, and the tastes which it forms, have a natural tendency to refine the mind'. Hence it is always possible for the educated mind erroneously to assume that refinement itself either constitutes or creates virtue. Ignorance can then be redefined as a moral evil, and its eradication by learning becomes therefore both the means and the definition of moral goodness. Written only in 1826, Newman's remarkable sermon 'On some popular mistakes as to the object of education' contains in embryo virtually all the educational ideas that he was to work out in so many different situations throughout his life. From the outset Newman held that knowledge, as one of the aims of education, is ambivalent. It can lead to pride rather than to God. He points out that in a civilized and sophisticated society like that of first-century Corinth, or nineteenth-century England 'Wealth and learning are necessary (by God's appointment) to protect and recommend the Christian doctrine.'

Yet 'the temptation of human learning ... led [the Corinthians] to prefer gifts to graces – the power of the intellect to moral excellence'.[134] It is impossible that people should hope to become or remain religious in an intellectually sophisticated world, he says, if they themselves have no education at all. Yet there is a tension between the desirability of knowledge on the one hand, and its possible opposition to virtue on the other, which Newman brings out clearly in his preaching. The first error concerning knowledge which Newman identifies is 'the mistake ... of supposing that in proportion as men *know* more, they will be *better* men in a moral point of view; and therefore a good education is *the* remedy for all the evil in the world'.

In a sermon from 1827 he says that, 'the very best means for advancing us in holiness *might* prove the very best for advancing us in sin – that everything depended on the state of mind worked upon'. This idea of 'state of mind' Newman saw as a vital element in religious and moral formation. Mere knowledge was not enough to form a character for love of God, saying 'It is one thing to know the truth, quite another to love it'.[135]

Now knowledge is a good thing, says Newman, or else, 'why should Christ have set up the Christian Church at all? For what is [the Church] but a school of education for the next life? ... the object of education is to *write the divine law upon the heart*.'[136] This, then, would seem to demand that not only religious education, but *all* education should have a religious end or purpose. Newman would agree. But he would not therefore demand that all education must be explicitly *about* religion. He certainly did not disdain the use of subjects other than purely religious ones in education. Rather we can characterize his attitude to education as a holistic one. All education is ultimately concerned with the final end of human life. 'The end of education', he said, 'is to affect the heart.'[137] Any form of education which ignores or contradicts that end is dangerously false.

The Tamworth Reading Room

Newman was given an opportunity to expound his view of the nature of moral education and the dangers of certain contemporary theories in January1841 when Sir Robert Peel opened a library reading room in Tamworth. In his opening speech Peel adopted a utilitarian view of religion, and suggested that reading would bring myriad wonderful facts to people's minds, and that knowledge would make them appreciate the wonder of the Creator who produced all these phenomena, which in turn would make them all become good and virtuous citizens.

It was Newman's response to his address however, that makes the occasion famous.[138] He argued that Peel's stated aim was quite inadequate as an account of the relationship between knowledge and virtue. Peel had hoped on the one hand that increased knowledge would promote Christianity, and yet on the other suggested that discussion of religion should be excluded from the Reading Room, on the grounds that religious doctrine is divisive. Peel claimed that 'in becoming wiser a man will become better', meaning by wiser that such a man will 'rise at *once* in the scale of intellectual and *moral* existence' and 'will feel the *moral dignity of his nature exalted*'. He thereby also implied the idea of secular knowledge as a substitute for religion. Newman publicly excoriated Sir Robert Peel for his surrender to religious liberalism and his approbation of the utility of education. Peel was approving an education that did not address the fundamental issue of moral development and for Newman this was simply no education at all. Knowledge without conscience was not likely to lead to religious awe and love, but to human pride and arrogance. Behind Peel's argument Newman recognized the moral optimism of Lord Brougham: 'Human nature wants recasting, but Lord Brougham is all for tinkering with it'.[139] Newman explains Peel's view:

Human nature, he seems to say, if left to itself, becomes sensual and degraded. Uneducated men live in the indulgence of their passions; or, if they are merely taught to read, they dissipate and debase their minds by trifling or vicious publications. Education is the cultivation of the intellect and heart, and Useful Knowledge is the great instrument of education. It is the parent of virtue, the nurse of religion; it exalts man to his highest perfection, and is the sufficient scope of his most earnest exertions.[140]

Newman believed that Peel's aim was to provide a training towards a merely utilitarian end.

Newman also identified another weakness in the utilitarian understanding of moral motivation; viz. that it is not grounded in the reality of the human condition. To Peel's contention that 'in becoming wiser a man will become better', Newman replies that 'to know is one thing, to do is another'. He gives examples:

A man knows he should get up in the morning – he lies a-bed ... A labouring man knows he should not go to the alehouse, and his wife knows she should not filch when she goes out charing; but, nevertheless, in these cases the consciousness of a duty is not all one with the performance of it.[141]

Newman the pastor knew human nature well; both the weaknesses and the moral potential of those in his charge were familiar to him. He knew that moral reform was beyond the power of the unaided human will. No one can become a better or more virtuous person simply by learning more facts, or by grasping intellectually that one should behave in one way, or avoid behaving in another. As he shows by his understanding of the true nature of conscience, only a sense of fear arising from our being answerable for our deeds to a divine judge can have that effect. Hence he concludes this passage by saying that 'if virtue be a mastery over the mind, if its end be action, if its perfection be moral order, harmony and peace, we must seek it in holier places than in Libraries and Reading Rooms'.[142] In this way he acknowledges both the connection between holiness and fear, and the necessary dependence of morality upon them both.

The great danger against which Newman worked throughout his life was the denigration of the importance of religion in human life, and the correlative error of expecting that it could be replaced by intellectual enlightenment. Nothing better epitomized the new spirit of universal utilitarian education than the establishment of public reading rooms like Peel's. They were founded on the twin convictions that education was best served by prohibiting discussion of the fruitless controversies in religion and politics, and instead promoting the cultivation of 'Useful Knowledge [as] the great instrument of education.'[143] Knowledge, it was believed by many within the intellectual classes, had the capacity to make us better. The essential weakness of this argument is deftly exposed by Newman through his insistence on asking how 'these wonderful moral effects are to be wrought under the instrumentality of the physical sciences?' Under such closer scrutiny it emerges that no specific mechanism is envisaged beyond 'a mere preternatural excitement under the influence of some stimulating object, or the peace which is attained by there being nothing to quarrel with'.[144] Newman believed that

> apprehension of the unseen is the only known principle capable of subduing moral evil, educating the multitude, and organising society, and that, whereas man is born for action, action flows not from inferences, but from impressions, – not from reasonings, but from Faith.[145]

He concludes:

> Christianity, and nothing short of it, must be made the element and principle of all education. Where it has been laid as the first stone, and acknowledged as the governing spirit, it will take up into itself, assimilate, and give a character to literature and science. Where Revealed Truth has given the aim and direction to Knowledge, Knowledge of all kinds will minister to Revealed Truth.[146]

For Newman, secular knowledge was a tool of unbelief and he says:

> if in education we begin with nature before grace, with evidence before faith, with science before conscience, with poetry before practice, we shall be doing much the same as if we were to indulge the appetites and passions, and turn a deaf ear to the reason.[147]

Newman in his 'Tamworth Reading Room' letters was clear that the contemporary error espoused by Peel was to suppose that excellence in life comes from without, rather than that the virtuous life comes from within the individual. No one, according to Newman, can be taught morality as a simply intellectual exercise. Nor can secular knowledge equip students with virtue. Newman saw a very weak relationship between secular knowledge and moral action. He understood the power of imagination. He saw that science can describe nature to us, but it cannot infer religious truths from that description. Therefore morals do not come from a study of secular knowledge. Science may benefit society but it begins and ends in the material universe and the material universe provides no system of morality by itself. Consequently, the liberal who hopes for the moral and social effects of education, hopes in vain. When he returned to this subject in the *Idea* in 1852 he summed up his position in a typically trenchant metaphor:

> Quarry the granite rock with razors, or moor the vessel with a thread of silk; then you may hope with such keen and delicate instruments as human knowledge and human reason to contend against those giants, the passion and the pride of man.[148]

Moral Education and Conscience

Holiness and Learning

In his 1827 sermon 'On general education as connected with the Church and religion', Newman argued that all education is by its nature religious as regards its end or purpose. This end is to be found in man's relationship with his Creator, which is to be formed gradually during this life in preparation for eternal life. Newman not only understood just how important is the establishment of this relationship with God, but how delicate it is. Nothing in this all-important matter could be achieved too quickly. What Newman aimed for in education was the formation of 'holiness of heart ... into which we are in this life to be changed'.[149] Holiness is 'so indispensably requisite for our enjoying the future presence of God' that it is absolutely essential that it be acquired. Yet it is not a natural state, but one which we need to learn, not simply intellectually, but in actions and choices and by the action of God's grace. As he said, we need to be changed, and that change is gradual and not without certain difficulties of achievement. Holiness of heart

> is a state in which we act not from extraordinary heat and impulse, but calmly, rationally, naturally . . . it is a state of change indeed, but of gradual change intended to begin in childhood and continue till death, all the powers and faculties of the soul being in progressive amendment, and growing into a nearer and nearer likeness of the attributes and will of God.[150]

Both intellect and will, therefore, need careful guidance and there is a danger in being 'very eager to bring children on in schools'. By which he means 'we are desirous of doing much in a short time'.[151] The process of education therefore requires patience on the part of both teachers and pupils. This is because the formation of character cannot be achieved simply by the imparting of principles, but only by their gradual inculcation.

Newman taught that education to holiness can only be possible if there is already potentially in the human soul a seed capable of such growth. In the *Grammar* he explains that this seed is 'the Image of God' planted in every person.[152] The image of God is not a neutral idea, but one replete with authority. Children, for instance, are quite capable of apprehending the idea of God as their 'Sovereign, Lawgiver and Judge' who is 'the good God, good in Himself, good relatively to the child'.[153] Such ideas may be very incomplete in a young child, so that the child cannot explain or define the word 'God', but the ideas are nonetheless recognizably present. Newman is not here concerned with their origin, but with the fact of their presence. They are indications of conscience as an inner sense of God's presence and authority.

Whether the 'elements of [the image of God in us] latent in the mind, would ever be elicited without extrinsic help is very doubtful ... but so far is certain', he says in the *Grammar*, 'that by informations external to ourselves, as time goes on, it admits of being strengthened and improved'.[154]

But if God's image can be enhanced and its meaning made clear to a child, it is also true that it can be damaged or effaced. Once disobeyed, conscience loses its intensity, and if it is continually ignored or disregarded it can be virtually disabled. As he wrote in the *Grammar*: 'Men transgress their sense of duty, and gradually lose those sentiments of shame and fear ... which are the witnesses of the Unseen Judge'.[155] While some would regard the gradual loss of such a powerful voice as liberation from an unwelcome form of restraint, Newman saw it as posing the greatest danger possible to the moral health and safety of the individual person and of society. Yet even though conscience is fragile, and can be damaged, it can never be entirely eradicated. Newman realized that this final indestructibility of conscience was the cause of many attempts by men to overthrow it. He identified 'a resolute warfare against the rights of conscience ... Literature and science have been embodied in great institutions in order to put it down'.[156] Throughout his life as priest and teacher he therefore strove to strengthen and protect the power of conscience as a sure guide to action.

Conscience and Education

The fostering of the sense of conscience was one of his greatest aims in his series of Parochial and Plain Sermons, in his conception of his role as tutor at Oriel and in Dublin, and in the arrangements he made and personally administered for the boys at the Oratory School in Edgbaston. Newman not only sought to bring those under his care to share his profound understanding of theology, but also his penetrating analysis of the workings of the human mind and will. In both cases he did not aim at a simply intellectual apprehension of what he believed, but a shared living-out of their consequences. The purpose of all education for Newman is 'to create in the breast of man a living witness to the truth of God, a righteous monitor, a spiritual guide and counselor ... so that we may instinctively and without effort at once discern what is holy, and feel a desire and possess the ability to practise it'.[157] He will not even allow the word education to be used of the mere imparting of knowledge. 'The mere acquaintance with ... the wonders of human ingenuity ... the uses of various arts ... excellent as it is abstractedly ... is a poor substitute for education – it has no effect upon the heart to change it.'[158]

Personal Influence

One of Newman's first convictions is the belief that morality cannot simply be taught, for it is the result of personal association and the influence of other human beings. In the vital process of teaching and training, the personal qualities and influence of the teacher are essential. It is not sufficient for the teacher to inform the pupil's mind, but to reach his heart and change it. Therefore the teacher's own character must both possess and display those virtues that he wishes to inculcate. The idea of personal influence in education was so important to Newman that its absence seemed to him nothing less than disastrous. As he wrote in 'The Rise and Progress of Universities': 'An educational system without the personal influence of teachers upon pupils, is an arctic winter; it will create an ice-bound, petrified, cast-iron University and nothing else.'[159] On the other hand, a teacher's good example is not only instructive but exhortative. Whereas nobody is likely to follow the moral guidance of a teacher who acts contrary to what he teaches, a teacher who practises what he teaches should have a profound influence on his pupils. As Newman put it in the 'Tamworth Reading Room': 'Persons influence us, voices melt us, looks subdue us, deeds inflame us.'[160] Such a teacher imparts far more than mere knowledge, but is capable of inspiring both fear and love. The motto he chose as cardinal was a perfect expression of his method: '*Cor ad cor loquitur*' – 'The heart speaks to the heart'. The true teacher reaches the heart of those with whom he is communicating from his own heart.

When he set up his university in Dublin he appointed tutors who were both academic teachers and moral guides, just as he had himself briefly been at Oriel. The disjunction of these two roles of instructor and guide he regarded as 'the evil of the age'. In his *Historical Sketches* he wittily, yet acidly described how, when in Oxford, 'I have experienced a state of things in which teachers were cut off from the taught as if by an insurmountable barrier; when neither party entered into the thoughts of the other . . . when the tutor was supposed to fulfil his duty, if he trotted on like a squirrel in his cage . . .'[161] The personal influence of the teacher was then *both* a responsibility laid on him, and also the only truly effective method of reaching the pupil's heart.

Teaching is not a mechanistic process, especially where faith is concerned. Nothing of value can be imparted unless the whole person, not just the intellect, is engaged. 'The heart is commonly reached, not through the reason, but through the imagination.'[162]

Newman's *Paideia* (1): The Moral Training of Children

One vital element of Newman's view that we have already mentioned is the importance of the process of formation of conscience in the young. In the *Grammar* Newman describes how the child keenly understands that there is a difference between right and wrong, and how his mind reaches forward with a strong presentiment to the thought of a moral governor, sovereign over him, mindful and just.[163] Essential to the idea of conscience is that of God's holiness. It is not only his presence that God makes known to us through our conscience, but also his authority. Newman says that while the promptings of conscience are not in all cases correct in every person, the sense of a judgement being made of one's actions is indelibly present to everyone. In other words, the promptings of conscience as they may be developed by the intellect into an ethical code can go awry if not properly directed. It is the mind that needs to be carefully formed for this aspect of conscience as judgement. As Newman says,

> we cannot estimate the wretched state of him, who knows what is right, yet habitually and systematically neglects to follow it – who sins against conscience, and while he confesses that religion is the one thing needful, yet continues a careless and ungodly course of life.[164]

Newman also believed that education must take account of other dangers to the formation of the powers of discrimination in conscience. He says that the 'light of the soul' will quite probably fade away and die out 'from neglect, from the temptations of life, from bad companions, or from the urgency of secular occupations'. On the positive side, 'the image of God, if duly cherished, may expand, deepen, and be completed, with the growth of their powers and in the course of life, under the varied lessons . . . by means of education, social intercourse, experience, and literature'.[165]

To begin from the viewpoint of the moral formation of children, Newman saw education as providing the opportunity for them to grow gradually in virtue under the careful guidance of a teacher whose good character would both be an example to follow, as well as warding off dangerous influences and tendencies. Sermon V of the 'University Sermons', entitled 'Personal Influence the Means of Propagating the Truth', expounds precisely this importance of personal influence in teaching as a means of counteracting the attraction of error. Yet Newman did not believe that formal education was the only, or even necessarily the most important, milieu of education. That was the responsibility in the first place of parents. Newman therefore attacked the notion that the education of children could, or should, be left entirely to the schools. He upbraided those parents who failed to instil 'good principles into their children's minds while young; but suffer them to form their own habits and gain opinions from any quarter'. Similarly he admonished parents who 'sometimes as an indulgence permit [those things] in practices, which the strict rules of propriety forbid – and thus allow them to break through duties at home as a *reward* for observing them at school'.[166]

For Newman, parents are 'from the earliest infancy of their children . . . their natural guardians and instructors'. Consequently, he holds that 'sending them to school is merely an accidental circumstance, and but a part of education'. It is therefore not surprising that Newman also reproves the 'error of supposing that school is to be a place of mere instruction'.[167] He is concerned that too many people see schools to be places where children have their minds filled with many precepts and much information, which is to forget the real end of education. Both in terms of moral training and in intellectual formation Newman was opposed to too much matter being imparted with too little space for understanding and absorption. He was also similarly opposed to the idea that education is simply concerned with instruction at the cost of forming the habits and the views of a good character.

But Newman was not opposed to schools as one of the means of accomplishing education. He held firmly that general education is a good thing, but only if it leads to love of God and neighbour and prepares for the next world, for the Kingdom of Christ.

> True, education has reference to the temporal callings of men, but it does not rest there – we do not educate children, that they may *succeed* in their respective occupations, but that they may so fulfil them as to make spiritual profit to their souls ... calling into action habits of conscientiousness, uprightness, diligence, truth, disinterestedness and humility. We are preparing them to do good in their generation, to glorify God by their lives wherever they may be placed, and to spread the knowledge of the grace of Christ to their own circle ...[168]

Newman was especially called upon to put his theories into practice when he founded the Oratory School at Edgbaston in 1859. He well understood the danger posed to boys by their coming from the restraint of home to the relative liberty of school. Yet he always placed a premium on trust. It would be better for the boys' character formation that they should learn the value and method of self-discipline under watchful and caring eyes at school, than be plunged unprepared into the many pitfalls and temptations of the world beyond school. For boys who did transgress Newman took correction seriously, though he disapproved of treating them roughly. In 1849, over ten years before the Oratory school was founded, he wrote to Fr Faber, on hearing that a schoolmaster under his authority had pulled a boy's ears he wrote that '... it had better not be done ... I think [the boys'] persons should be sacred'.[169] Nonetheless, twenty years later Newman wrote that 'the good old punishment of flogging, is, in due moderation ... the most efficacious of all punishments ... It is done and over – there is nothing to brood over, nothing to create a grudge.'[170] Still, corporal punishment was rare, and was only administered by the headmaster or another priest.

Newman's *Paideia* (2): the Moral Education of Students

Newman in Oxford

Newman was concerned as a tutor at Oriel not only with the intellectual development of his students, but also their moral development.

Tutors had traditionally been seen as both lecturers and disciplinary officers since

> In theory, every public tutor in a college (at Oriel there were four) was supposed to be responsible for the training, in the fullest sense of the word, of the pupils entrusted to him by the college Head. In practice, this charge, owing to the indifference of the tutors on the one hand, and the indiscipline of the students on the other, amounted to nothing very much.[171]

For such long-established reasons, the tradition of tutoring did not usually involve any close relationship between teacher and pupil – quite the opposite. Newman wrote: 'a stiff manner, a pompous voice, coldness and condescension, were the teacher's attributes, and he neither knew, nor wished to know, and avowed he did not wish to know, the private irregularities of the youths committed to his charge'.[172] Newman set about overturning this state of affairs, immersing himself in a far more demanding role. He instituted a model for tutoring students that placed emphasis both on their academic and on their moral supervision and thereby sought to develop the 'pastoral' responsibility as well as the academic role of the tutors. What he meant by the term 'pastoral' was essentially an extension of the vow ministers of the Church of England made at ordination.

For Newman, just as there was no division between his being a clergyman and a tutor, neither did he see any division between his role as a teacher and as a personal guide. Of course, the Fellows of the colleges were exclusively drawn from the ranks of ordained ministers, though Newman added a new moral intensity to the role of tutor. He made himself available to his pupils at all hours, carefully directing their reading and study and watching over their moral development. He was known to be demanding. Yet although he strongly disapproved of the students' drunken revels, he sought to discourage them by his personal presence and example of life, rather than by the imposition of penalties. Typically, he tackled the custom of drunken parties on the night preceding Holy Communion services, not by trying to get the parties banned, but by seeking to remove the obligation on the students to receive the sacrament, thereby profaning it. It was certainly difficult in the mid-nineteenth century to influence the conduct of the gentlemen commoners in Oxford who effectively did as they pleased. Such control as might be exercised over the students was characterized not so much by moral guidance as by a disciplinary code, exercised largely through a complex system of fines for offences committed.[173] Newman's experiment was, therefore, short-lived, but was revived by others in new forms in the 1860s. Arnold and Newman, both Fellows of Oriel, could therefore be said to have influenced the development of the idea of the 'moral tutor' in universities.[174] Both believed that there had been a decline in the character of students and that what was needed was the Christian moral regeneration of the individual and society.

Newman in Dublin

However, Newman did eventually get the opportunity to put his tutorial aims into practice when he was at Dublin. Archbishop Cullen of Dublin, who was Newman's immediate superior in the establishing and running of the Catholic university, was hoping that the new university would be something akin to a theological college for lay people, ensuring the religious formation of its subjects both morally and intellectually. Newman, too, recognized that there were many dangers to the students' moral welfare in a great city, and resolved to protect them from unusual temptations, as far as possible, by establishing houses where they might live in smaller numbers under the watchful eye of a dean and other lecturers in the university who would be wise tutors.[175] This was in a way reminiscent of the origins of the medieval colleges of Oxford, especially since Newman planned that separate houses might be run by different religious orders for their own members, or even for different nationalities. He envisaged that each house 'should have its private Chapel (and the Chaplain might be the Confessor)'.[176] One of these houses which he set up he even ran himself. With eight pupils under his care he was dean, tutor, chaplain, bursar and general factotum even locking up the door at night after the boys were in bed. As Culler observes, 'it was a new experience for him, the first time he had ever "kept house", but in some way it was the realization of his wishes'.[177]

Yet there were differences between the Oxford Anglican Newman and the Dublin Catholic Newman. He now seemed less severe, or even fierce, than he had been as a young Tractarian. The discipline which in Oxford had 'a distinctly strained and monastic flavour' was characterized in Dublin by 'a wonderful lightness and informality'.[178] As is often the case when his Oxford and Dublin modes differ, we can see that he was influenced in the latter by the example of Louvain, on which model the Catholic University had been founded. He admired the management of student discipline at Louvain as combining freedom in the students with the safeguard of Catholic morality. Whereas in Oxford he had objected to an undergraduate debating society on the grounds of 'unbridled speculations', in Dublin he actually formed one. But, there again, in Dublin the university was Catholic. As Culler says, 'Where religion was secure of its place, the mind could run freely without danger of error, and this was the explanation of the whole spirit of freedom which Newman was attempting to foster.'[179] Although he planned to license a theatre in order to bring it under his control, this scheme was never realized. But he did provide a billiard room so as to prevent the students from going to commercial establishments where they might be introduced to gambling. Nor did he object to those who could afford it going hunting.

Now it was Archbishop Cullen's turn to be censorious. He complained that Newman was permitting 'young men ... to go out at all hours, to smoke etc.' On one occasion he complained for over an hour to Newman about these various dangers to the moral health of the young men, but Newman simply listened without saying a word and promised to think about it. Nevertheless, as Cullen complained, everything went on as before. But, argued Newman,

> we could not do worse than to continue the discipline of school and college into the University, and to let the great world, which is to follow on it, be the first stage on which the young are set at liberty to follow their own bent.[180]

Cullen, having been a seminary rector, saw the university as a kind of seminary, whereas Newman realized the importance of training in self-discipline for young men not destined for the priesthood.

As he explained to the bishops in his first report as rector of the university: 'the young for the most part cannot be driven, but, on the other hand, are open to persuasion, and to the influence of kindness and personal attachment'.[181] Newman was, of course, pointing to the principle of personal influence and also implying that for guiding youth, a spoonful of honey was more effective than a glass of vinegar. 'In consequence they are to be kept straight by indirect contrivances rather than by authoritative enactments and naked prohibitions.'[182]

Morality and Mixed Education

Newman's view was that for English Catholics in those times mixed education among Protestants was a necessity, given the practical difficulties in setting up an exclusively Catholic tertiary education system of a comparable calibre to Oxford and Cambridge. Moreover, as he said, 'all places are dangerous, – the world is dangerous. I do not believe that Oxford is more dangerous than ... London – and I think you cannot keep young men under glass cases.'[183] It was an argument against the excessive shielding of the students from undesirable influences which he had also used in Dublin. It was Newman's view that 'In a bad matter and in a choice of difficulties, I would rather have Catholic youths in Protestant Colleges at Oxford with a strong Catholic mission in the place, than a Catholic College.'[184] His reasoning for this conclusion, so opposed by his fellow-convert Henry Edward Manning, by then the Archbishop of Westminster, was that

> in a large University there are good and bad sets; and a youth has an opportunity of choosing between them. In a small exclusive body there is no choice; and one bad member ruins for a time the whole community. Thus the open University, when complemented by a strong mission, may be even safer than a close Catholic College.[185]

As was so often the case with Newman's theories, his preference for a Catholic Mission in Oxford was not based on abstract reasoning, but was founded in his practical experience of students from his days as an Oriel tutor and in Dublin.

Morality and University Education

When Newman discusses human morality, he contrasts the true nature of conscience, which is founded on the inner voice of God, with its counterfeit of 'taste' or 'sentiment', which is founded on human respect. In the same way he draws an analogous contrast between the virtues of a Christian and those of a 'gentleman'. Newman's idea of the gentleman seems to have several qualities. First, he is sensitive to others for, in Newman's words,

> he is tender towards the bashful, gentle towards the distant and merciful towards the absurd; he can recollect to whom he is speaking; he guards against unseasonable allusions, or topics which may irritate; he is seldom prominent in conversation, and never wearisome.[186]

Besides being sensitive, he is also a model of what today we would call 'civility'. By this Newman means that the gentleman 'is never mean or little in his disputes, never takes unfair advantage, never mistakes personalities or sharp sayings for arguments, or insinuates evil which he dare not say out'.[187] Being both refined and civil, it is important that the gentleman takes the long view of things, and exercises an almost stoical composure. Hence, Newman says that 'he is patient, forbearing, and resigned, on philosophical principles; he submits to pain, because it is inevitable, to bereavement, because it is irreparable, and to death, because it is his destiny'. Newman says that 'nowhere shall we find greater candour, consideration, indulgence; [the gentleman] knows the weakness of human reason as well as its strength, its province and its limits'.[188]

Newman was here describing the ideal character produced by the Oxbridge collegiate system and therefore referred to young Christian gentlemen, although Newman disliked the word gentleman on account of its associations with the criteria of taste as opposed to virtue. Newman was far more concerned with the education and formation of the Christian conscience than of refined civility and perfect manners. For however desirable such attributes might be *in* a Christian, to Newman they were of no value to a person whose morality was based not on conscience but on mere human respect. It was a notion of university defined as an exclusive teaching institution. Sheldon Rothblatt accurately sums up the purposes of an Oxbridge education in his commentary on Cambridge: 'Education in Cambridge was both university and collegiate, the former professional in its objectives, the latter concerned with character formation'.[189] Dons were expected to be engaged in both types of teaching.

Consequently, it must be questioned whether Newman's idea of a university has much of a modern resonance considering the great diversity that constitutes the student body in universities today. Students are no longer a well-defined group with common backgrounds and many courses are vocationally orientated. Nevertheless, most universities and colleges since Newman's time have actively sought the expansion of student residences, in part, to provide some form of this 'living teaching' tradition together with assisting students in their more general developmental and personal growth. Wardens and tutors in these halls of residence were once specifically selected for their personal qualities or character.

Newman commented that if he had to choose between two university courses, one non-residential, but intellectually challenging (the new University of London), and the other residential, but intellectually disorganized (the University of Oxford), he would prefer the latter. He explains his choice thus:

> when a multitude of young men, keen, open-hearted, sympathetic, and observant, as young men are, come together and freely mix with each other, they are sure to learn from one another, even if there be no one to teach them: the conversation of all is a series of lectures to each, and they gain for themselves new ideas and views, fresh matter of thought, the distinct principles for judging and acting, day by day ...[190]

Newman believed that this 'youthful community' represents a 'living teaching' that shapes both intellectual and moral character. He is, of course, speaking hyperbolically. He is anxious to explain that his preference for the intellectually disorganized university is based on his strong disapproval of teaching systems which dispense with personal influence and interaction. He believes that the formative interaction between students is of relatively greater value to their education than the mere absorption of information whether from a lecturer or from books. This is a hypothetical case, for in reality Newman would have recognized that both the formation of character and of intellect in a residential university without teachers may equally be for good or ill depending on the existing characters of the students concerned. For Newman, the moral formation of students positively required tutors who were themselves well formed both intellectually and morally.

Making these allowances, Newman believed that the residential character of the British college, as distinguished from the non-residential continental European university, provided the best context for moral formation.[191] The quality of the personal contact between the students and their teachers provided much of that formation. If teachers do not give evidence of their own good habits and character, it is unlikely that they will be able to provide any real moral guidance for their students, whether by example or by precept. Newman's view is that moral character cannot simply be taught, it is the result of personal association and influence – person to person, or, as he chose for his motto as cardinal, 'heart to heart'.

Therefore, although Newman sees that a liberal education can be an excellent means by which society gains refined and civil gentlemen, he denies that such an education necessarily imparts any explicit moral virtue. He warns against 'distracting and enfeebling the mind by an unmeaning profusion of subjects', pretending that 'a smattering in a dozen branches of study is not shallowness, which it really is, but enlargement, which it is not'.[192] All such quantitative accumulations distort students intellectually, suffocating them beneath an oppressive weight of disconnected trivia. In Newman's estimation, such people become intellectual dilettantes, whom he describes in the preface to the *Idea* as characterized by what he calls 'viewiness' – the state of being ready at a moment's notice with views on nearly every subject.

Having discussed Newman's description of a liberal education and of the 'gentleman' whom it forms and shapes, we may ask ourselves: what college or university would not want such a person as a graduate or indeed as a member of its faculty? Newman asserts that even the most excellent liberal education by itself falls short of making the

Christian. According to Newman, the gentleman's ethical sensitivity and intellectual training can be achieved completely apart from any religious belief or formation. After listing the qualities we considered briefly Newman goes on to say that if the gentleman is a non-believer, he nonetheless remains too refined to ridicule religion. He respects acts of piety and the ministers of religion, but still does not perform such acts or believe what the ministers preach. He is tolerant and open and does his best to remain objective. In other words, the liberally educated person may turn out to be a St Francis de Sales, a person of liberal learning but also of deep piety and religious commitment, or an Edward Gibbon, a sophisticated and worldly sceptic. Newman, the patristics scholar, reminds us that 'Basil and Julian were fellow-students at the schools of Athens; and one became the Saint and Doctor of the Church, the other her scoffing and relentless foe'.[193]

Conclusion

During Newman's long life he watched as education ended up more and more in the hands of the state. He saw the content and approach in education increasingly determined by secular consider-ations, the universities more and more influenced by utilitarian con-siderations of usefulness, and religion and the morality based upon it rejected. Even in his own city of Birmingham the National Educa-tional League successfully campaigned in the 1860s for compulsory non-denominational schooling for the masses.

When Newman says in the preface to the *Idea* that 'the object of a university is intellectual, not moral', he might be mistaken for an Enlightenment philosopher rather than a student of Aristotle, for whom any strong separation of the intellectual and ethical virtues is untenable. But in fact these statements belie his own deepest con-victions, as we can discern in one or two places in the *Idea,* and as becomes abundantly clear in the *Grammar* with its powerful argu-ments against any such separation. Newman never intended that an intellectual liberal education would be the only form of education the university student would receive. While Newman provides a theory of secular knowledge, via a liberal education, he distinguished between secular knowledge and religious teaching which leads to the practice of virtue.

In common with many other Christian intellectuals of his generation, Newman believed both in a transcendent order by which society was ruled, and in individual conscience. He believed that political problems, such as how to educate the masses, are also religious and moral by nature and that a narrow rationality cannot solve such educational problems. Newman's ideas were conservative in an age in which utility appealed to industrialists and in which an increasing confidence in rationality grew just as faith in religion declined. The spirit of the age was one of growing liberalism which saw the Reform Acts of 1832 and 1867, free trade, competitive individualism and popularized utilitarianism. Nevertheless, it was still an age in which Christianity was overwhelmingly viewed as a guide to personal moral behaviour.

For Newman the idea of liberalism was inseparable from 'private judgement', a term which he uses in a pejorative sense. Contemporary liberal theorists of course expected much from education. The core of the liberal credo was a passionate faith in human reason and a belief that education could change the behaviour of the masses and raise the moral tone of national life. This was a secular gospel which promoted the state control of schools divorced from religion, by prescribing what went on in them. Effectively, these liberal theorists, who formed part of what was called 'advanced opinion', campaigned for a compulsory state secular education which would help children abandon their parents' religious faith, while retaining their moral standards. Ethics would be founded in reason rather than revelation, and science would become the basis for altruism.

Newman predicted that the subsequent generation of children would eventually abandon not only their grandparents' religious faith but also their moral standards, and find the meaning of their lives in the pursuit of material satisfaction. Newman's protests against liberalism were drowned out by the utilitarian cry of 'the greatest good of the greatest number' and of the rejection of religion as the basis of morality. Newman argued that the acquisition of knowledge without the ordering influence of Christianity is likely to lead to an overweening pride in one's own accomplishments. In the absence of a higher spiritual restraint the inevitable human tendency toward self-aggrandizement would be given free rein. Moreover, he realized that this is no accidental consequence, but a virtual necessity of our nature.

In educational terms Newman could, in one sense, be called a traditionalist in moral education. He regarded it as the duty of each generation to ensure that the next generation knew the truth, loved what was good and did what was right. He believed that children should be taught reverence and respect for custom and tradition and held, like Plato and most of his Victorian contemporaries, a paternalistic model of schooling in that those with superior wisdom had the right and duty to decide for others what should be learnt. This view was based on ethical objectivism and was embedded in and reinforced by a Christian way of life which was articulated in scripture, enacted by liturgy, exemplified by the members of the Church, both living and dead, and underwritten by revelation and tradition. The purpose of education was to guide each individual towards this goal.

However it would be wrong to suggest that Newman was excessively deferential to tradition or that he simply believed in mechanically 'indoctrinating' the young. This was the man who advocated liberal education and wanted an educated, intelligent and theologically aware laity whose opinions would be taken into account by the bishops. Newman did not advocate unreflective formation of habits of behaviour, but rather a process of learning to guide one's actions by thinking morally for oneself. Therefore, his aim was not to limit his students' freedom, but rather to help them to think about the values they had acquired in growing up in the light of Christian revelation.

Newman, like so many moral philosophers from Aristotle through Aquinas and beyond, held that our innate sense of morality shaped our behaviour. Yet this idea that we are endowed with a natural moral sense had already been attacked and largely rejected by those philosophers, beginning with Descartes, who wanted to separate morality from intellectual and practical formation. This represented a break with the tradition to which Newman belonged.

Chapter 4

Liberal Education: The Ability to Think

The Historical Background to Liberal Education

It is often said that from the time of Plato to the Hellenic era *paideia* was humanism in search of theology. Pagan theology, being polytheistic, had a completely different conception of the relationship of man to the cosmos from the Christians who introduced into philosophy the idea of the importance and urgency of the relationship between mankind and the Creator. It was the Fathers of the Christian Church like Basil the Great and Gregory of Nazianzus who built their own Christian scholarship upon the foundation of their studies in Athens,[194] who were to provide this kind of theology. As previously education had been entirely secular, Christian thinkers now sought to bring that education to serve the purposes of faith.

The relationship between pagan philosophy and Christian revelation in the intellectual and moral spheres was, however, not immediately clear. It was not to be in Athens, but in another great seat of learning, Alexandria, that the relationship between pagan and Christian philosophy was worked out. In Clement of Alexandria Newman found a second-century Christian who tackled this problem in the midst of a sophisticated and cosmopolitan world. Many early converts, like Clement himself, were well educated in the pursuit of wisdom, which included far more than knowledge – it meant a way of life. But pagan wisdom was founded on reason or 'logos', while Christian wisdom was founded in a historical person, Jesus Christ. Clement took as his starting point the prologue of St John's Gospel that 'the Word (logos) was God ... and the Word became flesh' that is, incarnate as man, in Christ.[195] Clement articulated a theory of the logos or word of God, through whom, as St John says, 'all things were made'. Christ is therefore both the one who gives order and unity to all creation, and the incarnate summit of human wisdom, which can be seen imperfectly but really anticipated in the great pagan philosophers. The logos is present in the world He has made, and He gives unity and completeness both to creation and to human understanding of it.

This view appealed to Newman as a vindication both of the importance of secular human learning, and of its only true unity in Christ. But not only is the logos the source of unity in all creation, but by virtue of His Incarnation, Christ is the true educator of men, who gathers about Himself his disciples, the very meaning of whose name is 'those who learn'. Pagan philosophy and learning, for Clement, is the divine education of the world, preparing it for the coming of the incarnate word. That preparation, though real, is imperfect in its range and vision, and in its slavery to idolatry. Christ is the one, and the only one, who fully enlightens and liberates men with the fullness of the truth. Newman resonated with this approach, since he had always been convinced of the truth that lay in the pagan writers, and therefore the philosophy of the Alexandrian Fathers 'came like music to my inward ear'.[196] Newman 'had from the first made much of [the classics], as the Holy Fathers did, as being in a certain sense inspired moralists and prophets of truths greater than they knew'.[197] Clement argued that pagan philosophy renders the mind more subtle, agile and ready to understand higher realities. Newman says that he learned from Clement and the other Alexandrian Fathers that 'nature was a parable: Scripture was an allegory: pagan literature, philosophy and mythology, properly understood, were but a preparation for the Gospel'.[198]

Alexandria was also the home of another great Christian thinker, Origen, who in the generation after Clement further developed the synthesis of pagan and Christian learning. Origen, brought up a Christian, had been given a good secular education, but had at first abandoned secular learning in order to concentrate on scripture. He returned to secular study because he realized that it would enrich both his study and his teaching of the scriptures. As Vincent Blehl describes it, 'he began a sort of university, in which an introduction to all learning was offered as a preparation for the crowning study of scripture'.[199] The term university is not inappropriate because

Origen called his curriculum *encyclia grammata*, since it included the whole circle of sciences known to the ancient world.

Moreover, Origen made philosophy the head of all the other sciences, to give unity and form to the circle. His purpose was to enhance the assimilation of Christian teaching through the intellectual training provided by the classics. Thus his method 'aimed at the development of intelligence so that it might receive a deeper understanding of religious truths than mere catechetical instruction could provide'.[200] It was also to Alexandria that Newman reminds us we owe another great institution of the intellectual world: the library as repository of the accumulated wisdom of generations to which no one could have access except in written form.

By the fifth century, a synthesis of classical education in the liberal arts and a specifically Christian learning, primarily biblical and theological, had been achieved; and it is this synthesis which provides the foundation of medieval culture. Newman describes the preservation by the Church of the ancient learning during the era of barbarian invasions of Western Europe and its transmission first through the monasteries, and then also through various schools founded by powerful leaders like Charlemagne.[201] Newman was also fascinated by the way in which the universities emerged around the beginning of the thirteenth century. It was a phenomenon, he says, that could not happen 'without the rise of some deep and comprehensive philosophy'.[202] This he identifies as the coming together of larger numbers of students and teachers for the sole purpose of pursuing knowledge. He notes how this also manifests itself in the deliberate inclusion of all kinds of knowledge into 'a whole system of instruction, which demanded in addition a knowledge of philosophy, scholastic theology, civil and canon law, medicine, natural history and the Semitic languages'[203] alongside the so-called seven liberal arts, the Trivium and Quadrivium of the ancient curriculum.

But while it is important to be aware of the intramural conflicts within medieval Christianity, it is also important, for our purposes, not to lose sight of the essentialism of Christian theology and philosophy which underlay all theories of education. Although there was disagreement over means, and even more disagreement over how one was to live in the world, what was accepted generally was the principle that all were created by God, held in existence by His will, and were called by God to discover, choose, and follow a path to Him. The meaning of human life was there to be discovered, and the purpose of education was to assist that search. It was therefore not surprising that many within the Church saw education as a good in itself and cultivated learning for its own sake.

Sharing in this Christian tradition, Newman was also aware that while the heart and aim of a liberal education remain unaffected by the passage of the centuries or by circumstance and personality, some of the subjects studied under its auspices can be expanded and added to. Newman was also preoccupied with religion and theology in the *Idea* and was therefore concerned with a Christian liberal education. He was concerned with the question of how to integrate the Christian faith with the inherited classical liberal education. He understood this to be part of a 'continuous historical tradition' which seemed to validate the Greek notion of liberal education. The Christian liberal education was a variation on the Greek ideal.

The Ends of Education

As we noted in Chapter 2, Newman distinguishes the ends of education in the *Idea* according to the purpose for which education is undertaken, and the aim at which it is directed. Seen from the aspect of its final or ultimate end, the purpose of education is to achieve human fulfilment. Thus, as we have already observed, in the fullest sense of the word, Newman sees the ultimate aim of education as religious, in the sense that a person's fulfilment lies in developing his or her proper relationship with God. Yet, of course, Newman did not consider that all education was, or ought to be, specifically about religion. A great deal of the knowledge which is imparted in education necessarily concerns a vast range of subjects that are not explicitly religious. But Newman would say that, ultimately, all knowledge must be one, however varied its matter or method, since it is of reality, which is all one. Truth, by which knowledge relates to reality, must therefore also ultimately be one. This is why Newman uses the expression circle of sciences to denote their interrelationship and common origin.

Yet it is important to remember that this unity of all that is knowable cannot be perceived in one glance. We need the various views that the disciplines provide. It is therefore possible to ignore or mistake that underlying unity of all that is. Newman comments that this mistaken view is all too common, since 'men have lost ... a philosophical comprehensiveness, an orderly expansiveness, an elastic constructiveness ... and cannot make out why. This is why: because they have lost the idea of unity ...'[204] Therefore, in Newman's view, any principle of education which does not acknowledge the unity of all that exists can only lead men deeper into error.

Yet there are, of course, other ends of education, subordinate to the principal one. For instance, one general kind of education is undertaken for the sake of the use to which it can be put. Commercial or professional education, for instance, is conducted in order to impart a particular discipline or skill, or a range of technical knowledge which will assist a student to achieve a practical end or perform a certain kind of function. There is, on the other hand, a kind of education whose end lies not in some ulterior use, but in the benefit given simply by acquiring and possessing it. This is what Newman understands by the term 'liberal education': that which deals with knowledge considered as its own end. Newman is careful to point out that these ends are not necessarily to be identified with particular kinds of subject matter, as though only some subjects are open to being studied for their own sake, and others can only be studied for some ulterior end. A particular subject may at one time or in certain circumstances be studied for its own sake, or at other times the same subject matter may be studied for some other purpose. The distinction lies not in the subject but in the motive; a science is accounted 'liberal' only when it is studied as its own end.

Knowledge 'its own End'

Now to say that knowledge is liberal which is pursued 'as its own end' cannot strictly be true. After all, it cannot be for the sake of the knowledge *itself* that it is studied or acquired, but for the sake of the *one who studies or acquires it*. Newman states the classical philosophical view that the pursuit of knowledge of itself fulfils a human need. Typical of this view, he quotes Cicero's statement that knowledge, or the search for truth, is the first object to which we are attracted, after our physical wants have been satisfied.[205]

That, of course, does not account for any distinction between different kinds of knowledge, liberal or otherwise. Therefore Newman applies Aristotle's distinction concerning possessions to knowledge: 'those rather are fruitful, which bear fruit; those *liberal*, which *tend to enjoyment*. By fruitful, I mean, which yield revenue; by enjoyable, *where nothing accrues of consequence beyond the using*.'[206] From this it might appear that Newman holds that knowledge which is sought for its own enjoyment is intrinsically superior to other kinds of knowledge which are sought for the sake of the fruit they will bear. That is not the case, as he illustrates with the example of theology, which he has already placed at the centre of the circle of sciences. Theology may be cultivated as a contemplation, when it is sought for its own sake and is then liberal, or it can be studied for the purposes of, say, preaching or teaching, in which case it is no longer accounted truly liberal, but certainly no less meritorious or lofty for that.[207] It is the building up of the discriminatory powers and synthetic faculties of the mind, not the subject studied, that makes a particular study liberal.

Nor does Newman state or even imply that liberal studies can only be intellectual, or that commercial and practical studies are devoid of any valuable intellectual content. Some bodily exercise may be liberal if pursued for its own sake, such as the ancient Olympic Games; while a science that is useful may be profoundly intellectual, such as medicine. 'We contrast a liberal education with a commercial or a professional; yet no one can deny that commerce and the professions afford scope for the highest and most diversified powers of mind.'[208]

Liberal Education: The Perfection of the Mind

Newman sees the value of a liberal education in the effect it should have upon the mind. He says that the health or perfection of the mind is an end worth pursuing, and that this end can be understood as the gain or benefit that liberal education gives to the one who enjoys it. In other words, Newman is not altering his claim that liberal sciences are studied for their own sake, but stating that what follows from studying them is a state of mental acuity that is desirable and good in itself. Newman points out that we do not have an adequate word in English to express this idea. He says that whereas the word 'health' stands for proficiency and perfection of the body, and 'virtue' for the perfection of our moral nature, we do not have an analogous single term for intellectual proficiency.

He explores several terms to illustrate how they do not exactly fit his requirement: some of these he dismisses as belonging to the raw material of the intellect, such as talent, ability and genius; others apply to powers or habits bearing upon the exercise of the intellect, like judgment, taste and skill; others again to conduct, like wisdom; or finally to intellectual ideas, such as knowledge or science.[209] Some commentators have therefore expressed surprise that Newman does not decide to adopt the word 'culture', but although Newman does speak of 'mental culture' or 'culture of intellect', he means by those terms the contents of the mind, or the process of training it, rather than the hoped-for aim of that process. Newman is explicitly discussing a *state* of mind, whereas 'culture' tends to denote either an *activity* of the mind, or its *contents*, i.e. its knowledge.[210] So when he talks of the 'cultivation of the intellect as an end in itself', Newman wants us to envisage a state of excellence of mind which is brought about by a certain kind of mental training, analogous to that state of health and fitness in a body which is brought about by exercise. It is essential to bear this in mind in order not to be misled by the word which he uses 'in default of a recognized term': viz. *philosophy*. Newman is not here introducing the science of philosophy as such, but rather harnessing the term to his specific purpose of describing the state of mental excellence. He explains this choice of term further when he describes as 'the philosophical habit of mind' those 'qualities and characteristics of the intellect in which its cultivation issues or rather consists'.[211]

At the beginning of the *Idea* Newman speaks of 'real cultivation of mind' as the aim of his educational programme in the university. He is, of course, concerned that 'the characteristic excellencies of the gentleman' should be inculcated by a liberal education, but cultivation of the mind has nothing to do with that. It is, he says, bringing the 'mind into form, – for the mind is like the body'.[212] Just as boys need to learn their bodily strengths and weaknesses, and generally make great mistakes at first in their doing so, so it is with their minds. 'At first they have no principles laid down as a foundation for the intellect to build upon; they have no discriminating convictions, and no grasp of consequences.' The end or purpose of a liberal education, then, is the development of these powers of intellect as a habit. Clearly this process requires 'a great deal of thought in the compassing, and a great deal of trouble in the attaining'.[213] That thought and trouble are the action of the mind upon the raw material, the facts and knowledge with which it needs to be furnished in order to develop its powers.

Hence Newman speaks of the 'enlargement of mind' which, although it requires a great deal of reading and presupposes the acquisition of knowledge, cannot be reduced to a merely passive reception of fairly random ideas and impressions. This was one of the dangers which Newman had identified in the 'Tamworth Reading Room', that of confusing the exposure of the mind to many facts with the development of its powers of understanding. For a person who is acquainted with many facts but has not brought the powers of his intellect to bear on them can appear at first to be sophisticated and knowledgeable, while in reality he sees everything disconnectedly, 'like the shifting scenes of a show, which leave the spectator where he was'. Such a person seems to take all in his stride, to be able to react with equanimity at any novelty, while all the time 'he has no standard of judgment at all, and no landmarks to guide him to a conclusion'.[214]

On the contrary, for Newman enlargement of mind is, on the one hand, characteristically *energetic*: acting 'upon and towards and among those new ideas which are rushing in upon it ... it is the locomotion, the movement onwards, of that mental centre, to which both what we know, and what we are learning ... gravitates'. Enlargement of mind must also include a *synthetic* power, as he puts it, of 'viewing many things at once as one whole'; a *formative* power 'reducing to order and meaning the matter of our acquirements ... making the objects of our knowledge subjectively our own';[215] a *critical* and *discriminating* power of 'referring [many things] severally to their true place in the universal system, of understanding their respective values, and determining their mutual dependence'.[216] Newman says that 'a truly great intellect ... is one which takes a connected view of old and new, past and present, far and near, and which has an insight into the influence of all these one on another; without which there is no whole, and no centre'.[217] The philosophical mind will, however, not only be energetic in its activities, but also 'patient, collected and majestically calm, because it discerns the end in every beginning, the origin in every end, the law in every interruption, the limit in each delay'.[218]

A liberal education disciplines the intellect to the 'perfection of its powers, which knows, and thinks while it knows, with the elastic force of reason'.[219] In modern educational language we would say that this 'philosophy' involves the ability to draw conclusions from a body of information through applying, analysing, synthesizing, and evaluating from observation, experience, and reflection. Nevertheless, this does not mean that a liberal education, which is pursued for its own sake, lends support to the kind of relativistic elective system in which content is less important than the opportunity to develop critical thinking skills, by exercising the mind on whatever interests it. In fact, it is the possession of the knowledge of the mutual and true relations of things, and the power of 'impregnating' knowledge with reason, that constitutes Newman's 'philosophical habit of mind'.

Of course Newman recognizes that a liberal education cannot yield identical outcomes in all persons. It is hardly possible that everybody so educated will be accounted 'a truly great intellect'. Yet 'when the intellect has been properly trained and formed to have a connected view or grasp of things, it will display its powers with more or less effect according to its particular quality and capacity in the individual'.[220] In contrast with persons who 'can never see the point, and have no difficulties in the most difficult subjects', or those who 'are hopelessly obstinate and prejudiced, and, after they have been driven from their opinions, return to them the next moment without even an attempt to explain why', a person with a properly trained and formed intellect will generally be capable of 'entering with comparative ease into any subject of thought, and of taking up with aptitude any science or profession'.[221]

Liberal Education: Learning to Think

Newman recognizes that the philosophical habit of mind cannot be acquired without 'a great deal of thought in the compassing, and a great deal of trouble in the attaining'. We must now review the means by which he sees that process conducted. Newman opens Chapter 4 of 'University Subjects' in Part II of the *Idea*,[222] entitled 'Elementary Studies', with a fascinating and closely observed account of the development of an infant's power of perception. He describes the way in which a child begins with the impressions of a medley of colours and shadows which present no image, for an image implies a unity and a form. A baby must gradually learn how to connect part with part, to separate what moves from what is stationary, watching the coming and going of figures and mastering the idea of shape and perspective. As adults, we largely take this process for granted, since it was so long ago and so primitive. We cannot recall what it was like not to be able to interpret what we saw and felt, not to know how to construct ideas of reality from all that crowded into our senses. Yet to Newman it marks the emergence of the mind's powers which can, in time, lead to the maturity of the philosophical habit of mind. He says

> that one main portion of intellectual education, of the labours of both school and university, is to remove the original dimness of the mind's eye ... to give the mind clearness, accuracy, precision; to enable it to use words aright, to understand what it says, to conceive justly what it thinks about, to abstract, compare, analyse, divide, define, and reason, correctly.[223]

'The infant', he says, 'does not learn to spell or read the hues upon his retina by any scientific rule; nor does the student learn accuracy of thought by any manual or treatise.'[224] Learning, for Newman, therefore necessarily implies teaching. Nobody can be entirely self-taught, but all persons require direction and training. The business of educating children is 'a discipline in accuracy of mind', which requires a careful instructor.

Newman holds that in the matter of teaching children it is essential to train the child's mind in preparation for higher education. But teaching and learning are never mere mechanical processes, such as shaping wood or metal might be, since 'the mind of man is more subtle material to work upon'.[225] As we have seen, Newman's view of reasoning is that it is intensely personal, and therefore that no two persons ever exercise reason in exactly the same way. Even with the same teacher and curriculum, no two students' intellects will ever develop identically. Newman's view is that a teacher has to be aware of this and to respect the native differences of temperament and character and in his dealings with his students, even while he is attempting to guide them.

If it is to be effective as a *paideia*, school teaching must make demands on a child's abilities and stretch its powers. Newman, speaking of teaching young children in general, as opposed to specifically in preparation for higher studies, says that it is an error 'to be too eager to make every subject learned by children *easy and amusing*'.[226] If a child learns nothing difficult at school, 'nothing which requires self-command and the power of attention to master, he will not be fit to act his part in life – for to live well in the world is nothing else than the doing or suffering hard things'.[227] This idea was to be taken up again in the 'Tamworth Reading Room', when he said that it was a major error of the day that 'our true excellence comes not from within, but from without; not wrought out through personal struggle and sufferings, but following upon a passive exposure to influences outside'.[228]

Since the intellect requires both formation and raw material upon which to develop its elastic powers, Newman sees the training of the memory at an early stage of education as one essential preparation for liberal studies. 'For some years [a boy's] intellect is little more than an instrument for taking in facts, or a receptacle for storing them.' Yet Newman does not regard him as altogether passive. On the contrary, he draws the picture of a boy who 'has a lively susceptibility of impressions' and 'imbibes information of every kind'.[229] Newman insists that 'the first step in intellectual training is to impress upon a boy's mind the idea of science, method, order, principle, and system; of rule and exception, of richness and harmony'. He sees the study of grammar as best suited for this purpose, adding: 'nor can too great accuracy, or minuteness and subtlety of teaching be used

towards him, as his faculties expand'.[230] In the study of mathematics, which Newman says should follow grammar, he recognizes that
'there is exercise for his argumentative powers'.[231] Mathematics will
also 'give him a conception of development and arrangement around
a common centre'.

At this stage of his education a boy's capacity for memory will
inevitably outstrip his intellectual powers. Hence Newman says that
a schoolboy principally 'heaps up' the matter of his studies in geography, history, language and natural history 'as treasures for a future
day'. But Newman sees the importance of cross-referencing studies
as, for instance, in stating that 'Chronology and Geography are so
necessary for him, when he reads History, which is otherwise little
better than a storybook'.[232] Newman also recognizes the danger that
what is merely passively received will simply pass out of the mind as
soon as it has entered it. Therefore, he recommends not just reading poetry, but composing metrical verses, a skill requiring careful
attention to quantity, i.e. length of syllables, as well as to expression.
Newman carefully distinguishes here between the 'poetry' which the
student reads, and 'metrical composition' which has no pretensions
to artistic quality, but helps to fix in the mind the ideas and images
encountered in the classics.

But not only does Newman see the potential later intellectual benefit the young student gains from this accumulation of material and
mastery of method, but also from the moral habits which encourage
and assist his learning skills, such as 'diligence, assiduity, regularity,
despatch, persevering application'.[233] Newman also insisted that boys
should study with other boys, on the grounds that 'there were con-
siderable advantages in boys having to gain the power of abstraction
by studying with other boys', in order to strengthen their powers of
concentration amid distraction.[234] These habits, acquired early, will
clearly be invaluable in the prosecution of higher studies.

Throughout his work in school teaching, therefore, Newman was
accordingly especially careful in inculcating these qualities in his
pupils. He had learned how to work hard as an undergraduate, but
he had lost direction for lack of sound guidance. He was to say that
he wasted his time as an undergraduate, not like so many who do
little or no work, but paradoxically by doing too much work of the

wrong kind for the stage he had reached. He was still learning like a schoolboy, when he should have been developing the 'philosophical habit' of which he speaks in the *Idea*. Having learned from his own experience, Newman the schoolmaster aimed to get the boys to do 'a little, but well; that is, really know what you say you know'.[235] To encourage the boys at his school in those areas that he most prized in school education, Newman established the Norfolk Prize Competition, comprising six days of searching tests in Greek, Greek New Testament, Latin, Euclid and learning by heart.[236]

Newman devoted himself with great care to examinations. Since personal influence was above all the mark of Newman's style of education, this was especially the case in the end-of-term examinations, which were conducted by him and other teachers, viva voce. Newman also introduced regular tests on the grounds, he told a parent, 'that they impart self-confidence, they serve to bring home to a youth what he knows and what he does not, they teach him to bring out his knowledge and to express his meaning clearly'.[237] Nothing could state more clearly than that Newman's aim for training the boys' minds, not just in commitment of facts to memory, but in learning to think clearly.

The art of 'knowing what you say you know' is a vital step in the formation of the mind's powers. But a student needs to move on from what is known to what is unknown. Newman says that once he has gained 'this habit of method, of starting from fixed points, of making good his ground as he goes, of distinguishing what he knows from what he does not know ... he will be gradually initiated into the largest and truest philosophical views'.[238] In 'Elementary Studies' Newman gives us two contrasting and delightfully humorous scenes of two candidates for university entrance being examined viva voce in a Greek and a Latin text.[239] One of the boys is clearly utterly unprepared; he illustrates what Newman calls 'inaccuracy'. The other has prepared well, but is still capable of being led further by his examiner. He is a student who, 'whatever may be his proficiency, at least knows what he is about, and has tried to master what he has read'. The examiner is, in both cases, as kindly and patient as he is searching.

While these are fictional cases, there can be little doubt that they represent the way in which Newman himself conducted such exams.

It is interesting to see how carefully and patiently Newman the examiner deals with both his contrasting candidates in 'Elementary Studies'. At this level of education, between school and university, a student 'really knowing what he says he knows' is one who can give an
account of himself and of his reading that is accurate. Yet Newman
also wants to move the examinee onwards to new aspects of the material he already knows. The examiner presents the subject-matter from
unfamiliar angles, asking questions that the examinee will not have
thought about before, and which the examiner knows he has not
thought about, not in order to show up his ignorance, but in order to
encourage new ways of thinking about material that is already in the
mind, and of which the student already has a sure grasp. This scene
therefore recalls Newman's desideratum that 'critical scholarship is
so important a discipline for [the student] when he is leaving school
for the University'.[240]

In common with many educationalists of the nineteenth century,
Newman had a high regard for the Greek and Latin classics in the
curriculum at school and university level. On the one hand, some
believed that the classics in particular, and literature in general,
were useful principally for developing a sense of taste and high culture. Such a narrow and exaggerated view of the moral effect of
literature had been criticized by Newman in the 'Tamworth Reading
Room'. For Newman, on the other hand, the merit of the classics lay
not simply in their expressive force and clarity, but in their power to
provide 'the most robust and invigorating discipline for the unformed
mind'.[241]

He illustrates this understanding in the section of 'Elementary
Studies' entitled 'Old Mr Black's Confession of his search after a Latin
style', which is surely autobiographical.[242] Not surprisingly, given his
later achievements, Newman here tells us that he took a special interest in the subject of style in writing prose and verse. But although he
was able to write in various English styles, he did not understand what
was meant by good Latin style. He read that this or that passage was
'neat Ciceronian language', but not why or how it was so described.
He believed that it was simply using good phrases, and so noted them
down and used them in his own composition. Eventually he came
across Latin orations delivered before the university of Oxford by

Edward Copleston. From these he learned Latinity. He says 'I quickly found that I had a new sense as regards composition, that I understood beyond mistake what a Latin sentence should be, and saw how an English sentence must be fused and remoulded in order to make it Latin.'[243]

He had at least learned that Latinity lies in structure; that it was not sufficient to write a grammatically correct Latin sentence *while the whole sentence remained English*. He illustrates this by providing six utterly different Latin translations of the same English sentence.[244] He says that they may be 'more or less deficient in hitting the Latin idiom yet [they] evidently know what idiom is'.[245]

A close reading of these pages will show how Newman himself learned to analyse thought and language accurately through construing and composing in Latin, and how he used his own lesson in teaching others. Newman's point, of course, is not that the study of Latin is the only means whereby a student may learn how to think. He remarked that the same discipline of accuracy of thought is required in, and acquired by, having to construe any foreign language into your own; he also observes 'what a still severer and more improving exercise it is to translate from your own into a foreign language'.[246] Nor does he by any means exclude other sciences from being able to carry out this perfecting of the mental powers:

> what a lesson in memory and discrimination it is to get up ... any one chapter of history ... what a trial of acuteness, caution and exactness it is to master, and still more to prove, a number of definitions ... what an exercise in logical precision to understand and enunciate the proof of any of the more difficult propositions of Euclid.[247]

There may be more wonderful facts and brilliant discoveries to attract students to study the physical sciences, but the question is whether, like Latin, they are able to enlarge the mind and strengthen its faculties of discernment and precision. And so, he concludes: 'of any other science – chemistry, or comparative anatomy, or natural history; it does not matter what it is, if it be really studied and mastered ... The result is a formation of the mind – that is, a habit of order and system ...'[248]

It is not surprising, then, to find that although classics was the staple diet in the curriculum at the Oratory School, nonetheless, as at his own boyhood school at Ealing, Newman's school had a broader range of subjects than did most other English public schools of the day.[249] For instance, at Harrow School in the early 1860s, Latin and Greek consumed eighteen of the twenty-two hours of a boy's weekly class-time. Newman, on the other hand, introduced his first form boys not only to Latin, but also to algebra, geometry, English history and French. In the second year he added geography, and then German and Greek in the third. This curriculum was also more liberally inclined than that of the Catholic colleges, which reflected their bias towards preparation for the priesthood with an emphasis on the Church Fathers rather than on the classical authors. Newman's school, by contrast, was the first Catholic school specifically to prepare boys for the professions via the universities. He selected scholarly men as schoolmasters, conducting rigorous interviews in order to ascertain which candidates were not only academically able, but generally suited to classroom teaching.[250]

Newman's conception of the liberal in education was not restricted to the intellect, but included any ordinary pursuit which is 'sufficient and self-complete', meaning that it 'is independent of sequel, expects no complement, refuses to be *informed* (as it is called) by any end, or absorbed into any art' beyond the enjoyment and the stimulation that they give.[251] Accordingly, not all school activities were confined to the classroom or to the study. Newman staged an annual Latin play, in the preparation of which he enjoyed taking a dominant role. He made his own edition of four plays, two each by Terence and Plautus, and wrote a Latin prologue to them. He coached the boys in construing as well as in acting them, and to the end of his life attended rehearsals with great interest.[252] Typical also was his attitude to music. A very good violinist himself, Newman regarded music not only as an excellent social amusement and source of pleasure, but also as in some way akin to thought itself, or at least as demanding intelligence in understanding and care in execution. However, he also knew the limitations of schoolboys, and their reluctance to practise music if that meant losing playtime. He therefore restricted the teaching of a musical instrument only to those boys who showed some interest and aptitude.[253] In such ways Newman aimed to encourage as wide a range of abilities and interests as possible among the boys.

Liberal *versus* Utilitarian Education: The *Edinburgh Review* Controversy

At the beginning of the *Idea*, Newman speaks interchangeably of university education and liberal education.[254] Of all kinds of educational institutions, Newman sees liberal education as the particular province of a university in the pursuit of 'knowledge as its own end'. He takes it for granted 'that the true and adequate end of intellectual training and of a University is not Learning or Acquirement, but rather, is Thought or Reason exercised upon Knowledge'.[255] Newman asks whether *usefulness* to the student should be considered the purpose of university study.[256] He argues that there are two fundamentally different ends of education to be considered here: the acquiring of knowledge for its own end, and acquiring it for some other end. All knowledge is to be acquired for a purpose, but what should that purpose be? Here Newman alludes to a controversy which had been conducted some forty years before in the pages of the *Edinburgh Review*. One of the leading writers for that journal was Henry Brougham whose thought had influenced Peel's establishment of the Tamworth Reading Room in 1841. Brougham and other reviewers favoured political and educational reform and developed a policy of hostile criticism of English educational institutions. Between July 1809 and April 1810 the *Edinburgh Review* contained a series of articles that systematically questioned 'English' education, by which the reviewers principally meant the values and culture of Oxford University.

The Edinburgh reviewers focused on the classical education then mainly offered in Oxford and criticized the amount of time spent on the study of Latin and Greek and the accuracy of the texts in use. The reviewers claimed that Oxford's educational system was not relevant to the contemporary world and that its claims to excellence depended more on its financial endowment than on its intellectual prowess. Oxford was accused of being ignorant of advances in science, moral philosophy and European literature and that the limited education on offer produced 'a style of elegant imbecility' in the graduates.[257] Sydney Smith claimed that Oxford represented uniformity, ignorance, narrowness, parochialism, and an inability to encounter difference or intellectual nonconformity.[258] Scottish universities, by contrast, were open, diverse, democratic, useful, and relevant to the modern world. It was claimed that they were cosmopolitan and pluralistic institutions rooted in a democratic culture capable of producing diversity among their participants. Scottish universities were also well advanced in research and professional education. Oxford in contrast lacked the capacity to give autonomy to its participants and was narrowly homogeneous and socially elitist. Above all, the philosophy of education in the *Edinburgh Review* posited an intimate link between the intellectual life and the practical life.

At the time of the *Edinburgh Review* attack, Oxford's intellectual tradition was defended by Edward Copleston of Oriel College. Copleston had already begun a campaign for reform in Oxford, in which he fought the system of patronage, sinecures and academic laxity in the colleges and advocated that they should be brought back under the university's supervisory powers. He also worked for the reform of the Oxford curriculum and teaching methods. As we have already seen, it was Copleston who recognized Newman's abilities despite his poor showing in the Schools and had him chosen as a Fellow of his College in 1822. In his *A Reply to the Calumnies of the* Edinburgh Review *against Oxford*, Copleston offered a defence of the study of classics and theology, but did less well in defending Oxford's clerical traditions.

Newman builds on and extends Copleston's defence of Oxford's traditions in the *Idea* by introducing a specifically nuanced version of a liberal education. Not only were the values of liberal education being called into question by the *Edinburgh Review*, but also by the establishment of University College, London, under utilitarian principles, and by the various commissions into Oxford and Cambridge and the public and grammar schools in the 1850s and 1860s. There was a movement to redefine the education offered in schools and universities and this involved a battle over the intrinsic and extrinsic value of the curriculum provided. There had also been a great expansion of universities and of the university curriculum since Copleston wrote, which Newman took into account both in composing the *Idea* and in the constitution of his own university. Newman, in the *Idea*, does not defend liberal education by any appeal to extrinsic value or contemporary relevance, but focuses clearly on the intrinsic value of a liberal education. It must be remembered that Newman was able to reflect many years after the original controversy in the light of his own experience as a teacher in Oxford, and as the founder of a new kind of university in Dublin. His argument in the *Idea*, though supportive of liberal education, is not simply a defence of Oxford. In fact, in his other educational writings from Dublin, gathered together as the *Historical Sketches*, Newman makes his own criticisms of Oxford's educational practices and structure as a university,[259] which he strove to correct in the constitution and practice of his university in Dublin.

Because of his defence of liberal education in the *Idea* Newman is sometimes seen as the arch-conservative defender of the study of Greek and Latin classics against those who wished either to replace the classics as the principal subject of study at English schools and universities, or at the least add to them the study of other, more practically useful courses of study. On account of this view Newman is often mistakenly accused of being an intellectual elitist. This, however, only appears to be the case because he was writing in opposition to the triumph of utilitarianism as an animating philosophy of English social and political life. Yet he established departments and teaching posts in disciplines such as engineering, previously unrepresented at Oxford in his day.[260] He also raised the School of Science to be independent of the Arts faculty. Moreover, while it is true that Newman believed firmly in the importance and enduring value of liberal education, he was far from discounting other practical or 'useful' forms of education. The next chapter will show the ways in which Newman went to great lengths to provide such practical education at Dublin alongside liberal studies, and the great importance he attached to these studies and to the general education of their students.

Newman's integrated vision of a university education is concerned with theoretical knowledge. While Newman was against the compartmentalization of education, he recognized the modern need for a multiplicity of disciplines. Liberal education is therefore not tied exclusively to certain subjects such as philosophy, history, and literature – the so-called humanities. Newman was in effect advocating the Hellenic *paideia*, adapted by centuries of Christian insight and practice, and adjusting it for his own times. It should also be noted that studying the humanities is not the same thing as acquiring a liberal education. Newman believed that there were certain forms of knowledge that were good by virtue of the qualities of mind their study imparted to the individual. Persons can acquire a liberal education through the study of the sciences, as long as they do so not primarily to prepare for a profession, but rather to develop their capacity to think and to reason. In the liberal-arts tradition, scientific disciplines may be considered equally liberal, that is, equally capable of developing the powers of the mind. However, for Newman this only increased the necessity of a principle of order, governing the whole. It was necessary for the student to perceive each branch of knowledge in relation to the rest.

In order fully to appreciate Newman's praxis as well as his theory of liberal education, it is essential not to rely solely on the *Idea*, but to take into account also the *Historical Sketches*. These two works of his Dublin years are in some ways complementary. We have already seen that in the *Grammar of Assent* Newman identifies two ways of knowing which he labels 'notional' and 'real'.[261] In giving notional assent, the mind embraces the abstract form, whereas 'real' assent is only given to actual instances or examples of that form. Each form of assent requires the other for a fully comprehensive understanding. Newman holds that for an idea to take hold on the imagination, real instances of the form must be grasped alongside the abstract form. In the *Idea*, as the title suggests, Newman explores education and knowledge as they are found notionally in a university. In the *Historical Sketches* he gives historical accounts of the development of universities as they have arisen and succeeded, or failed. In other words, Newman expounds his view of liberal education theoretically, or notionally, in the *Idea*, whereas in the *Historical Sketches* he gives historical instances that actually, or really, illustrate his theories.

The 'Idea' of a University in its Essence:
The Sharing of Thought

The end both of a university and of a liberal education are, for Newman, not learning but 'Thought or Reason exercised upon Knowledge'. The aim of a university education can therefore be put succinctly as 'the ability to think'.[262] For Newman this means constructing well-formed judgements on the foundation of being able to reason well. The formation of this state of intellectual excellence is therefore dependent on the development of powers of evaluation and discrimination in handling arguments and different kinds of subject matter. Though it does not necessarily require a thorough acquaintance with all kinds of knowledge, it does convey the ability to enter into any topic with ease. Such an ability is developed through exercising the mind in argument, and in learning to think independently, in the face of errors, distortions and overemphasized truths. This, Newman argues, is exactly what the atmosphere of a university provides: the context in which many minds interact and help to strengthen each other's powers of reasoning. So much is this the case that Newman considers this interaction to be more truly constitutive of a liberal education than is university teaching.

He is prepared to consider a *reductio ad absurdum* to illustrate his point. In an example which we have already considered in the last chapter, Newman protests that if he had

> to choose between a so-called University, which dispensed with residence and tutorial superintendence, and gave its degrees to any person who passed an examination in a wide range of subjects, and a University which had no professors or examinations at all, but merely brought a number of young men together for three or four years, and then sent them away ... if I were asked which of these two methods were the better discipline of the intellect ... the more successful in training, moulding, enlarging the mind ... I have no hesitation in giving preference to that University which did nothing, over that which exacted of its members an acquaintance with every science under the sun.[263]

Of course, Newman does not in fact propose a university without any teachers, since he accords good teaching such importance both intellectually and morally. But even if Oxford were as bad as its Edinburgh critics had maintained, Newman believes that it would still provide a better environment for imparting a liberal education as he conceives it than a non-residential institution could do. How is this to be explained? Newman answers: 'I suppose as follows: when a multitude of young men, keen, open-hearted, sympathetic and observant ... come together and freely mix with each other, they are sure to learn from one another, even of there be no one to teach them; the conversation of all is a lecture to each, and they gain for themselves new ideas and views, fresh matter of thought, and distinct principles for judging and acting, day by day.'[264]

Moreover, Newman sees in this process of mutual influence the seed from which an institution can grow. The coming together of persons from different places and backgrounds, with widely different notions offers the possibility of 'much to generalize, much to adjust, much to eliminate ... interrelations to be defined, and conventional rules to be established, in the process, by which the whole assemblage is moulded together, and gains one tone and one character'.[265] Lest he be thought to be speaking only in the abstract, Newman elsewhere gives the example from history of the emergence of universities, particularly in Paris, in the early thirteenth century.

> Benefactors and patrons may supply the framework of a *Studium Generale*; but there must be a popular interest and a sympathy, a spontaneous cooperation of the many, the concurrence of genius, and a spreading thirst for knowledge, if it is to live.[266]

It is the comprehensiveness of a university which, for Newman, constitutes its grandeur and nobility. 'What an empire is in political history, such is a University in the sphere of philosophy and research.'[267] Yet Newman is not simply ascribing this imperial image to the university's occupation of 'the whole territory of knowledge', but rather to its authority over all the subjects and faculties which it contains. A university professes to assign to each study . . . its own proper place and its just boundaries; to define the rights, to establish the mutual relations, and to effect the intercommunion of one and all; to keep in check the ambitious and encroaching . . . to keep the peace between them all and to convert their mutual differences and contrarieties into the common good.[268]

In this way, a university not only brings together the teachers and students of many different disciplines so that they may be of mutual influence and benefit, but also helps to avoid the usurpations of one science upon another. Newman even describes what he sees as the pattern of interdisciplinary dialogue that he wishes to see established in his university:

Its several professors . . . represent their respective sciences, and attend to the private interests of those sciences respectively; and, should dispute arise between those sciences, they are the persons to talk over and arrange it, without risk of extravagant pretensions on any side, of angry collision, or of popular commotion,

which ideally flourishes when 'a liberal philosophy becomes the habit of minds thus exercised . . .' and produces 'a breadth and spaciousness of thought . . .'[269]

Newman gives two more or less complementary accounts of the meaning of the word 'university': the first being viewed from the aspect of what is taught there, the second from the aspect of those who constitute it and what they do. In the *Idea*, Newman first defines it as 'a place of teaching universal knowledge'.[270] Later, in *Historical Sketches*, he defines it as 'an assemblage of strangers from all parts in one spot . . . for the communication and circulation of thought, by means of personal intercourse'.[271] Together these definitions constitute what he calls a university 'in its essence'. He expands this idea by saying that 'the zeal for study and knowledge is sufficient indeed in itself for the being of a University'.[272] Such a body of students will

embody a specific idea, it will represent a doctrine, it will administer a code of conduct, and it will furnish principles of thought and action. It will give birth to a living teaching, which in the course of time will take the shape of a self-perpetuating tradition, or a *genius loci*.[273]

But he also recognizes a certain kind of danger inherent in any university that simply fulfils that end with no higher guidance or governance. He gives the example of Abelard, one of the most brilliant and original minds of the twelfth century, who attracted many admirers to his lectures in Paris and who 'illustrates the strength and the weakness of the principle of advertising and communicating knowledge for its own sake, which I have called the University principle ...'[274] Abelard had all the strengths and weaknesses of intellectually able men; an uncommonly fine and subtle mind, and overweening pride in his own ability, which he placed above authority. It was this, according to Newman, that made him a great but dangerous teacher, capable of leading lesser intellects away from the truth. Newman recognizes that university teaching needs a safeguard to protect its members from error. He observes that Abelard's weakness lay in 'spoiling by his own self-will what would have been done well and surely under the teaching and guidance of Infallible Authority'.[275]

The Idea of a University in its Integrity: Religious Authority

Newman therefore complements the essence of the university with this need for a higher principle of authority as its guide and governor, which he defines as its *integrity*. Newman defines the integrity of anything as 'a gift superadded to its nature, without which that nature is indeed complete, and can act, and fulfil its end, but does not find itself, if I may use the expression, in easy circumstances'.[276] At first the idea of religious authority can seem oppressive of the free exchange of thought that is of the essence of a university. Revealed truth would seem to be opposed in principle to unfettered intellectual exploration. Newman does not see it thus. While he does recognize that religious authority has a duty to govern the interchange of ideas, this is in order to protect it rather than to restrict it. His argument is that, precisely where new ground is being broken, the human intellect is capable of making erroneous judgements.

He illustrates this point by describing how certain early Christian theologians, (he gives Tertullian and Sabellius as examples), strove to confront and correct existing errors, and yet ended up themselves in error through their impetuosity. Such a person can 'anticipate to a certain point what [the Church] is about to say or enjoin, he states it incorrectly, makes it error instead of truth, and risks his own faith in the process'.[277] With the passage of time, the Church meets these errors 'with those divinely appointed correctives which [she] alone can apply ... when the time comes'. The common factor among heresiarchs, according to Newman, is *impatience,* which is a form of self-will. They have fallen away, he says, 'because the Church would not adopt their views, [and] would have found, had they but trusted her, and waited, that she knew how to profit by them'.[278]

Newman therefore holds that religious authority is the necessary corrective and brake on intellectual pride, which alone prevents an educational institution from falling, sooner or later, into error. It would be a mistake to assume that such an authority is an inanimate and inflexible principle. Instead, Newman sees it as living and developing organically according to the needs of the times. In Discourse IX of the *Idea,* he explains this principle more fully: even if a university were to recognize and profess the entire Catholic credal system, 'still this would not at once make such a University a Catholic Institution, nor be sufficient to secure the due weight of religious considerations in its philosophical studies'. For instance, the Spanish Inquisition was 'a purely Catholic establishment ... the stern foe of every anti-Catholic idea, and administered by Catholic theologians; yet it in no proper sense belonged to the Church. It was simply and entirely a State institution ...'[279] The crucial missing element, according to Newman, without which it finally came into conflict with the Holy See itself, was 'the direct presence of the Church'. Similarly, says Newman,

it is no sufficient security for the Catholicity of a University, even that the whole of Catholic theology be professed in it, unless the Church ... fashions and moulds its organization, and watches over its teaching, and knits together its pupils, and superintends its action.[280]

Newman would therefore see the Church's role in universities as the protector of freedom rather than as its oppressor. This position makes sense when we remember that for Newman the aim of intellectual endeavour and research is truth. The danger of liberal education unprotected by constant reference to revealed truth and the authority of the Church, is that it tends towards a 'mere philosophical theory of life and conduct, in place of Revelation'.[281] It is the natural tendency of the intellect to speculate and to recast revealed truth into our own image. 'A sense of propriety, order, consistency, and completeness gives birth to a rebellious stirring against miracle and mystery, against the severe and terrible.'[282] Although there cannot be any contradiction between physical science and revelation, since both come from the same divine author, nonetheless Newman recognizes that 'in matter of fact, there has always been a sort of jealousy and hostility between Religion and physical philosophers'.[283] Newman here mentions the case of Galileo as one of the most familiar cases of conflict between revealed truth and Church authority on the one hand, and unbridled free intellectual speculation on the other. Galileo was not content with reasoning in his own province, but 'went out of his way directly to insult the received interpretation of Scripture'.[284]

It is this tendency to usurp the authority of an area of knowledge that is outside one's proper sphere of competence that Newman recognizes as the principal danger in intellectual pride. He even says that 'physical science is in a certain sense atheistic, for the very reason that it is not theology'.[285] This is to restate Newman's argument that once theology is omitted from the circle of sciences its place is usurped by other sciences, and serious distortions to our understanding of the truth will surely follow. But, says Newman, God is not only the subject of theology, but its author as well. 'When Truth can change, its Revelation can change; when human reason can outreason the Omniscient, then it may supersede His work.'[286] The statement and defence of that principle is, in Newman's view, essential to the protection of all liberal knowledge and the proper exercise of reason within its own natural limits.

The Idea of a University in its Integrity:
Personal Influence

The danger posed in universities by unbridled speculation on the part of its lecturers, such as Abelard, requires a counterbalancing influence. Newman argued that the institution of colleges in universities went a long way to providing that need. We have already seen that he believed that colleges sheltered inexperienced students from moral dangers and temptations which they had not yet developed the strength and knowledge to resist. He also believed that colleges provided a shelter and protection to students not only against dangerous intellectual currents, but also in the process of guided study.

The mode of guardianship was the same in both moral and intellectual spheres, in the form of the personal tutor. A tutor knows the students who are entrusted to his care. He is appointed not only to exercise supervision of their moral welfare, but also to direct their course of reading. In order to discharge this duty it is necessary for him to get to know his students well. Newman recognized the individuality not only of students' characters, but also of their intellects. Therefore a tutor must adapt his approach to each one's individual needs, strengths and weaknesses; in other words he must be pupil-orientated, since what suits one student will not necessarily be good for another. Personal interaction characterizes Newman's view of the role of colleges as domestic environments, and of tutors as personal guides; personal influence is at the heart of Newman's pedagogy.

As far as Newman is concerned, it is *possible* for a university to exist without teachers, but it is not likely that it will survive for long without falling into intellectual and moral difficulties. He appeals once more to the principles he had adumbrated in the 'Tamworth Reading Room' when he says in *Historical Sketches*, 'Intellect is helpless, because ungovernable and self-destructive, unless it be regulated by a moral rule and by revealed truth.'[287] On these grounds he holds that 'the personal influence of the teacher is able in some sort to dispense with an academical system, but that system cannot in any sort dispense with personal influence'.[288] Newman sees this influence as a positive benefit, characterized not as distant authority but as personal knowledge. He castigates as the antithesis of this personal influence his recollection of his time in Oxford when 'the tutor was supposed to fulfil his duty, if he trotted on like a squirrel in a cage ... where a stiff manner, a pompous voice, coldness and condescension, were the teacher's attributes ...'[289] We have already seen how Newman set himself and his colleagues to reform the tutorial system at Oriel and how, despite being removed from the post after too short a time, his personal influence over those pupils he supervised was decisive. Newman had a particular abhorrence for the idea of a university devoid of personal influence, calling it 'an arctic winter' which 'will create an ice-bound, petrified, cast-iron University ...'[290] He maintained that we could not truly call a university an 'Alma Mater' if it were a 'foundry, a mint, or a treadmill', but only by reason of her 'knowing her children one by one'.[291]

There is another essential element in the tutorial system which Newman identifies and which also explains his suspicion towards educational institutions devoid of personal influence, such as the Mechanics' Institutes being set up at that time. It is the interactive process, which requires not only the tutor's guidance but also the student's responsiveness. In the address entitled *Discipline of Mind* Newman tells his students in Dublin that: 'you do not come merely to hear a lecture or to read a book, but you come for that catechetical instruction, which consists in a sort of conversation between your lecturer and you. He tells you a thing, and he asks you to repeat it after him.'[292]

Lest this should seem to be a merely mechanical requirement of the pupil he adds that the lecturer 'questions you, he examines you, he will not let you go till he has proof, not only that you have heard, but that you know'.[293] It is precisely because young people are inexperienced in the exercise of judgement that they need guidance from those who are experienced and wise. The wise tutor will judge when the right opportunity has come for him to introduce his pupil to particular books or ideas, and the order in which to bring them in, and then guide him into understanding them clearly, thereby enlarging his synthetic and discriminatory intellectual powers.

In Oxford Newman had championed the cause of reform in the selection of better-prepared candidates for admission and examination. Examinations which had been conducted *viva voce* were made more searching by the introduction of paper work, and a Greek composition prize was established. He also reformed the lecture system.

> The principle now introduced was that each Tutor should in the first place be responsible and consult for his own pupils, should determine what subjects they ought to have lectures in, and should have first choice as to taking those lectures themselves . . . Otherwise they considered the office of Tutor became that of a mere lecturer, and that teaching was not an act of personal intercourse, but an ungenial and donnish form.[294]

Newman had not only the opportunity to integrate his experience and understanding of the tutorial role into the university at Dublin, but in a large measure his insights were eventually adopted at Oxford long after he had left.

Conclusion

Newman, over the course of his life, was involved in almost as many kinds of educational institution as existed in his day. In all of them he tailored his aims to the ends of the institution and the needs of the pupils. In all of them he was innovative and often controversial. Personal influence both in moral guidance and in intellectual training were inextricably linked for Newman. Even when concerned with a person's liberal education, he did not ignore his moral character. Any form of education which divorces intellectual formation from moral is, in Newman's view, both false and dangerous. He embodied 'the Holistic Principle', wherein all aspects of education are integrated with the faith and related to it.[295] This is because, in Newman's view, all true education is concerned with the way persons live as much as how they think. A good educator, therefore, cannot be neutral with regard to the good of the whole person under his or her charge.

When Newman opened the Catholic University in Dublin, he invited his new students to a soirée in the refectory of the new university house the day before lectures began and asked them if they knew what they were there for. It was obvious, he said, that they were to prepare themselves for their respective professions in life; but they might be able to do that elsewhere. Professions differ, but the one kind of education which all of them should have in common and for which they especially come to this university is the kind which *makes the man*, for a man is able to a great extent to be master of himself. To be master of oneself is no less than to be able both to think well and to act well. Such maturity is both the aim and the fruit of a liberal education.

Chapter 5

The Vocational Dimension of Education

Training versus Education

As we have already seen, Newman understood that education has a variety of different aims, practical, moral, intellectual, and above all, religious. Not all those aims are necessarily pursued at the same time in the same institution. But as far as Newman was concerned, vocational or professional training undertaken on its own would be limited as a form of education. Newman made a careful distinction between instruction and education. Instruction is concerned with external and mechanical rules and results in the mere transmission, acquisition or acceptance of information or technical skills. Typically, such instruction takes place either in institutions specially created for the purpose, or in the place of work, which therefore does not require any study outside its own expertise. Such a kind of technical training, necessary as it must be for a profession, could not qualify as 'education' according to Newman, insofar as it is incapable of developing the higher critical faculties of the mind.

Not that such training was necessarily devoid of intellectual content. Newman notes that in ancient Greece many of the doctors were slaves, and highly trained;[296] but they did not necessarily have any broader intellectual formation. It is not that Newman denied the intellectual character of their learning, but that, of itself, it did not develop their mental powers. The limitation of professional training outside the context of a liberal education lies in its intrinsic narrowness. The more highly particularized a skill or habit is, the more difficult it is to apply its principles to other skills or disciplines. For instance, a well-trained carpenter can produce a fine practical demonstration of his skills, but even if he is capable of giving a good account of them, he cannot thereby the more easily apply them to any other mental or physical skill or discipline.[297]

Nevertheless, Newman did hold that 'no one can deny that commerce and the professions afford scope for the highest and most diversified powers of the mind'.[298] But for this to be possible, it is necessary that the student for the professions benefit also from what he properly considers to be education, which alone is capable of developing and extending those powers of mind. Therefore, although Newman recognized genuine tensions between liberal education and vocational training (professional preparation), it would be wrong to conclude that he viewed the liberal and the vocational as mutually exclusive activities. It is also a serious misreading of Newman to accuse him of antipathy towards professional training. We would argue instead that while Newman did not regard liberal education as completely opposed to training for the various professions, he certainly held that training for the professions was no substitute for a liberal education.

It is true, of course, that Newman was much influenced by the Athenian model of education, which was prevalent among educationalists of his day. This model separated liberal education and vocational training: a separation that first originated in the social division of classes in the Greek State of Athens. The model consisted of dividing men into two categories: the physical and the intellectual. The majority of human beings whose nature was considered to be dominated by their bodies were destined to be manual workers or warriors. The minority, those relieved from the necessity to labour for a living, were destined to increase in rational or intellectual powers that would enable them effectively to rule over the majority of the population. Liberal education in this context literally meant educating free men. Plato's aversion to excessive educational instrumentalism was grounded in the belief that true knowledge can only be achieved through transcending the mundane, and since vocational training deals with the mundane it is opposed to the true purpose of education.

Newman's writings are certainly influenced by these conceptions of education, but not dominated by them. It was because he favoured a more holistic notion of education which did not accept the absolute separation of the liberal from the vocational, or the physical from the intellectual, that he insisted that professional training should not be separated from liberal education. For Newman, the ideal preparation for an intellectually effective professional training is a prior development of the mental powers and moral character through a liberal education. He noted how this necessary interaction between liberal and professional education had developed in the Middle Ages. In *Historical Sketches* III he describes the expansion of the medieval university curriculum from the Trivium and Quadrivium (the liberal arts) inherited from the ancient world, with the arrival of the 'new sciences' of theology, law and medicine, and in subordination to them, of metaphysics, natural history and the languages.[299] But although the medieval universities were dominated by these 'superior' professional faculties, undergraduates were usually admitted only to the *Philosophia* (Arts and Science faculty) and were required to graduate here first before moving to the professional faculties. It is in this Christian tradition of first acquiring a liberal education, before undertaking professional preparation, that both Newman's writings and his practice at Dublin are principally located.

Professional Education and Usefulness

In considering Newman's approach to professional education it is important to consider not only what he wrote both in the *Idea* (he uses the word in the sense of 'ideal') and elsewhere, but also what he did. It is too often alleged that Newman was interested in liberal education exclusively, but it can be easily demonstrated that this is not the case. Indeed, much of the debate about Newman's idea about utility in education is confused and confusing. Not only was Newman definitely not opposed to the teaching of vocational subjects, but he even insisted that 'nothing can be more absurd than to neglect those matters which are necessary for (a student's) future calling'.[300] If one sets Newman's discourses from the *Idea* in the context of his work in setting up the Catholic University, and reads them in the light of his own performance as its rector, it is clear that he argues for the necessity of a fundamental interaction between the liberal and vocational dimensions of higher education.

We have already noted that Newman made a distinction between instruction and education. While instruction is narrow in conception, education is much broader, being concerned with formation both of the intellect and of character. Newman held that it is an error to suppose that 'the end of education is merely to fit persons for their respective stations in life – to teach them their several trades, and put them in the way to rise in the world'.[301] He held this to be true for everyone, not merely for those who had the intellectual gifts or freedom to benefit from a liberal education. This is because, for Newman, as we have seen, the ultimate end of all education is religious. It is directed towards the formation of human character and intellect in preparation for all aspects of life. For Newman what is taught does not matter so much as how it is taught. Education, he writes, is an action on our nature, and the foundation of character. He posited an ideal of humanist, liberal, holistic education, which by implication he contrasted with narrow, instrumentalist, servile instruction. In this understanding even any academic subject studied in the university carries the danger of being taught in a narrow and introspective way if it does not broaden the mind, in short, if it is not liberal.

He was, of course, opposed to an excessive emphasis on knowledge as productive and useful which at the time was associated with the Utilitarianism of Bentham, a philosophy which he traces further back to Bacon and Locke. In the *Idea* Newman was effectively answering what he calls Locke's 'fallacy' that only professional training is useful.[302] He castigates the judgement of Richard Edgeworth that 'the value of every attainment is to be measured by its subservience to a calling'.[303] The utilitarian criterion judges competence primarily according to performance. Only a 'useful' kind of 'education' is valued in the Utilitarian system insofar as it is 'confined to a particular and narrow end, and should issue in some definite work, which can be weighed and measured'.[304] Newman, by contrast, sees those occupations which exclusively serve the necessities or conveniences of life, and therefore bypass the mind's freedom and breadth of thought, as 'servile'[305] in direct contrast to whatever is liberal.

As we have already seen, Newman does not deny that there is a practical benefit in liberal education, but he does not identify it as a narrowly utilitarian one. He reminds us that 'what has its *end* in itself has its *use* in itself also'.[306] He also makes an important distinction, that although what is useful is not always good, what is good is always useful. He has already maintained that a liberal education is a good, so therefore it must also be useful. It is one of the characteristics of the very goodness of the state of a cultivated mind that it tends to diffuse, or share, itself and its benefits: 'I say that a cultivated intellect, because it is good in itself, brings with it a power and a grace to every work and occupation which it undertakes'.[307] The nearest he comes to acknowledging the value of university education beyond its own fruitfulness for the mind is his statement that: 'if, then, a practical end must be assigned to a University course, I say it is that of training good members of society. Its art is the art of social life, and its end, fitness for the world.'[308] In other words, the formation of character is a worthy end of education alongside the formation of mind, and a liberal education tends towards that end. Whoever benefits from such an education is himself a benefit to society, because his education

> shows him how to accommodate himself to others, how to throw himself into their state of mind, how to bring before them his own, how to influence them, how to come to an understanding with them, how to bear with them. He is at home in any society, he has common ground with every class; he knows when to speak and when to be silent; he is able to converse, he is able to listen; he can ask a question pertinently, and gain a lesson seasonably . . .[309]

Newman did not assume that those who argued for a utilitarian purpose and content in education were necessarily anti-intellectual. The reviewers in the *Edinburgh Review* had viewed some forms of practical knowledge as having an intellectual and theoretical component and did not accept that all practical knowledge was simply knowledge of how to perform a task. They believed that the study of medicine, pharmacy, and law, for example, required a reflective knowledge base and that such professionals were not merely trained functionaries, but educated persons. They complained of the backward state of mathematical education at both England's universities and about how they adhered to antiquated methods with an outdated curriculum. Oxford in particular was criticized for its narrow understanding of liberal education and for not providing its students with an education in the social, economic and political forces at work around them.

There was clearly a tension between supporters of the older metaphysical and moral sciences and those of the newer natural and physical ones. Edward Copleston in defending his vision of Oxford's classical humanistic education replied three times to the *Edinburgh Review* in 1810 and 1811. He said that the purpose of the university is to counter the effects upon the individual of gross materialism, and described the benefits of an Oxford-style liberal education in terms which influenced Newman: 'And thus, without directly qualifying a man for any of the employments of life, [a university education] enriches and ennobles all', and quoting John Milton he concludes that it 'fits a man "to perform justly, skilfully, and magnanimously, all the offices, both private and public, of peace and war"'.[310]

However, Copleston's replies were weak in that he did not address the questions and charges being made by the *Edinburgh Review*, being more concerned with countering any external criticism of Oxford. Instead he made general statements such as: 'Never let us believe that the improvement of chemical arts, however much it may tend to the augmentation of national riches, can supersede the use of that intellectual laboratory, where the sages of Greece explored the hidden elements of which man consists'.[311] Copleston simply denigrated any form of scientific study and training as mere utilitarianism. The Edinburgh reviewers were arguing for better scientific training in the universities. They wanted to improve and extend the professional understanding and practices of individual practitioners in the new and growing professions.

Copleston's reply was to use the concept of liberal education in a defensive way, that is, concerned as a *post factum* justification of the status quo. He also used a negative definition of liberal education – as that which is not useful or vocational. It is interesting to note, however, that as provost of Oriel College, Copleston was in practice the chief advocate of the reform of the Oxford system of education in his day, and actually addressed many of the *Edinburgh Review* criticisms. He of course advocated these reforms in private within the internal procedures of Oxford University. Newman, while borrowing much from Copleston's replies in writing the *Idea*, nevertheless attempted to go much further in bridging the divide between liberal education and vocational preparation, both in the *Idea* and in his organization of the Catholic University itself. Thereby he also argued more explicitly for the kind of reforms which Copleston had begun in Oxford, and which Newman was to take much further still in Dublin.

Newman was clearly not opposed to all of the Edinburgh critics' concerns. In a 'Memorandum on the Objects of the University and the Means for attaining them', addressed to the Irish bishops, he proposes 'to provide a Professional education for students of law and medicine; and a liberal education for the mercantile class'.[312] He therefore wanted professionals such as doctors and lawyers to be trained at his university, but he did not want to turn out mere practitioners, well versed in their expertise, but lacking a general view.

> I do but say that there will be this distinction as regards a Professor of Law, or of Medicine, or of Geology, or of Political Economy, in a University and out of it, that out of a University he is in danger of being absorbed and narrowed by his pursuit, and of giving Lectures which are the Lectures of nothing more than a lawyer, physician, geologist, or political economist; whereas in a University he will know just where he and his science stand.[313]

A professional educated at Newman's university should be a well-rounded practitioner who can see the larger issues that arise in the practice of his profession. This broader view comes about by 'the very rivalry of other studies', from which he has gained 'a special illumination and largeness of mind and freedom and self-possession, and he treats his own in consequence with a philosophy and a resource, which belongs not to the study itself, but to his liberal education'.[314] In other words, he wanted to educate such a person to the level of a critical understanding and independence of mind as well as to enter a profession.

Therefore, while professional training had its proper place for Newman, it clearly presupposed a broader education of the whole person. Even though the teaching of applied disciplines is not the end, or purpose, of a university, that does not imply that such applied sciences should not be taught there. Newman has already established that the very definition of a university involves in some sense the idea of teaching all knowledge: 'What indeed can [a university] teach at all, if it does not teach something particular? It teaches *all* knowledge by teaching all *branches* of knowledge.'[315] Moreover, not only must a university teach all branches of knowledge if it is to be what it claims to be, but it is the only arena which can impart professional education in a context which is not narrowly utilitarian.

Newman warns against what he perceived to be Edinburgh University's rationalism in the liberal arts. He accepted that professional training contributed to greater professional efficiency and to the wealth of the nation. He quotes Copleston's observation that 'the more the powers of each individual are concentrated in one employment, the greater skill and quickness will he naturally display in performing it'.[316] However, Copleston believed that there is not merely a tension, but a direct opposition, between the contribution such an individual makes to the accumulation of national wealth on the one hand, and the extent to which he himself becomes more 'degraded as a rational being'. Newman here firmly endorses Copleston's argument that 'in proportion as his sphere of action is narrowed his mental powers and habits become contracted; and he resembles a subordinate part of some powerful machinery, useful in its place, but insignificant and worthless out of it'.[317]

Newman thus warns against a danger inherent in utilitarianism, that it tends towards the instrumentalization of persons through their occupations. He foresees utilitarianism leading to the measuring of the value of individuals' contribution to society largely by the extrinsic value of their work. As Newman observes of the Utilitarians: 'They argue as if everything, as well as every person, had its price; and that where there has been a great outlay, they have a right to expect a return in kind.'[318] Such an approach poses dangers to human dignity as 'the advantage of the community is nearly in an inverse ratio with his own'.[319] This assessment of value to the community rather than to the individual also corresponds to Newman's rejection of a 'mechanical' approach to education, comprising the idea that competence or skills are simply concerned with measurement and assessment – rather than with knowledge, reflection or understanding.

But Newman is more nuanced than Copleston. Where Copleston declares that the utility of knowledge to an individual varies inversely with its utility to the public, Newman follows another older Oriel Fellow, John Davison, who had argued instead that liberal education was in any case 'far higher even in the scale of utility than what is commonly called a Useful Education'.[320] In other words, Newman is unwilling to agree that there is a sheer antithesis between liberal and professional education, so long as it is truly *education* that is meant, and not merely professional training. For the usefulness of education lies in 'its being a real benefit to the subjects of it, as members of society, in the various duties and circumstances and accidents of life'.[321] Newman, of course, is happy to acknowledge the usefulness to society of a liberal education, so long as that is not understood to be its principal justification, much less its only one. Such usefulness to society is a fruit which follows from a greater good, which is the intrinsic good of the person who enjoys the fruits of a liberal education, namely the excellence of his mental faculties.

It is perhaps easier to illustrate what Newman means by contrasting the opposite case: the effect on society of those who have been only trained in their own profession. Newman once again quotes Davison: 'now of all those who furnish their share to rational conversation, a mere adept at his own art is universally admitted to be the worst ... if he escape being dull, it is only by launching into ill-timed, learned loquacity'. Newman puts it even more clearly at an earlier place in the *Idea* when he says that those who are defective in intellectual training 'have no difficulty in contradicting themselves in successive sentences, without being conscious of it ... have their most unfortunate crotchets, or hobbies, which deprive them of the influence which their estimable qualities would otherwise secure'.[322]

Therefore 'useful' training according to the utilitarian criterion may indeed have an intellectual content, but if it has not formed the mind's faculties beyond its own immediate professional sphere, it renders its practitioners less useful to general discussion, the pursuit of truth, and of the organization of civil and social life. Newman describes this as the 'great ordinary means to a great but ordinary end' of a university training, that

> it aims at raising the intellectual tone of society, at cultivating the public mind, at purifying the national taste, at supplying true principles to popular enthusiasm and fixed aims to popular aspiration, at giving enlargement and sobriety to the ideas of the age, at facilitating the exercise of political power, and refining the intercourse of private life.[323]

Following Davison, Newman therefore sees a tension between increasing specialization in education and the proper development of mind. He allows that anyone who makes a business of one pursuit is in the right way to eminence in it, and that divided attention rarely gives excellence in many pursuits. But there is a danger in doing this too early, before a general education has been given. It is a bad preparation for a person to excel in one pursuit if his early studies are fettered and the development of his mind cramped. Consequently, according to Davison, while 'a man of well-improved faculties has the command of another's knowledge, a man without them has not the command of his own'.[324]

Hence, as we have already seen, Newman's attitude to the school curriculum was to maintain a broad range of subjects especially in order to develop the interconnections between them. Specialization for professional training would follow after the mind had been thoroughly trained by a liberal education. It may appear at first that Newman contradicts himself by saying that a broad range of studies is helpful to the mind's development on the one hand, and that studying too great a range of subjects can lead to superficiality on the other. But this is not so. What matters is the manner of their introduction. This is one of the tasks of the tutor in university and the teacher in school: to judge the best way of introducing the student to new material, or new perspectives, so that he will enlighten rather than confuse the student's knowledge and understanding.

Accordingly, Newman sees that if 'different studies are useful for aiding, they are still more useful for correcting each other; for as they have their particular merits severally, so have they their defects . . .'[325] But this effect of mutual correction and illumination is activated only in a mind that has been carefully trained beforehand, so that it can subsequently benefit from juxtaposing varied disciplines, by comparing and analysing them. Thus Newman observes that history, philosophy and poetry each have certain tendencies to distort what they represent. History shows the 'morals and interests of men disfigured by all their imperfections of passion, folly and ambition; philosophy strips the picture too much; poetry adorns it too much'. Yet these three modes of representing 'things as they are' can be mutually enlightening and correcting in a mind which has been trained to read them critically side by side, and that 'the concentrated lights of the three correct the false peculiar colouring of each, and show us the truth'.[326]

As well as seeing the danger of over-specializing in individuals, Newman also foresees the danger of increasing specialization in universities, if this should lead to a lack of real understanding between disciplines, and arrogance or narrowness of mind on the part of their respective practitioners. We have already seen how he discusses the possibility of a professor of physics, for example, suppressing the idea of volition, or free will. Newman allows that the professor's definitions, principles and laws might still be correct with reference to his own sphere of research, but his error would be in considering his own study to be the key to interpreting everything else, so that 'it would not be his science which was untrue, but his so-called knowledge which was unreal'.[327] He concludes that

in making [the whole system of the world] identical with his scientific analysis, formed on a particular aspect, such a Professor . . . was betraying a want of philosophical depth, and an ignorance of what an University Teaching ought to be. He was no longer a teacher of liberal knowledge, but a narrow-minded bigot.[328]

Integrated Vocational and Liberal Education

Some forms of vocational training include the integration of theoretical knowledge, practical knowledge and experience. Technical skills are important, for without them we would not be able to achieve many of our highest and most admirable goals. Vocational training contributes to our ability to accomplish a great number of tasks both in the realms of paid employment and in the remainder of our personal and social lives. A liberal arts and science education is an important part of this training because it imparts a number of practical skills such as literacy and accuracy of expression in the many different ways that we communicate with one another. The extent to which elements of a broader liberal education have been, or ought to be, an integral component of what is ultimately a vocational degree, has been a subject of continuing debate. In the 'Tamworth Reading Room' Newman expressed the conviction that 'intrinsically excellent and noble as are scientific pursuits, and worthy of a place in a liberal education, and fruitful in temporal benefits to the community; still they are not, and cannot be, *the instrument* of education'.[329]

Vocational training can therefore only contribute to a liberal education if it avoids narrowness and is moulded within a broad perspective. To define professional training as the truly useful purpose of education is exactly that narrow utilitarianism which Newman rejects. Pelikan agrees with Newman that utilitarianism is 'short-term thinking'.[330] Professional training conducted outside the university tends to be tied to current practice – the short-term or utilitarian approach. In the university, on the other hand, professional training ought to be complemented by liberal education. After all, Newman states that a liberal education makes for 'taking up with aptitude any science or profession'.[331] This is clearly his aim in providing, as he said, a liberal education for the mercantile classes. Consequently, he favoured a liberal education prior to vocational training and insisted that all students should fulfil two years' study in the Arts' faculty before being allowed to transfer to another specialized faculty.

The only exception to this requirement which he permitted was to allow students to enter the Medical School without the prior two years' study in the Arts faculty. Given his critical attitude to premature specialization he was understandably reluctant to do this, and as a result of their lack of grounding in the Arts did not consider the medical students as 'regular members of the university'.[332] That he permitted this despite these misgivings is largely due to the fact that all medical training up to that point was in the hands of Protestant hospitals and colleges, and a Catholic school was clearly an urgent requirement for Newman and the Irish bishops. Because of the special nature of the circumstances and of this policy decision, the Medical School became the most flourishing department of the university after the Faculty of Arts. Yet although the medical students were not regular members of the university, Newman tried to incorporate them as much as possible into university life so that they might reap the twofold benefit of avoiding the moral dangers of living unsupervised in a city, and of associating with students in other disciplines. To this end he opened a medical lodging house for them and encouraged their attendance at the general lectures which he provided for the university students.

Apart from the question of the best possible provision for the medical students who had not the time first of all to enter the two-year course in Arts, we have noted how Newman planned to combine 'a professional training for students of law and medicine' with 'a liberal education for the mercantile class'. He decided that the core areas of knowledge that ought to be taught in a university are comprised in what he called the 'School of Philosophy and Letters'. He envisaged students entering the university at the age of sixteen, and spending two years studying 'classics, the elements of mathematics and logic, ancient history, etc.'[333] At this stage they would be examined for a kind of 'initial degree' which gave them the title of 'Scholar', corresponding in many ways to the Oxford responsions.[334] Thereafter he foresaw that most of the students would leave, 'which is compatible with having imparted a certain amount of liberal knowledge to those who are entering on the duties of their particular calling'.[335]

Newman was eminently practical in making this arrangement. In the first place, he was adapting to the fact that many of those who entered the university were much less well prepared than their contemporaries in Oxford and Cambridge. It was his aim, therefore, to make these two years, even though they obviously could not bring a student to the level of a Bachelor's degree, at least coherent in themselves as well as a suitable preparation for the degree course which followed. Secondly, Newman was submitting to the reality of the demands made upon these young men by their families and financial circumstances, which obliged them to enter the professions as soon as possible. Newman did not wish to lose such prospective pupils on the grounds that his university course was too long to attract them or persuade their parents to support them financially in their studentship. Yet he did foresee and hope that 'those who remain will give themselves for the space of a second two years to a course of modern history, political economy, law, metaphysics etc. which will terminate, at the age of 20, after an examination, in the degree of B.A'.[336]

Newman therefore judged that an appropriate mix of generalized and specialist content and skills should be integrated in a four-year course towards the first BA degree. The more detailed study of the second two years should only follow on from the foundation of the first two years' general study in the liberal arts. It is also clear that Newman did not assume that all specialization in the second two years would necessarily be ordered towards a profession, though obviously it might be so, especially if the specialization were to be in the 'school of useful arts, developing and applying the material resources of Ireland' which he projected would comprise such subjects as engineering, mining and agriculture.[337] He foresaw that some students might remain in the university beyond the BA degree to study over three years for the 'degree of M.A. or the Doctorate, to qualify themselves for a Profession or Professorship'.[338] Thus he appears not to rule out entirely the possibility of a professional course integrated into a liberal education. This second option can be achieved through critical reflection on the current practice of the profession, and by engagement in philosophical and moral thinking, especially through the varied evening classes which he and the other professors offered.

General Studies and the Evening Classes

Newman also instituted evening classes given by himself and by several of the professors in a variety of subjects as part of a general educational programme. Once again Newman was experimenting with a format that was unknown in the older English universities, and was still relatively new even in the recently founded King's College in London. They were offered to all comers partly as a showcase for the university, partly in order to counter the objection of some that there was no class of persons in Ireland who needed a university. Therefore Newman established them saying that 'we will give lectures in the evening, we will fill our classes with the young men of Dublin'.[339] Newman saw the evening classes in the form of an implicit mutual contract: '"I will speak, if you will listen" – "I will come here to learn, if you have anything worth teaching me."'[340]

Newman hoped by these means to provide a varied and stimulating intellectual environment for students studying a wide variety of disciplines, and for those 'employed in secular callings',[341] to bring them together to engage in a fruitful exchange of ideas. This he did, not so much by direct invitation, as, typically for him, by attraction. He was not aiming at attracting large audiences, but interested ones. If only a few turned up, he professed himself satisfied as long as those who came benefited. Therefore he did not 'rely on startling effects, but on the slow, silent, penetrating, overpowering effects of patience, steadiness, routine and perseverance'. In these lectures he sought only to exert his hearers' minds, so that they might make their own what they heard, 'by putting out [their] hand, as it were, to grasp it and appropriate it'.[342] He sums his aim up thus: 'An influence thus gradually acquired endures; sudden popularity dies away as suddenly.'[343] He hoped therefore that his audience would catch an interest in the character and work of the professors and pass on their enthusiasm by word of mouth, and imagines a conversation such as the following:

> By-the-bye, if you are interested in such a subject, go, by all means, and hear such a one. So and so does, and says there is no one like him. I looked in myself the other night, and was very much struck. Do go, you can't mistake.[344]

His object in establishing and in giving the Evening Public Lectures was therefore simply to teach as many as were prepared to come and learn about a great variety of topics. He believed that the great intelligence of the people of Ireland, and what he saw as their historical aptitude for philosophical speculation,[345] was not yet being matched by the level of their intellectual formation, so he resolved to set about providing the means. He also hoped to assist the intelligent Irish professional man in the street to use his native gifts both for the advantage of Ireland,[346] and for the greater understanding and defence of the Catholic faith 'especially at this day, when such a subtle logic is used against the Church, and demands a logic still more subtle on the part of her defenders to expose it'.[347] Note, however, that Newman was not merely offering courses in catechetics or apologetics, but expressing his confidence that by submitting themselves to such a curriculum of studies, evening after evening, with 'praiseworthy diligence', those who attended would be well versed in their religion, even though they might not be giving attention to the lectures with that view, but 'from the laudable love of knowledge, or from the advantages which will accrue to [them] personally from its pursuit'.[348]

Newman also planned practical short training courses for entrance to the civil service, civil engineering, Royal Artillery, and other professions which were offered to students by 1858.[349] The Catholic University was in many ways more practical than Trinity College, since, among other reasons, it needed to attract a greater variety of students. As Newman never succeeded in obtaining a charter from the government, his university could never grant degrees. Yet since so few students were able to avail themselves of the full university course this was not quite such a drawback in the event as it might at first have seemed. Therefore other kinds of courses not leading to a degree were deemed to be more useful and attractive.

Newman recognized to a certain extent the impact and value of the new Mechanics' Institutes to the class of people he was trying to attract, and of the encyclopedias and books of general knowledge such institutes promoted. Yet he also emphasized their limitations owing to a lack of personal influence and interaction between professors and students, saying that

a man may hear a thousand lectures, and read a thousand volumes, and be at the end of the process very much where he was, as regards knowledge. Something more than merely *admitting* it in a negative way into the mind is necessary, if it is to remain there.[350]

It was not professional subject matter as such, but the manner and the purpose of whatever kind of knowledge that was imparted which concerned Newman.

In many ways Newman was later to reproduce the same kind of arrangements *mutatis mutandis* for his schoolboys at the Oratory School. He was interested in a broad liberal education for the boys, supplemented with particular studies and coaching sessions which prepared them either for mercantile and similar occupations, or for entry into the legal profession, the Armed Forces or the Indian Civil Service.[351] Therefore, we need to understand his provision of secondary education as a preparation for vocational training. Since Newman always cooperated closely with parental wishes, he tended to prepare the boys at school for those professions favoured by the parents. Newman can at first sight give the impression from his writings, that at the theoretical level he hardly recognizes valuable forms of knowledge, especially practical knowledge, as true knowledge at all. However, we see in his practice as rector and teacher a full recognition of the importance of professional learning. There is no trace of dualism in his practice as an educator.

Vocational Preparation and Research

Newman clearly saw the usefulness of a university education in a variety of ways, and he speaks in passing of the importance of research activity in the *Idea*.[352] Just as it is mistaken to assume that Newman's idea of a university did not include professional training, so it is mistaken to assume that he eschewed research. From the outset he planned research in science, technology, archaeology, and medicine by setting up 'institutions, which will have their value intrinsically, whether students are present or no'.[353] As it turned out, several departments failed to attract students because of the requirement that all students fulfil two years in the Arts faculty before transferring to a specialization. Yet Newman was not dismayed that the departments of science and engineering remained without any students, and kept a complement of well-qualified faculty staff even in those departments in order to carry out research and so to contribute to the intellectual breadth of the university's life in the hope that these would eventually attract students by the sheer quality of their staff and work: 'This has been the case in the history of all Universities. Learned men came and opened schools, and drew followers.'[354]

Newman was accordingly explicit about the duty of the professorial staff to publish the fruits of their labours, saying that

> it is natural that men, whose occupations are of an intellectual nature, should be led to record the speculations in which their labours have issued; and that having taken this step, they should consider it even as a duty which we owe to society, to communicate to others what they have thought it worth while to record.[355]

He therefore published the *Atlantis* as a journal 'for depositing professorial work'.[356] Some of its readers complained that the journal was too dry, and that they looked there in vain for something more ornamental in style to please ordinary readers. Newman countered that 'ornamental writing is about as much out of place in the *Atlantis*, as *ormolu* clocks ... in Pump Court ...'[357] The *Atlantis* was designed instead to be a showcase of the university's higher intellectual researches and to put it on the international academic map. It was an advertisement of the breadth of Newman's faculty appointments.

Some of the posts he created were quite original and show Newman's independence of his Oxford past and his awareness of the particular local circumstances of Dublin. For instance, not only was the professorship of Irish history and archaeology the first such to be established in any Irish academy, but Newman himself regularly attended the professor's course of lectures. Similarly, he did not omit practical studies from his university and promoted areas of knowledge most relevant to the contemporary world of scientific progress. For instance, within the applied sciences he created chairs in physiology and pathology, disciplines that were hardly known in Oxford, but which existed in the Scottish universities.

Vocational Preparation: Newman and Modern Practice

Today, the idea of liberal learning for its own sake within vocational courses would not win many defenders. Nevertheless, Gordon Graham in *Universities: The Recovery of an Idea*, and Duke Maskell and

Ian Robinson in *The New Idea of a University*, both agree with much of what Newman wrote on higher education. For instance, Graham asserts 'the commitment to truth over usefulness as paramount'.[358] Yet they all recognize that, as Maskell and Robinson put it, the modern university in Britain has been remade 'not in defiance of Newman but in indifference to him'.[359] This is perhaps why they constantly refer to the 'old' idea of a university, thereby implying Newman's idea. In modern British universities the primacy is usually given to the economic value of education, requiring new kinds of people with new knowledge, skills and dispositions. That knowledge which is seen as 'product' or as having use as a 'commodity' is the most valued. This new knowledge is often specifically restricted to one particular context, it may well have a monetary value, and is short-lived within the particular organization. It is certainly not the liberal knowledge of which Newman speaks. If there are any institutions of education which come close to Newman's ideal today, they are probably the traditional American liberal arts colleges. Typically in these a broad curriculum of subjects is studied for four years leading to a Bachelor's degree. Only thereafter do the graduates proceed to detailed vocational studies, usually in other institutions.

Nevertheless, it can be legitimately argued that professional practice today requires active judgement in ways of seeing and understanding imaginatively amid rapidly changing circumstances. Such a critical judgement would be intelligent practice as opposed to mechanical practice. Oakeshott makes the distinction between technical knowledge in written text and practice knowledge that can be expressed in action and learned through experience.[360] Some would argue that practice possesses its own integrity. Newman's concern was whether professional schools, including medicine and law, can authentically participate in the university's principal purpose, which is the teaching of universal knowledge 'as its own end', for the health and development of all the mind's powers. Newman contrasts the educational philosophy of autonomous professional schools existing independently of a university and those schools which are integrated into the university's broader curriculum and mission. He warns of the increasing specialization of professional training and of professional education itself, abstracted from a university setting and context, and tending to focus on the particular at the expense of the universal. Professional training therefore has the potential to undermine the broader pursuit of the unity of knowledge at the heart of the university's mission. Nevertheless, Newman recognized that professional skills were increasingly necessary in the complexity of modern economic and political systems. In the *Idea* he says that 'the University, if it refuses the foremost place to professional interests, does but postpone them to the formation of the citizen'.[361]

Using the writings of Pring as a guide,[362] it is possible to construct an ideal typical contrast between liberal education and vocational preparation as conventionally understood. The chief goal of liberal education is to develop the ability to reason, to think critically and to appreciate that which is worthy of being appreciated.[363] In order to develop these capacities, the individual has to be 'initiated' into various intellectual disciplines, such as literature, mathematics, science and the arts. In the process of being initiated into such disciplines one acquires the essential concepts, intellectual skills, and habits required to cultivate the capacities of reason, critical thought and imagination. Pring says that the ultimate justification of all this is that cultivating the intellect is intrinsically worthwhile and is perhaps the supreme human good.[364] It has no other purpose and needs no further justification, although it is generally assumed that the intellectual improvement of individuals will benefit the wider society in some way. It is clear that Pring is here following the traditional account of the twofold usefulness of a liberal education as it was understood by Newman. First, liberal education is useful because it is its own end, and 'has use in itself'.[365] Second, because it 'tends to good, or is the instrument of good'.[366]

Pring goes further than Newman and sets up a model which indicates that liberal education ideally takes place in institutions which are insulated from the distractions of the world of business and utility. Pring develops his model by discussing the ideas of Michael Oakeshott and suggesting that schools and universities should ideally be like monasteries.[367] The control and direction of liberal education must be in the hands of those who are authorities in it, i.e. scholars, and 'certainly not government or industry or the community at large'.[368] In liberal education, the transaction between teacher and learner is shaped by considerations internal to the intellectual disciplines. However, Pring is critical of a narrow liberal education, as he construes it in his model, claiming that in such circumstances it leaves out whole dimensions of human experience, particularly the practical and the useful. Pring challenges what he terms the false dualisms that have grown up between academic and vocational, theory and practice, education and training, and between thinking and doing.[369] He claims that it is such dualisms that have fragmented the educational systems and impoverished the educational experiences of many within them. He seeks a balance and states 'there seems no reason why the liberal should not be conceived as something vocationally useful and the vocationally useful should not be taught in an educational and liberating way'.[370]

We believe that Newman would have agreed with this latter point. However, it seems that Pring is seeking to bring about some reconciliation between education and training simply by dissolving the distinctions between them. Carr certainly thinks so, as he believes that there are non-instrumentally valuable goals in education which have negligible vocational implications.[371] Or to put it another way, whereas vocational training can revisit the intellectual achievements of a liberal education and apply them afresh, a liberal education does not explicitly anticipate the content of vocational training. Carr adds that that while practical learning is as important as theoretical/academic learning, it is arguable that in education there lie certain forms of understanding which are in an important sense inherently theoretical or academic, to the significant exclusion of the practical. Carr's analysis appears to be closer to Newman's understanding of this dichotomy. It may also explain why many professional training schools located in universities today are accused of escaping the world of practical activity in order to justify the courses they teach by some kind of abstract theory. This has encouraged the notion of 'reflective-practitioners', who examine critically the basis of their everyday practice.

Pring is also concerned that liberal education has traditionally been for the few who have ignored the world of practice and had a disdain for the technological and practical mind. Of course, Newman would have seen liberal education as including all who could reasonably benefit from it. The difficulty is that liberal education is severely under threat within Western education systems as more and more focus is given to competence as the dominating ideal in vocational training. Professional training in medicine, law, accountancy, teaching, business, etc., has increasingly used the language of usefulness, meaning what works in practice, or implies the intrinsic utility of training, and often conceives of this training in narrow terms. If we are to seek 'vocationalizing the liberal ideal' as Pring suggests, then he is right to bemoan the lack of compulsory humanities in the English school curriculum after the age of fourteen years. A broader ideal of liberal education is needed in which, as Pring concludes, the student's 'capacity to become human is enhanced'.[372]

When education is conceived as vocational preparation, its chief aim is to develop competence in tasks which adults have to perform at work, home, or in the community.[373] It is assumed that the best way of developing such competence is by 'doing' under critical supervision, i.e. learning from directed experience. The ultimate justification for education, thus conceived, is that it gets people ready for the world of work and life. Vocational training is justified by reference to the needs of the economy and society, which require people to obtain specific skills and knowledge, with or without reference to their own individual needs. Crucially, in this way of thinking, education is not regarded as intrinsically worthwhile. Rather, its value is derived from its usefulness to the economy, to the individual, or to society. Newman did not argue that liberal knowledge is superior to professional knowledge, but he did question whether professional knowledge could in every case enlarge the mind liberally. Newman would not have considered behaviourist approaches to vocational training as part of the purpose of higher education. Such behaviourism employs criterion-referenced measures to gauge task-completion in complex jobs, such as, to take an example already mentioned above, carpentry. In this model the subject matter is broken down into discrete pieces and students are taken through specific skills, one at a time, and are then asked to demonstrate their competence in each. Newman would ask whether there are any conceptual or theoretical underpinnings to this approach? Can it really be considered as education? His answer in the case of carpentry would have been no. If the same approach is applied to the formation of teachers or doctors, then it has the potential to destroy a student's capacity to acquire new knowledge, and even worse, it can prevent critical reflection on what is being learnt.

Some would suggest that the ideal place for useful learning to take place is in the economic, social and everyday contexts in which the skills and competencies to be developed apply.[374] Traditionally, such learning took place through apprenticeship. However, for various reasons, traditional forms of apprenticeship are deemed to be no longer sufficient for developing the range of skills and competencies required of today's citizen and worker. Consequently, much vocational preparation today needs to take place in specialized educational and training institutions. However, these places of education and training should not be isolated from the practical world of work and life.

Newman provided a philosophically based and historically rooted defence of liberal education. He emphasized the intrinsic worth of liberal education and implied the extrinsic value of professional training. Professional training and liberal education can be viewed as standing at either pole of a single continuum, not necessarily in conflict with each other, but complementary. Newman clearly believed that schooling and university education must prepare students for their roles in society as well as develop their intellectual skills. He believed that an intellectual training will enable students to discharge their duties to society.

Newman also saw professional training within the context of relating to other studies within the university. For example, he believed that doctors and lawyers must gain from being exposed to other disciplines and their students. He would have said the same about students of history or economics. In order to become broadly educated persons, all students should benefit from wider academic studies, since intellectual breadth and depth require a well-balanced curriculum. Newman encouraged his professors to view their teaching 'from a height', meaning that each profession should be viewed within the larger 'survey of all knowledge'. Thus they can survey their discipline or professional training within a critical philosophical tradition. Within this perspective the structure and purpose of liberal education changes and some form of professional training can be viewed as having a share in liberal education. The relevance of Newman's vision of a liberal education within professional training needs to be rediscovered, since he explains how liberal education and vocational training should not simply co-exist, but can and should be integrated. Vocational training should refer back to, apply, and be enriched by, the intellectual lessons and skills acquired through liberal education.

Conclusion

Today there is a great expansion of professional education and training both inside and outside universities. Courses can either lead to a degree or certificate, or they can be studied and accredited by professional associations either in conjunction with universities or without them. This increased vocationalism or proliferation of professional courses in universities has, according to some, narrowed educational opportunity for students as they focus increasingly on future employment skills. This in turn can lead to narrow vocationalist conceptions of university courses which make integral connections between liberal education and preparation for work difficult. It does not help that within higher education there is a loss of educational consensus with little agreement about the true purposes of universities. This is not surprising since there is no single understanding of the kind of person an educated human being should be. There is only a set of competing visions between different disciplines whose advocates each claim to be educationally sufficient in themselves – an outcome that Newman predicted.

It may be that in the contemporary pluralist world of education it is no longer possible to have a unified university vision or even, as some might claim, desirable to attempt to find one. Liberal arts courses are often under threat or are declining in importance and are seen as old fashioned or irrelevant. There seems to be less appreciation of the benefits of a liberal education traditionally conceived. Even though contemporary universities differ from the vision Newman articulated, paradoxically it is still Newman's public rhetoric of a university education which often dominates conversations in higher education. This is ironic when the motivating force in curriculum changes and thinking in higher education are increasingly being led by the rhetoric of skills and competences. Newman's writings and practice therefore still provide us with a rich reservoir of resources to address intelligently many of the questions in contemporary higher education.

Notes

1. *Autobiographical Writings* (AW), p. 201.
2. Unpublished sermon 'On general education as connected with the Church and religion', 1827 (1827 Sermon).
3. cf. *Idea of a University* (*Idea*), p. 272.
4. v. Vargish, T. (1970), *Newman: The Contemplation of Mind*. Oxford: Clarendon Press.
5. *Letters and Diaries* (LD) viii, p. 546.
6. Copleston F. (1967), *History of Philosophy*. London: Search Press, Vol. 8, p. 279.
7. v. *Development of Christian Doctrine*, p. 33.
8. 'University Sermons' (US) no. X, p. 12.
9. *Letters and Diaries of John Henry Newman* (LD) Volume i, p. 219.
10. US XI, p. 1.
11. Ibid., p. 7.
12. US XIII, p. 7.
13. US XI, p. 1.
14. US XI, p. 15.
15. Ibid., p. 17.
16. Ibid., p. 18.
17. Ibid., p. 22.
18. Ibid., p. 23.
19. Ibid.
20. Ibid., p. 25.
21. US XII, p. 11.
22. US X, p. 26.
23. US X, p. 35.
24. Ibid., p. 42.
25. US XI, p. 25.

26. US X, p. 35.

27. Ibid., p. 7.

28. Ibid., p. 16.

29. US X, p. 38.

30. Ibid., p. 20.

31. LD xxv, pp. 35–6.

32. Copleston, op. cit., p. 276.

33. cf. Owen, H. P. (1969), *The Christian Knowledge of God*; Ferreira, M. J. (1980), *Doubt and Religious Commitment: The Role of the Will in Newman's Thought*. Oxford: Clarendon Press, and Newman, J. (1986), *The Mental Philosophy of John Henry Newman*. Ontario: Wilfrid Laurier University Press.

34. Copleston, op. cit., Vol. 8, p. 288.

35. Dulles, A. (2002), *Newman: Outstanding Christian Thinkers*. London: Continuum, p. 12.

36. *An Essay in Aid of a Grammar of Assent* (*Grammar*), pp. 9–10.

37. Copleston, op. cit., Vol. 8, p. 279.

38. *Grammar*, p. 99.

39. Ibid., pp. 99–100.

40. Ibid., p. 101.

41. Ibid., p. 102.

42. Ibid., p. 104.

43. Ibid., p. 117.

44. Ibid.

45. Nichols, A. (1990), *From Newman to Congar*. Edinburgh: T. & T. Clark, pp. 19ff.

46. LD xxiv, p. 375.

47. *Rise and Progress of Universities* ed. Katherine Mary Tillman (Tillman) v. Introduction, p. xxvii.

48. *Idea*, pp. 21–2.

49. Ibid., p. 114.

50. Tillman v. Introduction, pp. lxxi–lxxiv.

51. *Idea*, p. 33.

52. Ibid., p. 41.

53. Ibid., pp. 42–3.

54. Ibid., pp. 39–40.

55. Ibid., p. 38.

56. Ibid.
57. *1852 Discourses, Idea*, pp. 446–7, v. in Culler, op. cit., p. 174.
58. Ibid.
59. *Idea*, p. 56.
60. Ibid.
61. Ibid.
62. Ibid., p. 57.
63. Ibid., p. 59.
64. Ibid., p. 61.
65. Ibid., p. 63.
66. Ibid.
67. Ibid.
68. Ibid., p. 65.
69. Ibid., p. 66.
70. Ibid., p. 67.
71. Ibid., p. 69.
72. Ibid., p. 71.
73. 1827 Sermon.
74. *English Journal of Education* edited by Revd George Moody. The fascicles date from the first in 1843 until February 1845. Out of 26 issues, 24 survive and the covers bear Newman's signature. It is possible to deduce which articles he consulted from the pages which have been cut.
75. Unpublished sermon, 'On some popular mistakes as to the object of Education' 1826 (1826 Sermon).
76. Ibid.
77. Shrimpton, Paul (2005), *A Catholic Eton? Newman's Oratory School*. Leominster: Gracewing, p. 179.
78. Ibid., p. 90.
79. Ibid.
80. Ibid., p. 217.
81. Ibid., p. 180.
82. LD xviii, p. 319.
83. Ibid., p. 332.
84. *Sermons Preached on Various Occasions*, 1870, p. 14.
85. Shrimpton, op. cit., p. 182.
86. LD xxi, p. 51.

87. v. Culler, A. Dwight (1955), *The Imperial Intellect: A Study of Cardinal Newman's Educational Ideal*, pp. 166–7.
88. LD xv, p. 85.
89. Culler, op. cit., p. 167.
90. Ibid.
91. LD xvii, p. 440.
92. *Idea*, p. 272.
93. Ibid.
94. Ibid., p. 304.
95. Ibid., p. 305.
96. Ibid., p. 306.
97. Ibid., p. 308.
98. AW, p. 259.
99. *Present Position of Catholics in England* (*Present Position*), p. 390.
100. AW, p. 259.
101. LD xxi, p. 217 (Newman's emphasis).
102. Papal Brief of 26 November 1847 (translated from the original Latin).
103. LD xiii, p. 50.
104. LD xiii, p. 95.
105. *Present Position*, p. 390.
106. AW, p. 259.
107. Hughes, Gerard (2001), *Aristotle on Ethics*. London: Routledge, p. 19.
108. Aristotle, *Nicomachean Ethics*: II 6, 15.
109. AW, p. 82.
110. cf. Ephesians 4.13.
111. Romans 7.15.
112. cf. Romans 8.15.
113. Sermon, 'On some popular mistakes as to the object of education' 1826 (1826 Sermon).
114. *Apologia*, p. 18.
115. cf. *Grammar*, pp. 102ff.
116. 'A Letter to the Duke of Norfolk', in *Certain Difficulties felt by Anglicans in Catholic Teaching Considered*, Volume II, pp. 247–8.

117. *Grammar*, p. 103.
118. 'A letter to the Duke of Norfolk', p. 247.
119. Ibid., pp. 248–9.
120. cf. *Grammar*, p. 102.
121. 1826 Sermon.
122. 'A letter to the Duke of Norfolk', p. 250.
123. Ibid., p. 258.
124. Ibid.
125. *Idea*, p. 162.
126. Ibid., p. 165.
127. Ibid.
128. Ibid.
129. Ibid.
130. *Grammar*, p. 103.
131. *Idea*, p. 167.
132. Ibid., p. 170.
133. *Grammar*, p. 104.
134. 1826 Scrmon.
135. Sermon, 'On general education as connected with the Church and religion' 1827 (1827 Sermon).
136. 1826 Sermon.
137. Ibid.
138. 'The Tamworth Reading Room', *Discussions and Arguments* (DA), pp. 254–305 (also reproduced in original letter form in LD viii, pp. 534–561).
139. DA, p. 277.
140. Ibid., p. 255.
141. Ibid., p. 262.
142. Ibid., p. 268.
143. Ibid., p. 255.
144. Ibid., p. 265.
145. Ibid., p. 304.
146. Ibid., p. 274.
147. Ibid., pp. 274–5.
148. *Idea*, p. 111.
149. 1827 Sermon.
150. Ibid.

151. 1826 Sermon.

152. *Grammar*, p. 112.

153. Ibid., p. 111.

154. Ibid., p. 112.

155. Ibid.

156. 'A Letter to the Duke of Norfolk', p. 249, *Certain Difficulties felt by Anglicans in Catholic Teaching considered Vol II*.

157. 1826 Sermon.

158. Ibid.

159. 'The Rise and Progress of Universities', *Historical Sketches* III (HS), p. 74.

160. DA, p. 293.

161. HS, p. 75.

162. DA, p. 293.

163. cf. *Grammar*, pp. 104, 112.

164. 1826 Sermon.

165. *Grammar*, pp. 112–13.

166. 1826 Sermon.

167. Ibid.

168. Ibid.

169. LD xiii, p. 27.

170. LD xxiv, p. 216.

171. Bouyer, L. (1958), *Newman: His Life and Spirituality*. London: Burns and Oates, p. 85.

172. HS, p. 75.

173. v. Chapter 1, pp. 23–5.

174. v. Delaura, David J. (1969), *Hebrew and Hellene in Victorian England, Newman, Arnold and Pater*. Austin and London: University of Texas Press.

175. v. Culler, A. Dwight (1955), *The Imperial Intellect: A Study of Cardinal Newman's Educational Ideal*, p. 164.

176. *My Campaign in Ireland (Campaign)*, p. 273.

177. Culler, op. cit., pp. 164–5.

178. Ibid.

179. Ibid., p. 166.

180. *Campaign*, p. 37.

181. Ibid., p. 36.

182. Ibid.
183. LD xxiiii, p. 101.
184. LD xxvi, p. 110.
185. Ibid., p. 76.
186. *Idea*, p. 179.
187. Ibid.
188. Ibid., p. 180.
189. Rothblatt, Sheldon (1976), *Tradition and Change in English Liberal Education*. London: Faber and Faber, p. 247.
190. *Idea*, p. 130.
191. v. Culler, op. cit., pp. 166ff.
192. *Idea*, p. 127.
193. *Idea*, p. 147.
194. *Historical Sketches* (HS), pp. 35, 37–8, 45–6.
195. Jn. 1.1–14.
196. *Apologia*, p. 36.
197. *Autobiographical Writings* (AW), p. 82.
198. *Apologia*, p. 36. v. also: Vincent F. Blehl, 'Newman, the Fathers and Education', *Fordham University Quarterly*, Vol. xxv, no. 177, Summer 1970 (Blehl), p. 197.
199. Blehl, op. cit., p. 205.
200. Ibid., p. 206.
201. HS v. especially Chapter 13, pp. 150ff.
202. Ibid., p. 157.
203. Ibid., p. 159.
204. *Idea* (1852 Discourse V), p. 423.
205. Ibid., p. 98.
206. Ibid., p. 102.
207. Ibid., p. 101.
208. Ibid., p. 100.
209. Ibid., p. 113.
210. For a discussion of this point v. Ker, *Achievement*, p. 9.
211. *Idea*, p. 115.
212. Ibid., p. 10.
213. Ibid., p. 97.
214. Ibid., p. 122.
215. Ibid., p. 120.

216. Ibid., p. 122.
217. Ibid., p. 121.
218. Ibid., p 124.
219. Ibid., p. 123.
220. Ibid., p. 11.
221. Ibid.
222. Ibid., pp. 272ff.
223. Ibid., p. 273.
224. Ibid.
225. cf. Sermon 'On general education as connected with the Church and religion' (1827).
226. Ibid.
227. Ibid.
228. *Discussions and Arguments* (DA), p. 266.
229. *Idea*, pp. 115–16.
230. Ibid., p. 12.
231. Ibid., 115–16.
232. Ibid.
233. Ibid.
234. Shrimpton, Paul (2005), *A Catholic Eton? Newman's Oratory School*. Leominster: Gracewing, p. 175.
235. *Idea*, p. 275.
236. Shrimpton, op. cit., p. 198.
237. *Letters and Diaries of John Henry Newman* (LD) xxvi, p. 26.
238. *Idea*, p. 13.
239. Ibid., pp. 275–84.
240. Ibid., p. 12.
241. Ibid., p. 222.
242. Ibid., p. 298.
243. Ibid., p. 301.
244. Ibid., pp. 295–8.
245. Ibid., p. 297.
246. Ibid., p. 403.
247. Ibid.
248. Ibid., pp. 403–4.
249. For a full treatment of Newman's curriculum see Shrimpton, op. cit., pp. 171–3.

250. Ibid., p. 197.
251. *Idea*, pp. 100–1.
252. Shrimpton, op. cit., p. 199.
253. Ibid., p. 200.
254. *Idea*, p. 19.
255. Ibid., pp. 124–5.
256. Ibid., p. 94.
257. Sydney Smith in *Edinburgh Review*, 1809 (ER), p. 211.
258. ER, 15 Oct. 1809, pp. 45–6.
259. v. HS, pp. 228ff.
260. Culler, op. cit., p. 159.
261. v. chapter 2, pp.57–9.
262. Culler, p. 203.
263. *Idea*, p. 129.
264. Ibid., p. 130.
265. Ibid.
266. cf. HS, p. 157.
267. *Idea*, p. 370.
268. Ibid., p. 369.
269. Ibid., p. 371.
270. Ibid., p. 5.
271. HS, p. 6.
272. Ibid., p. 177.
273. *Idea*, p. 130.
274. HS, p. 195.
275. Ibid., p. 194.
276. Ibid., p. 180.
277. Ibid., p. 193.
278. Ibid.
279. *Idea*, p. 184.
280. Ibid., p. 185.
281. Ibid.
282. Ibid., p. 186.
283. Ibid., p. 188.
284. Ibid.
285. Ibid., p. 189.
286. Ibid., p. 191.

287. HS, p. 49.

288. Ibid., p. 74.

289. Ibid., p. 75

290. Ibid., p. 74.

291. *Idea*, p. 129.

292. Ibid., p. 394.

293. Ibid.

294. AW, p. 99.

295. v. Arthur, James (1995), *The Ebbing Tide; Policy and Principles of Catholic Education*. Leominster: Gracewing, esp. pp. 227–33.

296. v. *Idea*, p. 100.

297. cf. Erb, Peter C. (1997), 'Newman and the Idea of a Catholic University', *Occasional Paper in Catholic Intellectual Life* No. 2. Emory University, Atlanta: Aquinas Center of Theology, esp. p. 10.

298. *Idea*, p. 100.

299. *Historical Sketches* III, pp. 170–1.

300. *Idea*, p. 140.

301. Sermon 'On some popular mistakes as to the object of education' 1826.

302. *Idea*, p. 146.

303. Ibid., p. 148.

304. Ibid., p. 135.

305. Ibid., p. 99.

306. Ibid., p. 142.

307. Ibid., p. 146.

308. Ibid., p. 154.

309. Ibid., pp. 154–5.

310. Ibid., p. 148.

311. Copleston, E. (1810 and 1811) *A Reply to the Calumnies of the Edinburgh Review Against Oxford*. Oxford: Collingwood.

312. 'Memorandum on the Objects of the University and the Means for attaining them', 29 April 1854. (Memorandum) LD xvi, p. 557.

313. *Idea*, pp. 145–6.

314. Ibid. p. 146.

315. Ibid., p. 145.
316. Ibid., p. 147.
317. Ibid.
318. Ibid., p. 135.
319. Ibid., p. 147.
320. Ibid., p. 148.
321. Ibid., p. 150.
322. Ibid., p. 11.
323. Ibid., p. 154.
324. Ibid., p. 151.
325. Ibid., p. 153.
326. Ibid.
327. Ibid., p. 62.
328. Ibid., pp. 62–3. For a full account of Newman's view of this danger, see the discussion in Discourse III concerning the unity and mutual corrective role of the Circle of Sciences, pp. 51–71.
329. *Discussions and Arguments*, p. 304.
330. Pelikan, J. (1992) *The Idea of a University: A Reexamination*. New Haven, CT: Yale University Press, p. 149.
331. *Idea*, p. 11.
332. v. Culler, op. cit, p. 159.
333. 'Memorandum' LD xvi, p. 561.
334. v. Culler, op. cit., p. 160 for a full account of the content of these examinations.
335. 'Memorandum' LD xvi, p. 561.
336. Ibid.
337. Ibid., p. 559.
338. Ibid., p. 561.
339. *Idea*, p. 387.
340. Ibid., p. 396.
341. Ibid., p. 392.
342. Ibid., p. 394.
343. Ibid., p. 397.
344. Ibid.
345. Ibid., p. 391.
346. Ibid., p. 388.
347. Ibid., p. 391.

348. Ibid., p. 392.
349. Ibid., p. 441.
350. Ibid., pp. 392–4.
351. v. Shrimpton, op. cit., pp. 211–12.
352. *Idea*, p. 370.
353. 'Memorandum', p. 559.
354. Ibid., p. 558.
355. *Atlantis* II, *My Campaign in Ireland*, p. 433.
356. v. Katherine Tillman's introduction to *Rise and Progress of Universities and Benedictine Essays*, pp. lxx to lxxiv for a fuller treatment of Newman's arrangements for research at the Catholic University.
357. *Campaign*, p. 374.
358. Graham, Gordon (2002), *Universities: The Recovery of an Idea*. Exeter: Imprint Academic, p. 122.
359. Maskell, Duke and Robinson, Ian (2001), *The New Idea of a University*. Exeter: Imprint Academic, p. 25.
360. Oakeshott, Michael (1962), *Rationalism in Politics*. London: Methuen.
361. *Idea*, p. 146.
362. Pring, Richard (1995), *Closing the Gap: Liberal Education and Vocational Preparation*. London: Hodder and Stoughton, pp. 51–66; pp. 184–8.
363. Ibid., p. 184.
364. Ibid., p. 185.
365. *Idea*, p.142.
366. Ibid., p.143.
367. Pring, ibid., pp. 186–8.
368. Ibid., p. 55.
369. Ibid., p. 134.
370. Ibid., p. 183.
371. Carr, D. (1998), 'The Dichotomy of Liberal versus Vocational Education: Some Basic Conceptual Geography', *Proceedings of the Philosophy of Education Society*, p. 1.
372. Pring, ibid., p. 195.
373. Ibid., p. 187.
374. Ibid., p. 188.

Part 3

The Influence and Relevance of Newman's Work Today

Chapter 6

Newman's Challenge to Some Modern Educational Trends

Introduction

As we have seen already, liberal education is presented by Newman in the *Idea* as the 'philosophical habit of mind', by which the student is trained to grasp ideas accurately and so to be able to evaluate and arrange them in order to form judgements and reach well-reasoned conclusions. Good judgement, like wisdom, both depends upon a thoughtful and rather extensive acquaintance with many areas of study, and requires the ability to think independently, in the face of pressures, distortions, and overemphasized truth. In modern educational language we would say that this philosophy involves the ability to draw conclusions from a body of information through applying, analysing, synthesizing, and evaluating from observation, experience, and reflection.

Nevertheless, such independence of mind does not mean that the idea of a liberal education lends support to a relativistic elective system in which students choose their own content in a fragmented or haphazard manner. Such an approach lacks the opportunity to develop critical thinking skills. Newman denied that the imparting of skills and competencies alone can be a sufficient end of education and learning. Today many believe that education in schools and in universities should be primarily about the acquisition of skills – skills of thinking, learning, judgement and so on. Newman taught that skills of any sort in education are by-products of learning any particular discipline, whether it is geography, Latin, English, mathematics or history. To learn skills therefore requires the transmission of information for the mind to work on and come to a judgement.

While Newman was against the compartmentalization of education, he recognized the modern need for a multiplicity of disciplines. We have seen that Newman was in effect advocating the Hellenic *paideia*, adapted by centuries of Christian insight and practice.[1] Nevertheless, Newman recognized that each discipline would eventually enlarge its own perspective in isolation from other disciplines. Newman insisted on the absolute integrity and unity of all knowledge and the need of the human mind to reflect on that integrity. For Newman, the unity of the sciences derives from their common object of investigation, the truth. The omission of any one science or relying exclusively on any one view of a thing makes the attainment of the entire truth impossible.

Contemporary Educational Thought

Secular exclusion of Religion

Today religious commitments in education are treated with suspicion and mistrust, and they have generally been replaced by the idea that it is impossible to know the answers to life's most important questions. Educational philosophy has largely been perceived as a 'value-free' enterprise motivated by a supposedly disinterested search for knowledge and understanding in education. We can identify two major problems in contemporary culture with respect to education. The first is the widespread scepticism about our ability to know truth at all. The second is relativism, the view that one opinion is as good as another. Consequently, much contemporary educational thought excludes Christianity from any general consideration of the aims and purposes of education. In modern educational thinking the emphasis has been on freedom from tradition, authority and revelation, and from all *a priori* strictures and standards. The emphasis has been on promoting individualism, critical scepticism and of course a certain kind of secular rationality.

Many modern educational theorists claim to be largely concerned with the clarification of concepts and the development of the rational, critical and autonomous individual according to a secular model which excludes religion. Newman did not object to the 'rational, critical and autonomous' in the individual, but he understood this in a radically different way. He emphasized the enlargement of mind and personal freedom which a liberal education specifically based on Christian principles gives. As he said, 'to educate is to work together with God in the salvation of souls'.[2]

Newman did not see education as the cure for the world's ills, as a process to make people morally 'better', or as a system to perfect humanity in some way. Even in the early nineteenth century he protested against a growing tide of opinion that the purpose of education was not merely to fill the heads of the young and old with lifeless knowledge or to provide skills for success in employment. Nearly two centuries later, the trust in competence-based learning which reduces individuals to mere functionaries and the belief in the perfectibility of human nature through knowledge, both of which he opposed in education, have become even stronger, but seem unable to fulfil their goal. Newman clearly saw why this is so. He perceived and warned against the desire for education set free from Christian doctrine, knowing that without Christianity education totally fails to address the 'passion and the pride of man'.[3] Because he saw education as a process whose ultimate goal is to prepare us for the next world, Newman argued that children should be 'taught to view all things in a religious light'.[4] Yet he did not ignore either the present world or the need to educate the young to live well within it, drawing attention to this duty when he said that

> education has reference to the temporal callings of men, but it does not rest there – we do not educate children that they may *succeed* in their respective occupations, but that they may so fulfil them as to make them the means of spiritual profit to their souls, that their worldly trades and professions may affect them as they ought, may be instruments of good to them, calling into action habits of conscientiousness, uprightness, diligence, truth, disinterestedness and humility – we are preparing them to do good in their generation, to glorify God by their lives wherever they may be placed, and to spread the knowledge of the grace of Christ to their own circle ...[5]

Newman was equally firm in his emphasis on the duty of parents to educate their children. Once again, he seems to identify and address issues which are still of profound significance today. Parents, according to Newman, should not think of surrendering the education of their children to schools, but 'should consider that from the earliest infancy of their children they are their natural guardians and instructors; that sending to school is merely an accidental circumstance, and but a part of education . . .'[6]

Newman perceived both in himself and in his contemporaries a temptation to strive after intellectual excellence at the expense of moral goodness. As he said of his own time: 'we live in an age in many respects parallel to that in which the gospel was first preached' when the Corinthians 'were seduced by the temptation of human learning and the refinements of an unmanly luxury' which led them 'to prefer gifts to graces – the powers of the intellect to moral excellence – to look indulgently on vice, as weakness rather than a sin – to aim at outward elegance rather than inward purity'.[7] This was said in an age in which Christianity was still the major motivating factor in education. Yet Christianity was being reinterpreted by many contemporary educationalists as primarily a moral code of manners and respectability. For example, Thomas Arnold drew inspiration from Newman's idea of the 'gentleman', yet paradoxically the idea that Arnold adopts is the one that Newman criticizes: the man of taste, education and manners. This idea was more ethical than religious.

He also rejected 'mechanical teaching and learning' and the reductionism he saw in education and schooling as 'false philosophy'. He regretted that many contemporary educators 'insist that Education should be confined to some particular and narrow end, and should issue in some definite work, which can be weighed and measured. They argue as if everything, as well as every person, had a price, and that where there has been great outlay, they have a right to expect a return in kind.'[8] Since Newman eschewed instrumentality as a chief aim of education together with bringing 'children forward rapidly' by cramming their heads with information, he would therefore be critical of our present school and university systems. Instead he sought to work with the natural learning process in every child, which requires careful shaping and stimulation adapted to the needs and character of each, and is based on the Christian understanding of human nature which takes into account both our moral and our intellectual frailty.

Accordingly he judged as ill founded 'the inordinate endeavour to educate many at once and by the same process' and urged instead the need to 'take children separately' and 'address ourselves to them almost one by one'.[9]

Contemporary Relevance

Too often academics and even supporters of Newman selectively extract from his writings a variety of passages that they think are relevant to education and call this his educational theory. This inevitably leads to historical misrepresentation. Therefore we need to be careful about trying to systematize Newman's thoughts on education. As we have seen Newman throughout his life wrote about ideas that are directly relevant to contemporary philosophical questions in education, including the following: What is faith? How are faith and belief related? What is the relation of religion to culture? For what purposes do we educate? What does it mean to know? What does it mean to learn? What is the relation of teacher to pupil? What part should parents play in education? Some modern educationalists object to Newman's answers to these questions on the grounds that he wrote in the nineteenth-century context of secondary and university education as the province of the social elite, controlled largely by the Church of England and mainly for men. This may at first seem to disguise the relevance of Newman to today's democratic and secular education system. Nevertheless, among all the areas of education that Newman addressed and we have discussed in this book, there are a further three in contemporary education that have immediate suggestive relevance: the purpose of a religious education; the concept of teaching; and the idea of the learner.

Religious Education

Religious education is a broad term encompassing education within any faith tradition, but Newman thought in terms of Christian religious education. This involves an integration of cognitive understanding and personal growth in a living faith relationship with Jesus Christ. In fact Newman did not use the phrase 'religious education', which is really the product of progressive education combined with liberal theology. This liberal theology has rejected the teaching of doctrine in favour of a more illusory general education that emphasizes process over content. This results in a deconstruction of claims to religious truth. The supposed neutrality of secular education has produced a professionalism in teaching which inculcates in pupils the principle that different religions are equally valid and even complementary paths to religious fulfilment. As a teaching method it fails to produce in students any genuine understanding of, or respect for, religious differences.

Regarding the purposes of modern religious education, Newman helps us to recognize that, whatever tradition we work from, relativism which purports to prepare children for a 'pluralistic' society, is inadequate to human needs. Newman also rejected a dualistic approach to education in which two distinct activities are conducted within it – when the secular and religious aims of education are separated, not only in teaching and practice, but also in the minds of both teachers and learners. In this approach two distinct realities are set alongside each other; the one specifically religious, the other secular – the religious being considered the less important since it is seen as additional or optional. Newman demands a critical synthesis between education and religion in which there is a holistic approach to teaching and learning. In this model there is one single vision which unites teacher and learner in a religious conception of education inspired by their faith. Such a conception of education does not have many supporters within contemporary educational thought, which, in practice, has largely abandoned the search for an ultimate foundation for knowledge, but Newman's approach has contemporary relevance to different faith communities involved in educational institutions.

Religion in education and schooling is today very much a contested idea, when the emphasis is rather on the primacy of experience over beliefs and doctrines as the substantive content of religious teaching. Doctrinal formulations are considered secondary. No longer is it seen to be the goal for schools to seek to inculcate Christian commitment or assent to Christian doctrines in their students. Religion has a private role in education and it is a voluntary activity. The private is often equated with the personal and represents a separation from the mainstream in education and from meaningful participation in the general world of education. Newman, on the contrary, emphasized that the content of faith was coherent, objective and public and had a legitimate role in common education for all. While he also carefully balanced the intellectual and propositional aspect of the faith with its proper assimilation by the imagination and the heart, nowadays faith is often presented as subjective and as feeling at the expense of its doctrinal and objective dimension.[10] Newman wanted the objective truths of the faith taught and the believer to arrive at a personal assent to them. Most Western educational systems have largely marginalized religion in schools or simply omitted it altogether from the curriculum. When it appears it is often reduced to some sociological study of religious practices. In fact, what is taught instead is a kind of secular liberal confessionalism which challenges religious intolerance, and in doing so actually destroys religion by denying any objective content to it.

In the context of teaching religion, Michael Hime believes that Newman's *Grammar* assists us to understand that

> communicating the faith is not primarily a matter of supplying propositions and information (although that is part of the faith) but rather of evoking and naming experiences. The teacher of faith should help his learners examine their experience and offer categories to them for understanding that experience. Teaching faith is, in a sense, offering people a hermeneutic for interpreting what they experience within and around themselves so that disparate parts of their experience begin to connect and emerge as a meaningful whole.[11]

Hime adds that the implicitness and lack of clarity of these processes are 'sometimes more fruitful ways of knowing and believing than the clarity of what is explicit'. Hime actually appears to say the opposite of what Newman maintained, for he overestimates the role of the teacher in providing categories for the student. Hime's approach also appears to lack sufficient intellectual subject matter or content, in its preference for process over content. Not that Newman had no interest in the process of teaching, for he provided a stronger structural formation for his pupils' mental powers. In the *Idea*, for instance, Newman was explicit about a developmental model in which he recommends that intellectual training should begin with grammar. However, Newman did not accept the limitation of religious teaching to a process, or hermeneutic of experience, on the grounds that there was much content in the Christian faith that is not directly available to personal experience, e.g. the doctrines of the Trinity and the Incarnation, which can only be learned from Revelation.

Teaching

The second area of application of Newman's educational thought concerns teaching and the formation of teachers. On teaching, Newman says

> We cannot teach except by aspects or views which are not identical with the thing itself we are teaching. Two persons may each convey the same truth to a third, yet by methods and representations altogether different. The same person will treat the same argument differently in an essay or speech, according to the accident of the day of writing, or of the audience, yet will be substantially the same.[12]

Newman's idea of teaching and learning recognizes the uniqueness of each and every individual learner together with the uniqueness of the mind of the teacher who communicates with the learner's mind amid constantly changing circumstances. The contemporary idea that teaching can be narrowly based on producing quantifiable learning outcomes, which in turn constitute the major criterion of teaching competence, would be anathema to Newman. The teacher, for Newman, is not simply one whose contribution is limited to the systematic transmission of knowledge. By concentrating on practical teaching skills and methods – the mechanics of teaching – it is possible to produce a mechanistic teacher who is able to manage a class and instruct students with a fair show of competence. The emphasis here being on what the teacher can minimally do (a trade), rather than what the true teacher should be and can become (an educator). For Newman wanted a teacher to be an educator – one who helps form human beings, by seeing teaching in the perspective of larger theories of human development. Newman sought out teachers for his school who were cultured, were aware of the larger social setting, had the flexibility to anticipate change, and to adapt their methods to new demands. To produce such teachers it is necessary to strike a balance between a focus on the development of competence on the one hand and raising the teachers' awareness about the meaning of their task on the other. For Newman, good teachers sense the importance of acquiring a larger and deeper perspective on human values and thus they help develop the child's personhood. To accept a model of the teacher as one who only systematically *transmits* knowledge is to reduce the formation of teachers to the production of skilled technicians comparable to the proliferating variety of computer experts.

In his treatise *On The Teacher*, St Augustine expresses what Newman practised:

> For do teachers profess that it is their thoughts which are perceived and grasped by the students, and not the sciences themselves which they convey through thinking? For who is so stupidly curious as to send his son to school that he may learn what the teacher thinks? . . . Those who are pupils consider within themselves whether what has been explained has been said truly; looking of course to that interior truth, according to the measure of which each of us is able. Thus they learn, and when the interior truth makes known to them that true things have been said, they applaud . . .[13]

Newman saw teaching as above all a self-giving enterprise concerned with the betterment or good of students. Ultimately, teaching is an act of humility, as is learning. Teaching involves a complex set of beliefs and knowledge which are appropriate for teachers to hold, and the teaching by which those beliefs and knowledge may be communicated to students. Accordingly, in order to avoid a merely mechanistic transfer of information from teacher to pupil, it is essential that teachers themselves hold those same appropriate values which they should inculcate in their pupils. Values are an integral part of teaching, reflected both in what is taught and also in how teachers teach, and interact with, students. Parents provide a model for this kind of interaction. This is why Newman held that teachers act *in loco parentis*. Students spend the greatest amount of their daily time with teachers, who therefore have significant opportunities to influence them. The time spent by students in the company of teachers ought, therefore, to be personal and formative. As Newman says, 'It is the living voice, the breathing form, the expressive countenance' which teaches.[14] Good teachers are connected to their students, in the sense that, whether intentionally or not, teachers shape the character of their students, for at the heart of the practice of education is the relationship between teacher and student. It is this relationship that sets the tone for all else in the classroom and Newman insists upon it. Hence his denunciation of the aloofness of the tutors in his time at Oxford:

> I have experienced a state of things, in which teachers were cut off from the taught by an insurmountable barrier; when neither party entered into the thoughts of the other ... where a stiff manner, a pompous voice, coldness and condescension, were the teacher's attributes ...[15]

It was this state of things which he had striven to change first at Oriel, then in Dublin where he lived among his students. Newman's approach to tutoring was more than a revival of discipline, for he wished to influence his pupils with the presence of his own good example. He understood the power of personal influence and how it is essential to good teaching, and wanted teachers both to discard distant authoritarian attitudes and to be open and available to their students. Newman believed that what was vital in education was not only what is taught, but how it is taught. He gave great emphasis to tutors and students living in community residences as an integral part of a university education. Many universities have followed this model with tutors acting as moral guides to their students. Yet in contemporary universities and schools teachers and lecturers have largely abandoned the idea of influencing their students' moral attitudes through their teaching and personal example. Personal influence in education was a theme Newman returned to again and again and he preached on it at St Mary's in 1832 – 'Personal Influence: the means of propagating the truth'. For Newman the essence of education is inseparable from the personal influence involved in teaching and includes one's own personal way of reasoning. J. F. Crosby stresses Newman's emphasis on the personal:

> Newman had a definite pastoral reason for his fascination with real assent. He realized that we human beings are so constituted as to be moved to action much more through the imagination than through the intellect. If our apprehension of the world is mediated too much by universals and general notions, we are left in the position of spectators. But the more we apprehend the world and other persons in their concreteness, the more engaged we become with them, the more capable of acting towards them, and so the more we live as persons.[16]

Increasingly, within education, questions seem to be turned into objective problems to be solved, and the belief that for every objective problem there is some sort of technical fix appears to be gaining ground. Consequently, questionable assumptions go unquestioned. The characteristics that differentiate and define teaching do not necessarily imply the criteria for good teaching or successful teaching. Successful teaching simply brings about the desired learning in narrow subject terms. Good teaching is harder to discern and is, therefore, open to wider interpretations. It has long been accepted that good teaching is much more than the transmission of knowledge. The idea of the 'good teacher' implies one who is capable of helping students to develop their own individual mode of reasoning, which Newman called the 'illative sense', and respecting their diverse experiences and aptitudes.[17]

The Learner

The third area in which Newman has particular relevance for education today concerns the way we learn. Newman states that the human mind is made for truth and that through the perception of different

aspects of the truth it can apprehend the unity of an idea. Newman further elaborates the 'unity of an idea' in his explanation that
knowing is more than merely comprehending information. Learning
consists 'not merely in the passive reception into the mind of a number of ideas hitherto unknown to it, but in the mind's energetic and
simultaneous action upon and towards and among those ideas'[18] an
educated mind is one 'which knows, and thinks while it knows, which
has learned to leaven the dense mass of facts and events with the
elastic force of reason'.[19] However, this 'unity of an idea' is difficult
to achieve because of the fragmentation of knowledge. Newman suggests that an interdisciplinary approach to knowledge is necessary to
avoid the increasing tendency towards fragmentation brought about
by too narrowly specialized disciplines. He wrote that the disciplines
within a university must 'complete, correct and balance each other'
and that they should also 'respect, consult, and aid' one another in
putting together the connected view of things.[20] Since the modern
university lacks a core defining purpose there seems little chance that
a connected view of things is practical.

Michael Oakeshott, a modern exponent of liberal teaching and
learning, provides some of the most sophisticated articulations of
traditional conceptions of liberal education. Oakeshott believed that
to teach is simply to bring the learner to understand and remember something of worth which the teacher intends to be learned.
This may be achieved in numerous ways, including: 'hinting, suggesting, urging, coaxing, encouraging, guiding, pointing out, conversing,
instructing, informing, narrating, lecturing, demonstrating, exercising, testing, examining, criticizing, correcting, tutoring, drilling, and
so on – everything, indeed which does not belie the engagement to
impart an understanding'.[21] Oakeshott believed that contemporary
education is deformed by rationalism and post-rationalist modernity.
It would appear from this that he and Newman have a great deal
in common. Yet the difference, though not at first easily detected, is
really quite profound, for Oakeshott's approach leaves aside the core
of Newman's *paideia*, which is the formation of the Christian mind
and heart. Even a Christian writer like Jaroslav Pelikan accepts that
Newman, stripped of the theological element of his thought, can still
be relevant to education today.

Learning involves change, and affects both behaviour and knowledge. All human beings have the capacity to grow to maturity by reflecting on the range and depth of their experiences of life. They become educated by learning through that reflection. Education is a lifelong process and can never reach a terminal point before death. Newman understood learning as the forming and re-forming of ideas in the mind, which is an 'active' process capable of producing critical and thinking learners. Learning implies personal formation as well as intellectual development. Therefore all genuine learning is active, not passive. It involves the use of the mind, not just the memory, and it is essentially a process of discovery that stimulates both the imagination and the intellect. For Newman the 'enlargement of mind' is not the passive reception of facts. G. H. Bantock was one of the first philosophers of education to draw attention to Newman's logical method based upon a view of mind and of reason as 'active'.[22] Take for example one of Newman's finest pieces of rhetoric: 'The heart is commonly reached, not through the reason, but through the imagination, by means of direct impressions, by the testimony of facts and events, by history, by description. Persons influence us, voices melt us, looks subdue us, deeds inflame us.'[23] This both provides a richer understanding of the interaction of teaching and learning and it also gives greater importance to the role of the imagination in learning.

Newman provides an excellent justification for 'experiential learning' or 'self-activity' on the part of the learner. This means that the child or student engages his mind in study and thinks for himself, thereby becoming an active participant in the learning process. It also means that the student discovers knowledge when the subject matter becomes material for exploration rather than a mere body of knowledge to be presented and remembered. However, this discovery does not happen by accident. The role of the teacher is vital, for he carefully selects the subject matter for the student to discover. Teaching also aids the student when it is conducted by asking questions and leading discussions – the Socratic mode of teaching. Newman himself was also a student-centred teacher who wanted his students to take responsibility for their own learning. In Newman's judgement, it is a false view of education 'to be very eager to bring children on in schools', by which he means both trying to do too much in a short time and reducing education to an instrument of worldly ambition.[24]

Newman disagreed profoundly both with those who wished mechanically to fill pupils' minds with facts and with those who undervalue the content of teaching at the expense of process. Newman sought students who were open-minded and who were able to advance their own point of view and develop as persons, while having assimilated and made their own the content of what has been taught to them. Newman made it clear that neither teachers nor anyone else can perform these activities for students, but rather teachers must guide their students so that they may learn to do this for themselves.

Conclusion

Newman's educational thought suggests a multi-layered approach to the process of improving the mind. It begins with the mental preparation of the learning person, first of all through the acquisition of knowledge, then also by acquiring and practising basic skills such as reading, writing, speaking, listening, observing, estimating and calculating. From the interaction of knowledge and skills arises the enlargement of mind, which brings to birth in the learner's mind an improvement in critical judgement and an enhancement of imagination. This model of mental development that Newman outlines applies equally to school and university levels of teaching and learning. It also leads to a sophisticated conception of teaching in which persons interact with developing persons. It is clearly a far richer understanding of the role of teacher and learner than that for which contemporary education often allows. Newman also wrote that we must not pursue our studies disconnectedly and that we must feed our minds with what is important. As he said

> It is . . . education which gives a man a clear, conscious view of his own opinions and judgments, a truth in developing them, an eloquence in expressing them, and a force in urging them. It teaches him to view things as they are, to go right to the point, to detect what is sophistical, and to discard what is irrelevant.[25]

Although Newman does not offer us a systematic theory of education, he does provide a *paideia* by which we can educate the mind
and form the character. For Newman, then, the education of the
human mind is not a sufficient end in itself, but it must be part of
the total formation of the human person. The fully mature human
person, in Newman's view, is one who has come to know his place
in the world and understand his religious destiny and purpose. In
his own phrase, education is the means to 'prepare us for a divine
citizenship'.[26]

Notes

1. v. supra chapters 2 and 3.
2. Sermon, 'On some popular mistakes as to the object of education', 1826 (1826 Sermon).
3. *Idea*, p. 111.
4. 1826 Sermon.
5. Ibid.
6. Ibid.
7. Ibid.
8. *Idea*, p. 135.
9. Unpublished sermon 'On general education as connected with
   the Church and religion', 1827 (1827 Sermon).
10. v. *Idea*, p. 43.
11. Hime, M. (2004), 'Communicating the Faith: Conversations and
    Observations'. Boston College: unpublished paper, p. 11.
12. *Development of Doctrine*, pp. 55–6.
13. Augustine of Hippo, *De Magistro*, Chapter XIV.
14. *Historical Sketches* III (HS), p. 14.
15. HS, p. 75.
16. Crosby, J. F. (2002), 'Newman on the Personal', *First Things*, 125,
    pp. 43–9.
17. for the illative sense v. chapter 2, pp. 59–60.
18. *Idea*, p. 120.
19. Ibid., p. 123.
20. Ibid., pp. 94–5.

21. Fuller, T. (ed.) (1989), *The Voice of Liberal Learning: Oakeshott on Education*. New Haven, CT: Yale University Press, p. 70.
22. v. Bantock, G. H. (1952), *Freedom and Authority in Education*. London: Faber and Faber.
23. *Discussions and Arguments*, p. 293.
24. 1826 Sermon.
25. *Idea*, p. 154.
26. 1827 Sermon.

Appendix A

Note: Newman numbered all his sermons in order of composition and this one is No. 128. It was first given at St Clement's, Oxford on Sunday afternoon 8 January 1826. This sermon was number 12 in a course of sermons entitled 'Obedience to the law and the purpose of education'.

Sermon 12: On some popular mistakes as to the object of education

I Cor viii. 1

> '... *Knowledge puffeth up, but charity edifieth.*'

The Church at Corinth to which these words were addresst [*sic*] by Saint Paul, had been formed a very few years – yet even in them had run its course of degeneracy, and was corrupt even while miraculous gifts were found in it, and before the civil power had given Christians that security and those temporal privileges, which were the occasion of its supineness and unfaithfulness in after ages. It was overcome by another sort of enemy – not wealth but false philosophy. The first promulgation of the gospel took place in one of the most refined, enlightened, and luxurious ages which the world has seen – Society was in its last stage, about to break up and commence its race anew. It was intended (as it seems) by the great Author of Christianity to plant His religion in the very constitution of Kingdoms and governments – So the new doctrine was preached just before a ploughing time of all nations, that the seed might be ready when the spring-season came.

But being *first* preached in the last age of a previous system it was exposed to corruption from the peculiar vices and errors of that age – these were false learning, self-conceit, profaneness and luxurious self-indulgence.

Doubtless in so wide a field as that in which the Christian Church was planted the varieties of the soil were great – society had in some places advanced much more than in others – and was never nearer its dissolution – whereas in some places the Apostles preached to *Barbarians*. Thus it would in different places be more or less exposed to corruption. And again the occasional *persecutions* of the Church would do much to preserve it from corruption. In Corinth however, in the Apostles' time, there seems to have been no external means of preservation – and as Christians were afterwards corrupted by wealth and power, so were they then at Corinth by false philosophy.

Wealth and learning are necessary (by God's appointment) to protect and recommend the Christian doctrine, just as miracles were necessary for its introduction – and when they are made more of than this and are used, not to countenance religion, but to do its work, wealth begets hypocrisy, and learning infidelity.

The Corinthians then, were seduced by the temptation of human learning and the refinements of an unmanly luxury, led to prefer gifts to graces – the powers of the intellect to moral excellence – to look indulgently on vice, as a weakness rather than a sin – to aim at outward elegance rather than inward purity: to range themselves under different leaders, from a conceit about their powers of discrimination and judgment – nay further than this to dishonor the ordinances of the Church by a profaneness which seems to us almost unaccountable.

It is plain many of these faults are the faults of the Christian Church at the present day – for we live in an age in many respects parallel to that in which the gospel was first preached. For instance, the maxim in the text is particularly appropriate to our case. Nothing is a more common error now than that of exalting human knowledge over Christian love or piety – and of attempting to put knowledge in the place of sound religious principle, as a more than sufficient practical substitute. The mistake takes various forms – One of the most common whether avowed or concealed is that of supposing, that in proportion as men *know* more, they will be *better* men in a moral point of view; and therefore a good education is the remedy for all the evil in the world.

Education, if conducted on right principles, is an inestimable blessing – if it were not, why should Christ have set up the Christian Church at all? for what is it [but] a school of education for the next life? – But, if conducted on wrong principles, it is a great evil – This seems plain enough and yet it is necessary to enforce it – for men assent to general proposition, without being able to apply it in practice, more than if they had never heard it. Having then last week spoken of the error of considering education everything – I will now remind you of one or two errors in the mode of applying it – All education should be conducted on this principle – that it is a means towards an end, and that end is *Christian holiness*; the knowledge imparted is intended to make us 'wise unto salvation <2 Tim. 3> – a knowledge leading on to love – for knowledge by itself 'puffeth up but love edifieth' (I have before this had occasion to mention the state of the Corinthian church when the Apostle wrote his first Epistle to it) Corinth was at that time one of the most flourishing cities of Greece (a country celebrated for mental cultivation and literary pursuits). It happened then, as it is always likely to happen among a highly civilized people, that the Christians there fell into the error of preferring *knowledge* to that warm and spiritual *charity* or love (for the same is meant by either word) which is the fulfilling of the law. Instead of seeking each other's edification, they learned to pride themselves on their intellectual attainments – and perverted <abused> the miraculous gifts which were bestowed on them for the good of the church to the gratification of their own vanity and selflove.

Hence Saint Paul is urgent in exhorting them to humility and love of each other – and throughout his Epistles (as in the text) presses upon them the immense superiority, in a religious view, of charity over knowledge. 'Knowledge,' he says, 'puffeth up – but love edifieth –'

I have said there is always a tendency among a civilized people to prefer knowledge to love – we need not then be surprised if we find this error very prevalent among ourselves at the present day. The period we live in is remarkable beyond all others for general education. There have been times when even to be able to read was considered a mark of superior attainments – now on the contrary we are almost surprised to find individuals who cannot read; while numbers in the common ranks of life are advancing far beyond the mere elements of letters, and are devoting some portion of their leisure to scientific pursuits. This is all well, as far as it goes – were it not for the mischievous error just mentioned – Knowledge has puffed up.

It may be useful to consider this common mistake as to the use and purpose of education with some attention – for ideas on this subject are closely connected with soundness in religious faith.

It can never be too often repeated that the object <use> of education is to *write the divine law upon the heart* – to create, in the breast of man a living witness to the truth of God, a righteous monitor, a spiritual guide and counsellor – to be the instrument of the Holy Spirit in giving us a right judgment in all things, so that we may instinctively (as it were) and without effort at once discern what is holy, and feel a desire and possess the ability to practice it. Education is to prepare the heart for the gospel of Christ – it is to lead us to correct views of our own state and a knowledge of our own hearts – it is to train us and win us over to habits of practical godliness – to accustom us to deny ourselves, to govern our passions, to fix our affections on God, and to trust Him with a humble and implicit faith – In short, it is to make us see our need of a Saviour and a Sanctifier, while at the same time it discloses them both to the young mind as it is able to bear it.

This being the great end of education, let us consider

1. the error of those who think education does everything, if it teaches to *read*. How many are there who conceive that the object of schooling and instruction is accomplished, when a child has learned to read fluently – as if reading were a good in itself independently of the use made of it – as if there were not bad books to read as well as good. The mere ability <(power)> to read is no more good than wealth is in itself a good – every thing depends on the way we use it. If riches are spent wickedly or wantonly, they are an *evil* – and if a person takes advantage of his learning, to read bad books, reading is an evil. So far then is skill in reading from being the *end* of education, that it is but the *beginning*, the *first step* – we read *in order to* [?] something beyond – we read *that through* reading we may learn our duty towards God and man. We should

never suspect that a person called in a physician merely in order that he might take medicine – as if taking medicine was in itself a desirable object. whereas it is taken *in order to* gain health – and in like manner a child learns to read, not as if that were all, but that *through reading* he may be introduced to the revealed word, the gospel of his salvation.

2. It is an error of somewhat similar nature to suppose that the end of education is merely to fit persons for their respective stations in life – to teach them their several trades, and put them in the way to rise in the world. Men talk of instruction as a fine thing – and point to those who through it are prospering in life, while the uneducated are wasting <living> in ignorance or vice. Thus education is robbed of its religious character, and made the mere instrument of worldly ambition. My brethren, if the end of schooling is only to make expert and intelligent traders or farmers, I know not how Sunday schools can escape the guilt of profaning the Lord's day – If to teach is to prepare for *this* world alone, surely we are abusing the season of holy rest to the purposes of an earthly convenience. How are ministers concerned in education, if it is altogether for this world? How is Christ's Spirit, whose kingdom is not of this World? True, education has reference to the temporal callings of men, but it does not rest there – we do not educate children, that they may *succeed* in their respective occupations, but that they may so fulfil them as to make them the means of spiritual profit to their souls, that their worldly trades and professions may affect them as they ought, may be the instruments of good to them, calling into action habits of conscientiousness, uprightness, diligence, truth, disinterestedness and humility – We are preparing them to do good in their generation, to glorify God by their lives wherever they may be placed, and to spread the knowledge of the grace of Christ to their own circle, be it small or large – We are tutoring them for a heavenly calling, and for the enjoyment of a divine citizenship and the employments of an eternal life.

3. Again there are many who lose sight of the necessity of training their children at home considering *school* the only place for education, as if it were impossible to carry on the work elsewhere. Hence they never think of instilling good principles into their

children's minds while young; but suffer them to form their own habits and gain opinions from any quarter – and when at a proper age they send them to school, they think they have done all that can be required of good and wise parents. Nor do they trouble themselves about their children's advancement in the *intervals* <(between the times)> of schooling – but by allowing them to do as they will, when they come home, undo all that is done at school. Nay they sometimes as an indulgence permit them in practices, which the strict rules of propriety forbid – and thus allow them to break through duties at home as a *reward* for observing them at school (a procedure similar to that of that Eastern false prophet, who proposes as a reward for restraining sensual passions *here* the permission of indulging them without restraint *hereafter*). But parents should consider that from the earliest infancy of their children they are their natural guardians and instructors; that sending to school is merely an accidental circumstance, and but a part of education – that to them it is intrusted to train their young minds and store them with all things useful and honest: to watch over them to lead them to God even the Father of our Lord Christ, and to see that the grace given to them as members of the Church be not bestowed in vain.

4. Here too let us notice the error of supposing that school is to be a place of mere instruction. It is too common (and we need much to be reminded of the mistake) to be very eager to bring children on in schools. Forgetting the real end of education we think it a great thing to store their minds with many precepts and much information – we are desirous of doing much in a short time, and try to educate (if I may so say) by mechanism. <(Davidson)> But that truly would be a wonderful machine which would at once and with certainty instil right principles and holy feelings into many minds, and open the heart to receive the gospel as easily as it can make the tongue to repeat it – Far from this summary method must be our procedure, if we would really call down the blessing of the Spirit upon our labours – we must know each – we must address ourselves to them almost one by one – we must press upon them the necessity of personal holiness, and the uselessness yea, the guilt of knowing the truth without practising it.

The opposite course is very mischievous – to learn will be considered every thing, and if a child is quick and understand readily, he will answer every expectation. Alas, to know the Truth and to love it, are quite different things – it often happens that those who enter into the meaning of the Christian doctrine most readily, feel it least. And knowledge puffeth up – it excites vanity, self-esteem and contempt of others – it cherishes pride and selfindulgence – makes the heart sensual and unbelieving – and is thus the very instrument of Satan, yea Satan transformed into an angel of light <2 Cor. 2> – and hence the meaning of the Apostle may be seen when he says to the Corinthians in the verse following the text – 'If any man think that he knoweth any thing, he knoweth nothing yet as he ought to know.' For then only we know as we ought, when we feel that holy love is the end of the commandment and that *we* are far, very far, from fulfilling it, as our duty is.

Education then is not merely to teach reading or writing – not to fit us for the successful performance of our worldly calling, nor to inculcate the bare principles of belief and practice; it is not to impart barren lifeless knowledge; but to work together with God in the salvation of souls. It should never be prosecuted without prayer – It is a work of faith and labour of love <1 Thess.1> – and is only then acceptable to God when it is done for His sake and in the name of Christ.

Knowledge puffeth up but love edifieth – My brethren, I would that in the case of children only a preference of knowledge to substantial godliness were visible among us – Would that, when we became men, we put away childish things <1 Cor. 13> – but, alas, the error in question is one of universal prevalence. And I doubt not that there are some persons in this parish influenced by it.

What shall we say to those who profess a zeal for the Lord and love to hear the voice of His servants, and yet do not His will? Are there not those (in almost every part of England we come to) who speak much about religion (religious objects, religious works, religious societies, who are given to wander after preachers) and almost pride themselves on their knowledge of salvation; who yet are making but feeble efforts in the great work of sanctification and suffer vanity or selfishness or a worldly spirit to have a great portion of their heart? – Are there not very many, who more or less, in a greater or less degree, answer to this description? and are not such, in the same proportion as they thus live, preferring a barren knowledge to the open-hearted, lowly and holy spirit of Christian love?

Are there not others amongst us who think it enough to read good books, and to understand the ten commandments and the creed and their duty towards God and their neighbour, and to come regularly to church; and who profess to know their Bible well, who yet put up with a form of knowledge without feeling the power of godliness – Yet what can it profit a man to say <vid James 2> he believes in the divine nature of Christ, in His incarnation, in His sacrifice for sin, and in the doctrine of the Trinity, if these high subjects make no impression on his heart? Can such a faith save him? – Is there any merit in the mere act of believing difficult doctrines? Is not the great object of faith to convey these doctrines with power to the soul and through grace to renew it in holiness after the image of God? Here again, I would say, do not be content with feeling that you are not *altogether* such an one, but let each ask himself is he in *any* degree thus preferring knowledge to a Christian spirit; whether the doctrines in question produce their full effect upon him, whether the world of God has free course within him and is glorified by a consistent and holy life. <2 Thess. 3>

It is not difficult to account for our proneness to prefer knowledge to practical religion – the desire of knowledge is a feeling natural to us, and though right and commandable [*sic*] <praiseworthy> within proper bounds, is not necessarily connected with spiritual feeling. It is no task to many minds to inquire, to learn and attain – and there is a satisfaction in possessing knowledge, a self-complacency in surpassing others in understanding, which more or less is felt by all men. But to regulate the heart, to discipline the affections, to govern well the passions, to set heaven before us, to wake from the sleep of sin and stand alive and active to do the will of Christ, to humble ourselves in His sight, and to depend solely on Him for salvation, who finds this an easy undertaking? who that ever set about it in right earnest, will speak triumphantly of his progress in this narrow walk that leadeth unto life? Surely it is the Holy Ghost and none else, who thus enables us to prefer love to knowledge, who opens our eyes to see the beauty of holiness, and weans us from sin, and strengthens us unto habits of virtue and active obedience.

My brethren, no words can adequately express the importance of this subject – We cannot estimate the wretched state of him, who knows what is right, yet habitually and systematically neglects to follow it – who sins against conscience, and while he confesses that religion is the one thing needful, yet continues a careless and ungodly course of life. Alas, alas, how soon will his hour of trial be over, and he called to meet his Judge, the infinite and all-knowing God! (How do the years roll away, we are now even commencing another year – and when we look back upon that just passed, do we not recollect those who a twelvemonth ago were alive, and now are in the other world? – they thought, conversed and acted and were full of life then, but where are they now?) (How forcibly do the events of every day call upon us to prepare for death! how many things happen in the course of Providence to remind us that we may be suddenly called away from this world! – and if that summons should find *us* us who are here assembled unprepared, if when brought into God's presence we can give no reason why we should be saved, if we discover *then* before His throne an ignorance of our own hearts, an ignorance of our own sinfulness and our secret faults, can we doubt that our doom will be dreadful? – We shall assuredly find in that day that a knowledge – and that words and fine sentences and the knowledge of hard names or acquaintance with many books, or a power of disputing and arguing, are in themselves nothing worth.) May we then all be stirred up of God to seek after that fruitful knowledge of Christ which leadeth to salvation; that we may know Him not from mere hearsay and in a barren way but from His actual work within us – not from the mere instruction of others, but by His living in our heart to sanctify and bless it all our life long – not from the mere word of Scripture, but from its power and spirit dwelling richly in us – that (if) <whenever> it shall please God to take *us* from this world (before another year comes round) we may be found of Him in peace, without spot and blameless. <2 Pet. 3>

Appendix B

Note: Newman numbered all his sermons in order of composition and this one is No. 162. It was given at Well Walk Chapel, Hampstead on Sunday morning, 19 August 1827. The national school on behalf of which this sermon was preached would have been, not a state school, but a parochial school belonging to the 'National Society for the Education of the Poor in accordance with the Principles of the Established Church'. Newman placed a note on this sermon after preaching it: 'This sermon got me into a scrape with the Hampstead people, who said it required charity to hear the charity sermon.'

On general education as connected with the Church and religion

(for National School)

Acts xx. 28

> **'Take heed therefore unto yourselves and to all the flock over the which the Holy Ghost hath made you overseers to feed the Church of God, which He hath purchased with His own blood.'**

That holiness of heart, which is so indispensably requisite for our enjoying the future presence of God, and into which we are in this life to be changed, is no mere transient feeling, but a state of heart – a state in which we act not from extraordinary heat and impulse, but calmly, rationally, naturally – it is a state of change indeed, but of gradual change intended to begin in childhood and continue till death, all the powers and faculties of the soul being in progressive amendment, and growing into a nearer and nearer likeness of the attributes and will of God.

And as this process of spiritual conversion is to be continued on all through our lives, never perfected but always in progress, so all our lives are passed in external circumstances admirably calculated to promote this conversion – trials and temptations of various kinds, which at first sight indeed may raise an inconsiderate murmur, but which, soberly contemplated, are the very best outward means for maturing our souls in holiness and virtue.

Such was the substance of what I had to lay before you last week. Yet I then granted, or rather I was cautious to warn you, that the very best means for advancing us in holiness, *might* prove the very best for advancing us in sin – that every thing depended on the state of mind worked upon.

How then must we obtain that previous state of mind which is thus to sanctify the troublous events of life into means of grace to the soul? The answer is evident 'by a judicious training in early youth' – and thus as this life altogether is a season of discipline for another, so is the period of youth a season of discipline for this life, nay a discipline by the very same means – for the events of life discipline and train us to virtue by pleasure and pain, and children are trained by pleasure and pain also.

The great importance of early education is at once seen – it is necessary to make this world have its right and due effect upon us – without it trial and temptation will have (it is to be feared) precisely the reverse effect of that intended by Providence.

Yet it must not be supposed that education is of any service to us without the influence of God's grace – human efforts are nothing without the aid of that Holy Spirit which Christ was exalted to send down upon earth.

Thus inward help, outward training, both are necessary for learning to act our point well here, for profiting by the events of life, and being by them prepared for heaven. Now doubtless Christ might give His inward grace and injoin upon us outward training independent of any observable system or arrangement – He might impart the influences of His Spirit without regard to any system of operation which human understanding can follow – and again He might have injoined no express regulations on the subject of education, the duty being left incumbent upon individuals only, no reference being had to a general plan of procedure. But in His wisdom He has otherwise determined – Here, as in every work of nature, He has made use of *means* – means of inward grace, means of outward teaching. He has founded a Church with whom He has lodged both grace and teaching – To the Church of Christ belong the means of *grace*, such as the sacraments, ordinances, and the weekly worship of God – and to the Church belong the means of instruction, such as schools and other places of education.

By 'the Church' is meant the public body of Christians associated according to certain rules and governed by certain officers – and when it is said that the means of grace and instruction belong to the Church, it is meant that God has not promised his grace in the sacraments or his blessing on teaching to private individuals standing by themselves separating from and independent of other Christians – that He has willed His followers to be *one body* – that His promises are made to them *as a body* – and hence that all means of grace, all Christian plans or instruction must be *public* – not self-originating from isolated individuals, but the deed of the general body.

Every community must have governors – and Christ has appointed overseers to His Church – His ministers – to these He has given (for the good of all) the office of presiding over all the means of grace – and hence, as being the more immediate instruments of God's mercy, they are sometimes called exclusively the Church – but properly the church is the whole body of Christians – and they but shepherds of the flock, over which (in the solemn words of Saint Paul which I have taken for my text) the Holy Ghost has made them overseers, that they may feed that church which God has purchased with His own blood.

The Catholic Church of God then, as being that whole body of Christians to whom Christ has made the promises, is the appointed mother and nurse of every individual Christian, from his first admittance into it at baptism – the earthly source of all spiritual good from the Apostles' days to our own, the guardian and expounder of the word of God, and the minister of His Spirit.

The immediate subject to which I shall presently direct your attention will not allow me to enter into the Scriptural proof of these articles of our faith – 'the holy Catholic Church, and the communion of saints' – I only stop to remind you that Saint Paul seldom mentions the gift of the Holy Spirit without attaching it to the *body* of Christ, of which individuals partake as being members – and on the other hand that he speaks of religious training as no private work but as proceeding from that church which had apostles, prophets, evangelists, pastors and teachers, for the perfecting of the saints, for the work of the ministry, for the building up of the body of Christ – <Eph 4>

That with the church are deposited the sacraments and ordinances of inward grace few among us perhaps doubt ... But the outward means through education and instruction, that these according to the will of God are to be provided by the church, and the ministers of Christ as pastors and nourishers of the flock are to preside over all schools and places of <for> religious and general knowledge, this, though I am persuaded most thinking men among us would on consideration admit it, is very frequently forgotten. To this subject I shall this morning address myself – indeed I am particularly invited to it on the present occasion, when I am to advocate the system of instruction adopted by that branch of the Universal Church planted in this country, and to recommend to your support a particular school under its superintendence –

When the great end of education is borne in mind, viz to prepare us for acting and feeling religiously in all that befalls us in the course of our lives, it seems to stand to reason that to educate the young is as much a part of a minister's parochial duty as visiting the sick or preaching. And this applies not only in the case of those poorer classes of the community whose education being what is merely necessary has almost entirely a religious character, it is equally true in the case of those who have a fuller and more liberal education. For all branches of knowledge should be viewed in a religious light – all things should be made to tend towards religion and their relative value ascertained by religion – Let the subject before us be metaphysics, physics, moral or political philosophy, rhetoric, history or general literature, a spirit of faith and Christian principle should leaven them all. It seems indeed to be a fundamental mistake in a system of education, when the instructors of youth in general knowledge are not also their religious instructors. To exclude religion from education, is to rob it of a just and most salutary right. Not to state other and obvious bad effects, this at least will be its effect upon the minds of both teacher and scholar – it will lead them to consider that religious faith has its definite province, and must be confined to that – that theology is (but) one particular *science* and the Christian ministry (but) a certain *profession* – while the glorious world of general knowledge is left religionless, the assigned property of infidelity, deprived of that new birth into holy uses which is conferred on it by Him who made all things new.

If then it is expedient, nay a duty, that men should be taught to view all things in a religious light, it is doubtless expedient and according to the will of Christ that the church should preside over *all* education, and that those who are set apart for religious offices should be connected with institutions not only of directly religious but also of general knowledge.

The primitive church certainly thought so – its Fathers were the most learned men of their day in secular knowledge – and some of them were teachers in those branches of literature then most in esteem.

The Church of England has followed this example (vid No. 122) considering it the duty of the clergy to provide for the education of the great body of the people – and considering instructor of every kind either as acting with them, as parents – or under them, as other teachers. Hence in the Canons it is provided <Canons 77, 78, 79> that 'no man shall teach either in public school or private house, but such as shall be allowed by the Bishop of the diocese ... being found meet as well for his learning and dexterity in teaching, as for sober and honest conversation and also for right understanding of God's true religion' and a preference is expressly given to the incumbent of each place (should he be willing) to be a teacher of the youth of his parish, and again – that '*all* schoolmasters shall teach ... as the children are able to bear, the larger or shorter catechism ... And as often as any sermon shall be ... within the parish where they teach, they shall bring their scholars to the church where such sermon shall be made, and there see them quietly and soberly behave themselves, and shall examine them at times convenient, after their return what they have borne away of such sermon.' And that the youth of the upper classes as well as of the lower were contemplated in this provision is evident by the frequent directions which present themselves in the Canons as to the religious discipline of Colleges in our Universities. This is sufficient to shew the intention at least of our Church that all education should be in connexion with ministerial instructions and superintendence.

And in great measure this intention has been actually realized. The clergy have the general education of all ranks of the community from our colleges down to our parochial schools; and it is considered as almost part of their character to be the most learned body of men in the country. And here I must repeat, the clergy are not to be considered as controlling education in their own right; but as representatives and instruments of the general body of Christians, for whose good God has appointed them to the office of superintendence: to feed the flock of God which He has purchased with His own blood.

So much then generally, on the connexion between education and a Church system. I proceed to make some observations on the subjects in which it is desirable children should be instructed.

Now the end of education is the same to rich and poor – to *affect the heart* – If this end were kept in view, we should have little of that hesitation, which many of us now feel, in deciding on the relative merits of various modes of education. Above all we should not hear of that portentous mistake, into which numbers in the present age are in such danger of falling, of supposing that education is the *imparting mere knowledge* – The present age is an age of inquiry – and so far an age of promise – for the acquisition of knowledge viewed in all its bearings and with reference to its ultimate effects on the mass of society must be a good – But the same spirit of inquiry is attended with great local and temporary evils – accidental indeed, still great and serious. It is a serious evil, if we allow ourselves to believe that mankind will be at all the better or happier in having their minds filled with the knowledge of various facts in natural philosophy or general science – The mere acquaintance with the phenomena of matter, the wonders of human ingenuity the events of history, the uses of various arts and pursuits, excellent as it is abstractedly, and excellence too practical in its proper place, is a poor substitute for a good education – it has no effect upon the heart to change it. A man is not likely to conduct himself better in his social, political, moral or religious relations by knowing all the secrets of earth and heaven. Though he have all knowledge he is nothing without Christian love – and such a course of instruction as I am referring to has no tendency to encourage the principle of Christian love. Nay, on the contrary in most cases it is a positive evil – for knowledge, mere knowledge whether religious or secular, 'puffeth up' – It was the old promise of the Evil one 'Ye shall be as gods, *knowing*' – and the temptations which prevailed with uncorrupted nature, has a strong accession of influence when addressed to nature fallen. And if the acquisition of knowledge, when made a disproportionate object of education, is an evil, how much more dangerous a procedure is it, with some ingenious writers, to hold out as a lure to the improvement of the understanding the *gratification resulting from knowing what others do not know*! Far be it from us, my Brethren, brought up in the principles of the Christian faith, to encourage by such pernicious excitements that price, self-conceit and self-importance that impatience of restraint and government of the natural heart, which it should be the very office of education to repress and eradicate. The duty of Christian teachers is a far more difficult task – it is comparatively easy indeed to excite in the minds of others a desire for knowledge – for that desire is natural, innocent and praiseworthy and is strengthened moreover by various motives natural too, but <though> corrupt and irreligious – But it is hard indeed to rouse the mind of child or man to look at the world and life in the light of sober truth – to raise the mind to its Maker, to make men acknowledge the evil of their hearts and that prospect of bad promise which the idea of a righteous Judge should present to them – to make them see the hand of God arranging all things in the world distinctly though silently, and His voice speaking to them in the volume of revelation – To make them listen patiently when that voice addresses them as criminals, as self-destroyed, as miserable wretched sinners – in no soft accents of praise or commendation, but as so fallen, so odious in the sight of divine purity that only a mercy great as God's and a wisdom profound as His could save them from ruin – moreover when it warns them that, though graciously and wonderfully pardoned, they cannot enter heaven without a [thorough] and laborious change of heart – to make them (I say) acknowledge and feel all this, who does not see the vast difference between this Scriptural education in the deep principles of faith and holiness, and that superficial colouring of the mind, which many advocate, which veils it perhaps with the outside show of cultivation but in reality inflames the corrupt affections and desires which lie within it?

It is a great end then of a Christian education to teach children practically their duty – and to connect the performance of that duty with those notions springing from faith and love which Scripture injoins upon us – A second object of education is that, not merely of *teaching*, but of *training* – to lead children to live as Christians – to make them read as Christians, whatever be the subject of their reading – to view all subjects of knowledge as Christians – to look upon their present duties as Christians – and their worldly calling, for which they are preparing, as Christians. For the habit of Christianizing (if I may so say) the subjects on which as children they employ their minds, when they come into the world, may under God's grace be transferred to the more serious employments of life – In like manner industry, attention, teachableness, obedience, generosity, modesty, mutual yielding to each other, forgiveness of injuries, and other Christian graces may more or less be begun in the soul by a judicious education – True the best endeavours will in numberless instances fail, still we must attempt great things – and in many cases we shall at least sow the seeds of holy habits which the events of life may mature instead of destroying. (vid No. 128).

Here then I am led to notice an error into which I conceive we sometimes fall of being very eager to bring children forward *rapidly*. Forgetting the real end of education, which can be effected but slowly and gradually we often seek short ways of advancing children in *knowledge* – But short ways as there may be to *knowledge* no short way will there ever be found for *renewing the* heart – Providence has pointed out by the weakness and immaturity of the body the time He intended for the education of the mind – and though children *may* be forced forward prematurely into a fitness for the particular trade or profession they are destined for, it must be remembered they have a part to act as *men*, as Christians, a much nobler part – and it is a short-sighted policy indeed to sacrifice their interests as immortal beings to their petty views as members of an earthly community. It is a second error (as it seems to me) to be too eager to make every subject learned by children *easy and amusing* – *All* extremes must be bad – If a child learns nothing difficult at school, nothing which requires self-command and power of attention to master, he will not be fit to act his part in life – for to live well in the world is nothing else than the doing or suffering of hard things. Another danger closely connected with the foregoing to which modern systems of education are liable, is the inordinate endeavour to educate many at once and by the same process – Of course I speak, as before, for the inordinate endeavour, the extreme – Now dull matter, governed by invariable laws, the metal and the stone, may be formed and moulded by this mechanical process – But the mind of man is a more subtle material to work upon – and truly it must be a wonderful machine which can at once and with certainty instil right principles and holy feelings into many minds and open the heart to *receive* the truth as easily as it can make the tongue repeat it. Different indeed must be our procedure, if we would really call down the blessing of God's grace upon our labours. We must take children separately – we must know each – we must address ourselves to them almost one by one – we must press upon them the necessity of personal holiness, and the uselessness, nay the guilt of knowing the truth without practising it. The opposite course is very mischievous – to *learn* will appear to a child to be all that is required of him – and if he is quick and understands readily, he will seem to himself to answer every expectation of his teachers. Alas! To know the truth and to love it are not the same. It often happens that those who enter into the meaning of the Christian doctrine most readily, feel it least. And (to repeat an important text) 'Knowledge puffeth up, but love edifieth. If any man think he knoweth any thing, he knoweth nothing yet as he ought to know.' <1 Cor. 8> – for then only we know as we ought, when we feel that holy love, gentleness, meekness, purity are the one thing needful, and that *we* are far, very far from having our hearts imbued with these holy dispositions.

Thus I have attempted to set before you the object of Christian education, its reference to the world and a future life, and its connexion with the Church. I must not be supposed to imply that our own Church is enabled to act up to the principles she herself acknowledges – or that there is no room for improvement in the mode, the matter or the instruments of her instructions. But it is much to have right principles – for they are the foundation – and if we have them clearly before us, we may under God's grace grow in practical wisdom, and gradually assimilate our measures and plans to the pattern we set before us.

This morning, my Brethren, we are called upon to show our conviction of the necessity of a national education and our willingness to promote it by contributing to the school for the instruction of the poorer classes of the community – Let very one then here present consider himself as a member of the Church whose duty it is, as a body, to provide for the instruction of every of the <its> meanest member. You are called to a work of love – to administer to the necessity of saints – of the young household of God, those who have been made Christians in baptism and who need your assistance that the grace received through baptism may not be quenched and lost.

You are called to a *direct* duty – no extraordinary work of charity, no work of doubtful expediency, but a plain simple act of religious obedience. My brethren I might flatter you with some splendid panegyric on your benevolence, on its disinterestedness, beauty and worth. I will deal more plainly with you – You are *not* doing an act of free unrequired liberality in supporting schools of this kind – you are paying a debt which as members of the Church you have incurred – The Church I repeat has baptized the children whose cause I am advocating – she had admitted them as members of Christ under the express promise and stipulation to the Lord to whom she presented them that they *should* be educated. <(vid No. 124)> To baptize and not to educate is a grievous sin – it is quenching grace – it is like profaning the Lord's supper by coming to it unworthily. The minister before baptizing requires a solemn pledge from those who bring the infant that it *shall* be brought up 'virtuously to lead a godly and a Christian life'. Nor has he any authority to baptize without it. As a body then we have admitted these children to baptism, as a body we shall sin if we neglect their education.

Moreover, you are thus acknowledging that debt of gratitude to Christ your Saviour, which though you can never pay, it should be your joy and delight to proclaim – You are in your several stations assisting to feed those lambs which have been purchased by the same blood that bought you. What you do to them, you do to Christ – He on earth invited the little children to come unto Him, and now He bids you rear them for His sake – Nor is this only a labour of *love*, it is also a work of *faith*. In assisting in the education of these children, we gain no *immediate* or *visible* advantage either to this place or the church at large – But we give our aid as looking into the future, and providing for an increase of piety in a generation which many of us may not live to see – we are sowing what we probably shall not find here, nor till after *many days* – what we do not expect to find, till the end of days when at the judgment the secret things of this world and all the intricate working and complicated influence of our actions here will be unravelled and brought to light – We look for a glorious reward then in the sight of hearts changed and souls saved who (humanly speaking) but for us would have lived without the knowledge or the spiritual blessings of the gospel of Jesus Christ.

Lastly, I bid you beware of forgetting your own salvation while you are engaged in advancing the salvation of others. We are all in danger, all in proportion as our office is to teach others, of neglecting to teach ourselves – Beware then of placing your personal hopes of acceptance with God, not on the evidence of His spirit within you, but on the outward deeds of charity and mercy – Search your hearts and try them, whether you are more or less neglecting the state of your own souls – Suffer it not that even by a possibility these children whom you are educating may have Christian hearts rather than yourselves – If however you are watchful and are really seeking to please God in heart as well as deed, He doubtless is with you. He is pleased with you – He graciously accepts when you make your offering – accepts it whether greater or less, if made in love and faith and given as an offering to Christ – and He will doubtless recompense it even in the present life by a more abundant gift of His grace, and the comfort of His Holy Spirit.

Bibliography

Writings of John Henry Newman

Apologia pro Vita Sua, ed. Svaglic, Martin J. (1967) Oxford: Clarendon Press.

Autobiographical Writings, ed. Tristram, Henry (1956) London and New York: Sheed & Ward.

Certain Difficulties felt by Anglicans in Catholic Teaching Considered, Volume II (1876) London: Basil Montagu Pickering.

Discussions and Arguments on Various Subjects (1882), London: Pickering.

An Essay in Aid of a Grammar of Assent (1870), London: Burns, Oates.

An Essay on the Development of Christian Doctrine (1890), London: Longmans, Green.

Fifteen Sermons preached before the University of Oxford, 3rd edition (1872), London, Oxford and Cambridge: Rivington.

Historical Sketches Vol. III (1888), London: Longmans, Green.

The Idea of a University, ed. Ker, I. T. (1976), Oxford: Clarendon Press.

Lectures on the Present Position of Catholics in England; Addressed to the Brothers of the Oratory in the Summer of 1851 (1889), Longmans, Green.

Letters and Correspondence of J. H. Newman, Vol. 1 ed. Mozley, Anne (1891), London: Longmans.

The Letters and Diaries of John Henry Newman, ed. Dessain, Charles Stephen *et al.*, vols xi–xxii (1961–72, London: Nelson), xxiii–xxxi (1973–7, Oxford: OUP), i–ix (1978–2006, Oxford: OUP).

My Campaign in Ireland, Part I, ed. Neville W. (1896, privately printed).

Newman the Oratorian: His Unpublished Oratory Papers, ed. Murray OSB, Placid (1969), Dublin: Gill & Macmillan.

The Rise and Progress of Universities and Benedictine Essays, ed. Tillman, Mary Katherine (2001), Gracewing: Notre Dame Press.

Sermons Preached on Various Occasions (1881), London: Burns and Oates.

Secondary Sources

Arthur, James (1995), *The Ebbing Tide; Policy and Principles of Catholic Education*. Leominster: Gracewing.

Bantock, G. H. (1952), *Freedom and Authority in Education*. London: Faber and Faber.

Barr, C. (2003) *Paul Cullen, John Henry Newman, and the Catholic University of Ireland 1845–1865*. Leominster: Gracewing.

Barrie, John (1986), 'Bantock on Newman: a nineteenth-century perspective on contemporary educational theory', *British Journal of Educational Studies*, Vol. 34, No. 1, Feb.

Blehl, Vincent F. (1970), 'Newman, the Fathers, and Education', *Fordham University Quarterly*, Vol. XLV, No. 177.

Bouyer, L. (1958), *Newman: His Life and Spirituality*. London: Burns and Oates.

Briel, D. (1997), 'Liberal Learning and Professional Education in Newman's *The Idea of a University*', http://www.stthomas.edu/1997b/briel.html

Carr, D. (1998), 'The Dichotomy of Liberal versus Vocational Education: Some Basic Conceptual Geography', *Proceedings of the Philosophy of Education Society*.

Collins, Peter M. (1976), 'Newman and Contemporary Education', *Educational Theory*, 26, 4, pp. 366–71.

Copleston, E. (1810 and 1811), *A Reply to the Calumnies of the* Edinburgh Review *Against Oxford*. Oxford: Collingwood.

Copleston, F. (1967), *History of Philosophy*, Vol. 8. London: Search Press.

Corcoran, T. (1929), *John Henry Newman, Selected Discussions in liberal Knowledge*, Dublin.

Culler, A. Dwight (1955), *The Imperial Intellect: A Study of Cardinal Newman's Educational Ideal*. New Haven, CT: Yale University Press/Oxford University Press.

Crosby, J. F. (2002), 'Newman on the Personal', *First Things*, 125, pp. 43–9.

Delaura, David J. (1969), *Hebrew and Hellene in Victorian England, Newman, Arnold and Pater*. Austin and London: University of Texas Press.

Dessain, C. S. (1966), *John Henry Newman*. London: Nelson.

—(undated), 'Religion and education in J. H. Newman', Third Morley Lecture given to the Divinity Department of Bishop Lonsdale College.

Dulles, A. (2002), *Newman: Outstanding Christian Thinkers*. London: Continuum.

Erb, Peter C. (1997), 'Newman and the Idea of a Catholic University', *Occasional Papers on the Catholic Intellectual Life*, No. 2. Emory University, Atlanta: Aquinas Center of Theology.

Fennell, F. (1995), 'The Idea and Modern Ideas: Newman and Higher Education', in Sundermeier, Michael W. and Robert Churchill (eds), *The Literary and Educational Effects of the Thought of John Henry Newman*. Lampeter: Edwin Mellen Press.

Ferreira, M. J. (1980), *Doubt and Religious Commitment*. Oxford: Clarendon Press.

de Flon, N. M. (2004), 'A work to do: Edward Caswall and pastoral ministry at the Birmingham Oratory during the 1850s and 1860s', *Recusant History*, Vol. 27, No. 1, pp. 103–23.

—(2005), *Edward Caswall, Newman's Brother and Friend*. Leominster: Gracewing.

Ferreira, M. J. (1980), *Doubt and Religious Commitment: The Role of the Will in Newman's Thought*. Oxford: Clarendon Press.

Fuller, T. (ed.) (1989), *The Voice of Liberal Learning: Oakeshott on Education*. New Haven, CT: Yale University Press.

Garland, M. M. (1996), 'Newman in his own day', in Turner, F. (ed.), *The Idea of a University*. New Haven, CT: Yale University Press.

Gilley, Sheridan (1990), *Newman and His Age*. London: Darton, Longman and Todd.

Graham, Gordon (2002), *Universities: The Recovery of an Idea*. Exeter: Imprint Academic.

Hime, M. (2004), 'Communicating the Faith: Conversations and Observations'. Boston College: unpublished paper, p. 11.

Hirst, P. (1972), 'Christian education – a contradiction in terms', *Learning for Living*, Vol. 11, No. 4, pp. 6–10.

Hughes, Gerard (2001), *Aristotle on Ethics*. London: Routledge.

Ker, I. T. (1988), *John Henry Newman: A Biography*. Oxford: Clarendon Press.

—(1990), *The Achievement of John Henry Newman*. London: Collins.

—(1996), 'The Idea of a University', *Louvain Studies*, 21, pp. 203–15.

—(1999), 'Newman's Idea of a University: a guide for the contemporary university', in Smith, D. and A. K. Langslow, *The Idea of a University, Higher Education Policy 51*, London: Jessica Kingsley.

McGrath, Fergal (1951), *Newman's University: Idea and Reality*. London: Longmans, Green.

—(1962), *The Consecration of Learning*. New York: Fordham University Press.

Maskell, Duke and Robinson, Ian (2001), *The New Idea of a University*. Exeter: Imprint Academic.

Merrigan, T. (1991), 'Clear Heads and Holy Hearts, The religious and Theological Ideals of John Henry Newman', *Louvain Theological and Pastoral Monographs*. Louvain: Peeters Press.

Mulcahy, Daniel G. (1972), 'Cardinal Newman's Concept of a Liberal Education', *Educational Theory*, 22, 1, pp. 87–98.

—(1972), 'The Role of the Disciplines in Cardinal Newman's Theory of a Liberal Education', *Journal of Educational Thought*, 6, 1, Apr., pp. 49–58.

Newman, J. (1986), *The Mental Philosophy of John Henry Newman*. Ontario: Wilfrid Laurier University Press.

Nichols, A. (1990), *From Newman to Congar*. Edinburgh: T. & T. Clark.

Oakeshott, Michael (1962), *Rationalism in Politics*. London: Methuen.

—(1972), 'Education: the engagement and its frustration', in Dearden, R. F., *et al.* (eds), *Education and the Development of Reason*. London: Routledge and Kegan Paul.

Owen, H. P. (1969), *The Christian Knowledge of God*. London: Athlone Press.

Pearce, B. L. (1990), 'Newman and the Useful Arts', *RSA*, Vol. 138, pp. 847–9.

Pelikan, J. (1992), *The Idea of a University: A Reexamination*. New Haven, CT: Yale University Press.

Pring, R. (1968), 'The Aims of Catholic Education', in Tucker, B., *Catholic Education in a Secular Society*. London: Sheed and Ward.

—(1995), *Closing the Gap: Liberal Education and Vocational Preparation*. London: Hodder and Stoughton.

Reno, S. J. (1970), 'Religious Belief: Continuities Between Newman and Cirne-Lima', *Neoscholasatic*, Vol. 44, p. 506.

Roberts, J. M. (1990), 'The Idea of a University', in Ker, I. T. and A. S. Hill (eds), *Newman After a Hundred Years*. Oxford: Clarendon Press.

Rothblatt, Sheldon (1976), *Tradition and Change in English Liberal Education*. London: Faber and Faber.

Rule, P. C. (1995), '"Growth the only evidence of life": Development of Doctrine and the Idea of a University', in Sundermeier, Michael W. and Robert Churchill (eds), *The Literary and Educational Effects of the Thought of John Henry Newman*. Lampeter: Edwin Mellen Press.

Shrimpton, P. (2005), *A Catholic Eton? Newman's Oratory School*. Leominster: Gracewing.

Slee, P. (1986), *Learning and a Liberal Education*. Manchester: Manchester University Press.

Smith, S. (1809), 'Review of Professional Learning by R. L. Edgeworth', *Edinburgh Review*, 15 October, pp. 45–6.

Stevens, C. (1995), 'Moral education in the thought of John Henry Newman', in Sundermeier, Michael W. and Robert Churchill (eds), *The Literary and Educational Effects of the Thought of John Henry Newman*. Lampeter: Edwin Mellen Press.

Sundermeier, Michael W. and Churchill, Robert (eds) (1995), *The Literary and Educational Effects of the Thought of John Henry Newman*. Lampeter: Edwin Mellen Press.

Taylor, Brian W. (1993), 'John Henry Newman and a Catholic presence at Oxford', *Irish Journal of Education*, Vol. 27, nos. 1–2: Summer and Winter.

Tristram, Henry (ed.) (1952), *The Idea of a Liberal Education*. New York: Barnes and Noble.

Vargish, T. (1970), *Newman: The Contemplation of Mind*. Oxford: Clarendon Press.

White, R. (1986), 'The Anatomy of a Victorian Debate: An essay on the history of liberal education', *British Journal of Educational Studies*, Vol. 34, No. 1, pp. 38–65.

Index